Nuclear Weapons,
Deterrence, and Disarmament

Canadian Journal of Philosophy
Other Supplementary Volumes

New Essays in the History of Philosophy
Edited by Terence Penelhum and Roger A. Shiner

New Essays in the Philosophy of Mind
Edited by Terence Penelhum and Roger A. Shiner

New Essays on Plato and the Pre-Socratics
Edited by Roger A. Shiner and John King-Farlow

New Essays on Contract Theory
Edited by Kai Nielsen and Roger A. Shiner

New Essays on Rationalism and Empiricism
Edited by Charles E. Jarrett, John King-Farlow and F.J. Pelletier

New Essays on John Stuart Mill and Utilitarianism
Edited by Wesley E. Cooper, Kai Nielsen and Steven C. Patten

New Essays in Philosophy of Language
Edited by Francis Jeffry Pelletier and Calvin G. Normore

Marx and Morality
Edited by Kai Nielsen and Steven C. Patten

New Essays in Ethics and Public Policy
Edited by Kai Nielsen and Steven C. Patten

New Essays on Plato
Edited by Francis Jeffry Pelletier and John King-Farlow

New Essays on Aristotle
Edited by Francis Jeffry Pelletier and John King-Farlow

New Essays in Philosophy of Mind, Series II
Edited by David Copp and J.J. MacIntosh

The University of Calgary Press
Calgary, Alberta, Canada

Nuclear Weapons, Deterrence, and Disarmament

Edited by
David Copp

©1986 Canadian Journal of Philosophy

The University of Calgary Press
Calgary, Alberta, Canada

ISSN 0045-5091   ISBN 0-919491-12-X

*This volume
is dedicated to the memory of
our colleague and friend*

STEVEN C. PATTEN

Table of Contents

CANADIAN JOURNAL OF PHILOSOPHY
Supplementary Volume 12

STEVEN C. PATTEN
(1941-1985)

Steve Patten was born in 1941. He grew up in a subsidized housing project in Vancouver, Washington; attended art school in San Francisco; received all three degrees in Philosophy from the University of Washington; and assumed his first (and last) teaching position at the University of Lethbridge in 1968. He died in November 1985.

Intellectually as well as physically he was a man of substance. Physically he appeared to have a slightly lower centre of gravity than most people. This was due in part to slightly sloped shoulders and a girth with which he struggled during the last years of his life. So far this might sound like a pear-shaped individual, but he had too much height for that. His height gave him the appearance of solidity and stability.

He had large hands with thick fingers that made the things he handled look more substantial and more valuable than they might be whether it be a cigarette or a piece of sculpture. The way he put a plastic cover on a styrofoam cup of coffee made it look like a delicate container of holy water.

His life was pervaded with quality and substance, from the clothes he wore to the pen he wrote with, from the car he drove to the tires on which it rolled. Like the person, all had a kind of solidity about them: a good heft and a stable appearance. But he wasn't an ordinary upper middle class academic, though these observations might suggest it; he never forgot his early life in Vancouver, the tenderloin of San Francisco, or Jackson Street in Seattle. There was quality 'junk' food. He found a kindred soul in Calvin Trillin of *The New Yorker* magazine who wrote on the best rib joints in North America, the world chili contest and other similar phenomena.

Then there was his kindness. He had the American propensity to root for the underdog. He had a greater than usual sympathy for the South African or inner city blacks, chicanos, native Americans, and the poor. Besides the sympathy, there was almost an envy, not for the condition, but for the vitality that seemed to emerge from the survivors in their art, music, speech, and life style in general. In characteristic self-mocking humor he spoke of changing his name to 'Jesus' ('Hey-soos,' not 'Jesus') or 'Muddy' (after Muddy Waters). He went out of his way to help students who were loners, isolates or were 'sad.'

His life had a theme: life should be lived with intelligence, humor, intensity, and, above all, sensitivity. The intellect of the person who lived it was a very intense and narrowly focused spotlight. What it shined on, he examined in every detail. He turned a thing over and over, on its side, and inside out. And he examined it directly, sideways, and upside down. He stared at it wide-eyed to grasp the whole, and squinted at it in order to discern every detail so that he might properly assess its significance, often as not its significance in the grander scheme of things.

It didn't matter whether it was your face or gait when he first saw you in the morning, Thelonious Monk's *Criss Cross*, Milgram's experiments on obedience to authority, or the role of religion in history. All were subject to the same scrutiny. The result was, of course, that he often saw things that most people don't see or he saw them in a particularly illuminating way.

I don't intend the spotlight metaphor to mean that his intellect was narrow. It was narrow only in its temporary focus, the concentration of the beam. This gave the intensity that allowed this scrutiny. He shined the beam everywhere: people's appearances, and their lives, music, art, politics, junk food, history, science, and himself. *Everything* was subjected to the same intense scrutiny, and when he exhausted himself on the subject or activity, he moved on.

His career at the University of Lethbridge exhibited this characteristic. He involved himself in university affairs as faculty association president, member of the General Faculties Council ('senate' elsewhere), then almost as quickly as he came upon that scene, he left it, but not before exhausting himself and some of those around him on all the important issues and every aspect of them.

His teaching was similar. He worked hard at lectures and the skills involved, he worked with his students, and occasionally published articles under joint authorship − a phenomenon not all that common at an undergraduate institution. When lecturing he studied the faces of his students to see the slightest evidences of their involvement or lack of involvement − and he was sensitive to every expression of recognition, understanding, agreement, disagreement, as well as to every smile, yawn, or look of disinterestedness. Unequipped with some of the defenses others have, the very act of teaching exacted a terrible price: two-thirds of the way through a semester he would often be exhausted.

His friendships had the same character. They were all-consuming. Again the spotlight: one beam, one object illuminated at a time. One intense friendship with one person at a time. This is a bit of an overstatement, but not by much. One felt the spotlight, one knew that the slightest disagreement or disapproval would be picked up and turned over and over in his mind. There were few secrets from him. He was kind, generous, flattering, sensitive (overly so), demanding, occasionally manipulative, fun and good humored even when he felt terrible.

It is quite understandable that someone who was so sensitive, so perceptive, and so intense in his relationships with others and the world should wonder about his fit with them or it. And so it is not surprising that most of his work was on the self and its relation to the world. His Master's thesis was on one of the more difficult passages in Kierkegaard having to do with self-consciousness; his doctoral dissertation was on Kant and the transcendental deduction which involves the ego in a crucial way.

One can also see his subsequent work in this light: his critique of Hempel's application of the covering law model to explanations by reasons; his critiques of Milgram's experiments on obedience to authority; his discussion of deception in experimentation; and his scholarly work on Mill's utilitarianism and Hume's bundle theory of the self.

All of this work is the product of the same focused and intense intellectual labor. On a good day I can last an hour on whether a conclusion follows from some premises; he wanted to talk about it for five or six hours. If the conclusion didn't follow, he wanted to know why the author might have thought it did. Did he or she have a deep insight that was badly expressed? If the conclusion did follow, then he wanted to know why he or anyone else might want to deny that it did. Was there an insight there we might be missing? And when that was done there was the painful question of whether his conclusion on the matter was really worth anything to anyone. This method led to a thoroughness which I hope rubbed off on me. It also led to a strong intolerance and suspicion of glib, facile, quick, or witty philosophical work. Though I haven't read everything he wrote, I think part of this shows through, even though his attractive writing style made it look easy.

I do not believe he would ever have produced a philosophy, a *Weltanschauung*, had he lived any longer. The mental style I have tried to describe wouldn't make that possible. But we would have had much more sane, solid, and sound philosophical work on a variety of topics. Who knows where else the spotlight might have shone?

During the last years of his life he was concerned with one of the ultimate problems of the relation of the self to the world: the possibility of nuclear omnicide. Seeing that the arms build-up increased the likelihood of omnicide he agonized over the justification for deterrence theory as a justification for that buildup. In our last conversations on this topic, he was wondering what to do with the possibility of nuclear blackmail. I do not know if he came up with an answer. His last published paper on nuclear issues is published here and deals with the individual's role and responsibilities in preventing a nuclear holocaust. It is fitting, therefore, that this volume is dedicated to him.

RONALD M. YOSHIDA
University of Lethbridge

CANADIAN JOURNAL OF PHILOSOPHY
Supplementary Volume 12

Introduction: Deterrence and Disarmament

DAVID COPP
University of Illinois at Chicago
Chicago, IL 60680
U.S.A.

One cannot convey, in a few words, the nature of the tragedy nuclear war would be. The immediate death and destruction are not the only factors, yet they are the easiest to quantify; so consider the effect of exploding a single one-megaton nuclear bomb, a bomb seventy times the power of the Hiroshima bomb, over New York City. According to one estimate, over two million people would be killed right away, and almost four million additional people would suffer major injuries. New York would be reduced to rubble. The bomb would release approximately one thousand times the fallout of the 'worst conceivable' accident in a nuclear power reactor, severely contaminating more than one thousand square miles with radioactivity, and causing hundreds of thousands of additional

1

casualties over time. The United States and the Soviet Union possess thousands of bombs of one-megaton size. If a thousand bombs of this size were detonated in Europe, it has been estimated that over two hundred million persons would be killed in short order. A global nuclear war would be several times worse, and the trauma, pain and cultural loss would be immeasurable.[1]

People are understandably concerned about the likelihood of nuclear war. However, in a recent sober analysis, Paul Bracken argued that there is little danger in times of 'peace or minor tension.' The nuclear weapons of the Soviet Union and the United States are controlled by complex systems with layers of checks and balances that should be adequate to prevent an accidental war. However, Bracken argued, in a crisis situation where the systems of both sides are placed on a high level of alert, the interlocking warning systems of the nuclear powers may 'amplify' any mistakes, causing the political leaders to lose control, and leading to dangerous instability. 'Few people would disagree that operating nuclear forces at ... high states of alert in this environment could easily tip over into preemptive attacks and all-out war. Each nation might not want war but might feel driven to hit first rather than second.'[2] In a context

---

1 These estimates are taken from Harold Freeman, 'The Effects of Nuclear War,' in James P. Sterba, *The Ethics of War and Nuclear Deterrence* (Belmont, CA: Wadsworth Publishing Company 1985), 68-79, at 71, 79. Also see *The Effects of Nuclear War*, by the United States Office of Technology Assessment (Washington, D.C.: U.S. Government Printing Office 1979).

2 Paul Bracken, *The Command and Control of Nuclear Forces* (New Haven, CT: Yale University Press 1983), 48-73, especially 53-65. The quotations are from pp. 53, 58, 65. It is obvious that estimates of the risk of failure of complex systems are highly fallible. Two examples: first, two months before the April 1986 accident at the Chernobyl nuclear power plant, Vitali Sklyarov, the Ukrainian Minister of Power and Electrifications, was quoted as saying that the chance of a meltdown in a Soviet nuclear power reactor is one in 10,000 years. The Chernobyl accident was described as a meltdown in *Time*, May 12 1986, 35. Mr Sklyarov was quoted in the February 1986 U.S. edition of *Soviet Life*, according to *Maclean's* magazine, May 12 1986, 26. Second, studies of the chances of a fatal accident to the United States's space shuttle, an accident that would result in loss of the shuttle or the crew, 'resulted in widely contradictory results, ranging from one engineering estimate of one chance

of high military alert, war could be caused by what would not otherwise be a dangerous event.

Further, if a determined opponent launched a massive nuclear attack against one's homeland, using modern methods to deliver its bombs, there would be no adequate defense. The bombs would arrive in minutes. Air defenses cannot be one hundred percent effective, even in the science fiction of the American Strategic Defense Initiative, and a single nuclear warhead of one-megaton size would devastate any urban target. This is the peril in which we now find ourselves and which must somehow be eliminated or reduced.

It is not possible for either the Soviet Union or the United States to disarm the other by means of a pre-emptive surprise attack, for modern systems of strategic and tactical warning would make a surprise attack difficult; and anyway, each side has positioned its weapons in ways that make them difficult to destroy. Strategic missiles are based in 'hardened' shelters on land, as well as in submarines at sea; cruise missiles are widely dispersed and easily concealed; and the bomber fleets can be airborne in minutes. It would be even more difficult to achieve a disarming first strike if the opponent had a missile defense, even a porous one. For to disarm an opponent, one would have to destroy all of its weapons, or at least a sufficient number that one's own defenses could prevent any of the remaining weapons from getting through to one's cities. An opponent would be capable of massive retaliation as long as it retained enough weapons in working order to permit a few to penetrate one's defenses.

Each nuclear power has based its defensive strategy on its ability to retaliate for any attack. As long as neither side is capable of disarming the other in a first strike, then each side can use the threat of nuclear retaliation to deter the other side from attacking it.

Deterrence obviously does not require that the threatened response be viewed as retaliatory; it simply requires a threat that,

---

of disaster in every 100 flights to NASA's own estimate of one chance in every 100,000 flights' (*New York Times*, June 4 1986, 11). In light of the 1986 Chernobyl and shuttle disasters, it seems unlikely that the optimistic claims about safety were correct.

if carried out, would inflict damage on a scale that no rational opponent could risk. Under a 'counter-force' strategy, a nuclear power would respond to nuclear attack with a strike against its opponent's nuclear forces and command structure, in an attempt to reduce the scale of any subsequent attacks against it. The targets would probably include the opponent's capital city, site of its political command, at least in peace-time, as well as military installations in or near other cities; and so the effect would be massive killing and destruction of a magnitude comparable to what would result from an indiscriminate retaliatory attack. Therefore, the deterrent effect of planning a counter-force second strike would be indistinguishable from that of threatening a purely retaliatory strike; or, if it were not, the counter-force strategy would be supplemented, as it is in fact, by a threat of retaliation against civilian targets. For the underlying strategy is to deter attack by threatening a nuclear response that would kill millions of people. Accordingly, we may treat the counter-force strategy as simply a variation on the strategy of deterrence by threat of retaliation.[3]

Deterrence by the threat of retaliation would be lost if either side achieved a first strike capability, either by increasing the accuracy and penetration of its weapons, or by building an effective missile defense, such as S.D.I. is intended to be. All bets would be off if it seemed that one side were close to achieving the ability to disarm the other. The side facing this threat might be tempted to strike preemptively, and risk of this might prompt the stronger side to preempt. On the other hand, the drifting fallout from a massive nuclear attack, and the 'nuclear winter' that could result, would put every-

---

3 The basic strategic situation is not changed by introducing 'flexible response' or 'war-fighting' strategies that are intended to avoid the risk that any conflict with the opposing superpower will immediately escalate to all-out nuclear war. Bracken argues that these strategies are unrealistic because of command and control problems, and because of the serious risk of escalation in times of major crisis. See *Command and Control*, especially chapter IV. In any event, the threat of escalation would remain the major deterrent to the use of nuclear weapons, and the major incentive to end any war between the two superpowers as soon as possible.

one at risk.[4] In this respect, nuclear weapons are something like exploding blunderbusses, and we might hope that the risk of damaging one's own people constitutes something of a deterrent which would remain even if the threat of retaliation were lost.

For the present, the threat of retaliation is the major deterrent to war between the superpowers. Yet nuclear deterrence seems morally doubtful to many people. Deterrence is not simply a matter of threatening a potential attacker, for it involves threatening an entire people with nuclear attack in order to deter a subgroup of that people, its government or military. And the retaliation that is threatened would destroy many millions of persons, both citizens of the country under attack, and people in neighboring countries who would be subject to the effects of nuclear fallout. Most of these people are innocent, in that they pose no threat themselves. Does the right of self-defense extend this far? Can we justifiably threaten the lives of millions of innocent people in an attempt to save ourselves?

From a simple consequentialist perspective, the answer depends entirely on the relative magnitude of the risks. The threat would be justified, provided it sufficiently reduced the likelihood of war. That is, if there is a sufficient risk of attack in the absence of the threat, and if the threat sufficiently reduces the risk, then the threat can perhaps be justified on the ground that the benefits to us, in the form of an increase in our safety, exceed the cost to others, in the form of the increased risk to them. From this point of view, there is no problem of principle in justifying deterrence. The difficulty would lie mainly in estimating the probability of war under the various possible scenarios.[5]

---

4 Carl Sagan, 'Nuclear War and Climate Catastrophe: Some Policy Implications,' *Foreign Affairs* **62** (1983), 257-92. Also see 'Less Drastic Theory Emerges on Freezing After a Nuclear War,' by James Gleick, *New York Times*, June 22, 1986, 1.

5 A simple consequentialist perspective would seem to imply that nuclear retaliation cannot be justified. But a threat loses its point if it is not credible, and it is not credible if it does not appear sufficiently likely that it will be prosecuted. Therefore, a consequentialist justification of deterrence would have to

This consequentialist perspective can be criticized from at least two directions. On the one hand, some strategic thinkers would limit themselves to considering the risks faced by their own nation; they would insist that the risk to others is not relevant, and that deterrence is justified provided only that it increases the safety, and otherwise serves the interests, of one's own country. This could be called the 'realist' perspective. On the other hand, some moralists would argue, from a deontological perspective, that deterrence is wrong, regardless of its impact on the risk of war, because it involves the intention to use nuclear weapons against innocent persons. If it is wrong to attack innocent persons in time of war, as is implied by just war theory, then deterrence is wrong, for it involves the intention to attack innocent persons if war breaks out.

The essays in this volume mainly address moral issues about deterrence and disarmament, including issues about consequentialist reasoning, just war theory, and so-called realism in international affairs. The one exception is Ian Hacking's essay on the 'form' of scientific knowledge in the nuclear age. Hacking argues that the military financing of scientific research affects the kinds of questions that are asked by scientists, and therefore, the theoretical innovations that are made. The thrust and emphasis of science is altered, and, over time, our scientific knowledge will bear the mark of this. For, ultimately, what we know and how we understand it will be influenced by why we were pushed to discover it.

If Hacking is correct, then the military influence on our societies and cultures goes beyond the obvious. It is not simply that we risk suffering a horrible end, but even if we escape this fate, our understanding will have been shaped in quite subtle ways by the exigencies of the military. The history of science affects the form of our knowledge, for it affects the possibilities that we can consider, and the future paths that we can follow in our attempts to learn about the world. It is clear that the military funding of science leads to ever more sophisticated weapons, but it also has the often unno-

---

imply a justification for a system that makes it credible that there will be retaliation for a nuclear attack, despite the consequentialist objection to retaliation. See below, notes 11 and 12, and the related discussion in the text.

ticed effect that it creates the 'world of mind and technique in which those weapons are devised.'

Noam Chomsky's contribution to the volume is an analysis of deterrence and the barriers to disarmament. Chomsky regards war as inevitable, unless the relations among nations change dramatically. The probability of war is low at any given time, but it is likely that war will erupt at some time in the future. Despite the risk, we should not be optimistic about nuclear disarmament, for, as Chomsky argues, the system of deterrence has deep institutional roots; it is stable in the short term; and it is rational in a short term planning perspective.

The nuclear systems of the superpowers are part of what Chomsky describes as the Cold War system of global management. This is a system which has matured over the past twenty-five years or so, and which enables the United States and the Soviet Union to compete with each other in relative safety. Each side has a sphere of influence within which it pursues strategic and economic advantage, such as access to resources and markets. This pursuit occasionally requires military intervention, as in Afghanistan and Nicaragua, but the system of deterrence permits these interventions to take place with assurance that they will not lead to military confrontation with the other superpower, unless and until one side seeks to gain at the expense of the other. Arms control might be possible in this context, if it were designed to reduce the risk of war, but disarmament would undermine the means by which the powers ensure their superiority. For without mutual nuclear deterrence, neither power could be as confident that the other would not attempt to interfere militarily in its area of influence. The system of deterrence functions to protect the superiority of each superpower within its own realm; it does not merely function to deter unprovoked nuclear attack.

We have seen that deterrence can be criticized even when it is regarded as purely a means of defense. But it will seem still less palatable when it is recognized as part of a method by which the superpowers control their spheres of influence. For it is one thing to threaten people in order to protect one's existence; it is another to threaten people in order to secure one's power over others. This could hardly be seen as benign, except perhaps by a person who thought that one or other of the superpowers used its influence exclusively or mainly for good ends.

Onora O'Neill emphasizes the political nature of strategic discussions. She contends that our discussion of deterrence must aim to be *practical*, unless we refuse to enter a discussion of strategic military affairs at all, or unless we give up attempting to affect military policy. That is, we must aim to reason in ways that will be *action-guiding* and *accessible* for some audience with power to bring about change. O'Neil argues that individual persons, as such, mostly lack sufficient power, for military policies are the policies of nation-states, and only nation-states have the power to change them; consequently, we must address ourselves to nations.

O'Neill urges us not to let ourselves be distracted by skepticism about the agency of nation-states, for they are capable of acting and of processing information. In fact, the system of deterrence *requires* that the nuclear powers have these capabilities, for, in order to deter attack, a country must be able to process the information that reaches its warning and intelligence network, and it must be capable of nuclear retaliation. A more serious form of skepticism involves doubts about the relevance of moral considerations to decisions regarding 'national security.' A 'strict realist,' in O'Neill's usage, is one who denies that national decision making bodies can take moral reasoning into account in decisions regarding peace and war. A strict realist might hold that some form of 'national egoism' is inevitable.

One way to defend a type of 'realism' would be to invoke Hobbes's argument that in a 'state of nature,' where there is no sovereign power sufficient to bring about peaceful government, there is a 'warre of every man against every man,' and it follows that 'nothing can be Unjust.'⁶ If the international arena is an approximation to the 'state of nature,' then one could use a Hobbesian strategy to argue that there can be no injustice in international affairs. But while it is true that there is no world government, or world sovereign power, the international scene is dominated by the two superpowers,

---

6 See Thomas Hobbes, *Leviathan* ed. C.B. Macpherson (Harmondsworth, England: Penguin 1968), chapter 13, 188.

and this means that the situation is not closely analogous to Hobbes's state of nature, in which the many individuals are roughly equal in power; furthermore, there are an international culture, international trade and commerce, and international law, and so the global arena is not closely analogous to Hobbes's state of war, where culture, trade and law are absent, and where 'the life of man [is] solitary, poore, nasty, brutish, and short.'[7] Therefore, it is not at all clear that a Hobbist would be able to defend this form of realism in international affairs.

At least two other doctrines could be regarded as versions of the realism that O'Neill is concerned to address. One is the moral thesis that national decision makers have a duty to take into account only the interests of the nation, when they make decisions regarding national security. A second is a political thesis to the effect that national decision makers will in fact tend to take into account only the interests of the nation; if they tried to do otherwise, they would be replaced or countermanded. However, even if the latter thesis is true, there is no reason to believe that it must remain so. And there is little reason to think that national decision makers have no duties other than a duty to take into account the national interest. If a parent has moral duties that limit the pursuit of the family's interest; if a corporate executive has a duty to see that the corporation is a good corporate citizen, even when doing so does not maximize corporate profits; then a special argument would be needed to show why national decision makers are not obligated to take into account more than just the interests of the nation. O'Neill argues that if we can identify and address the basic premises in national thinking about nuclear strategy, we may be able to bring about a situation where ethical discourse can play a practical role. Most important, she argues, is to change the rhetoric of national and ideological confrontation and supremacy.

James Sterba dismisses the idea that 'national egoism' can replace morality, on the ground that morality is a 'requirement of reason.' Nation-states are not rational if they, or their strategic thinkers, ig-

---

7 Hobbes, *Leviathan*, chapter 13, 183-4 and 186

nore moral considerations when formulating war-making policies. Every nation has some moral values in areas related to security issues, such as views concerning national sovereignty, terrorism, and the like; simple consistency requires that they take moral considerations into account in matters of defense and war. But then, O'Neill would insist, these 'moral starting points' must be addressed, and efforts must be made to show how they commit nation-states to certain policies regarding nuclear strategy. Otherwise, moral discussion of nuclear issues risks failing to be practical.

Sterba discusses just war theory in relation to three approaches to morality: a social contract approach, a utilitarian approach, and an approach which incorporates the moral principle that it is wrong to do evil that good may come of it. Sterba argues in favour of the contract approach, and he argues that it yields a very close approximation to the traditional principles of just war theory. The approach is familiar from John Rawls's work. It involves evaluating moral principles in light of what would be chosen by rational persons who were choosing principles for their society from behind a 'veil of ignorance.'[8] Sterba claims, for instance, that rational persons behind a veil of ignorance would want the international community to accept a prohibition on 'directly intending' harm to innocent persons, either as an end, or a means to some end.

Sterba claims that the contract approach would also favour a 'just threat theory,' which prohibits the threatening of actions that are prohibited by just war theory. It follows that nuclear deterrence by the threat of massive retaliation is morally unacceptable, for it is plain that massive nuclear retaliation would involve harming innocent persons, and Sterba argues that it would involve *directly intending* to harm innocent persons, even, presumably, under a counter-force targeting policy. Now one might question various aspects of Sterba's thesis. It is not clear, for example, that rational persons behind a Rawlsian veil of ignorance would want to prohibit nuclear threats, if it appeared that deterrence offered the best chance of significant-

---

8 John Rawls, *A Theory of Justice* (Cambridge, MA: Belknap Press of Harvard University Press 1971)

ly reducing an otherwise appreciable risk of nuclear war. Be that as it may, Sterba argues that deterrence can be achieved by *bluffing* a massive nuclear retaliation. Unlike threatening, bluffing does not involve intending, so bluffing retaliation does not imply threatening retaliation. Therefore, bluffing retaliation does not violate the principles of just threats. Sterba favours deterrence by *bluff*.

The concept of threat is difficult, but I think, contrary to Sterba, that a threat does *not* require the intention to carry through with the threatened action. Suppose you point a gun at me and say that you will shoot unless I turn over all of my cash. Then you have threatened me, unless you have somehow indicated (perhaps by a wink or a smile) that you have no intention of shooting. If you are bluffing, you will attempt to hide your true intentions; and if you succeed in hiding them, you will have threatened me. For you will have announced an intention to shoot me if I do not turn over my money, and I would not be rational to ignore this in deciding whether to pay up. Similarly, it seems to me, the United States is threatening the Soviet Union with nuclear retaliation, even if its threat is a bluffing threat. A threat to commit violent action, accompanied by the manifest ability and the apparent willingness to carry through, does not cease to be a threat, and become merely a bluff, if the intention to carry through is removed.

A different criticism of Sterba's thesis is suggested by Michael Dummett, who argues that one cannot justify deterrence on the ground that it is mere bluff. Governments cannot bluff nuclear retaliation, for in order to make a bluff credible, a military system would have to be established with the capability of retaliating, and given the existence of such a system, a government could not ensure that the threat would not be carried out. If it tried to guarantee that retaliation would not occur, there would be a continuing risk of discovery by foreign intelligence. And even if the government told itself that it did not intend to retaliate, it would not remain in office indefinitely, and it would not be able to control subsequent governments.

Dummett maintains that deterrence demands an actual intention, even if only a conditional intention, to use nuclear weapons against civilian targets. He concedes that it may be permissible to intend conditionally to do something wrong, provided that one is certain the condition will not be satisfied. But no-one can be certain that the conditions the superpowers have set for the use of nuclear weapons will not be satisfied. In the absence of certainty about this, and given that the use of nuclear weapons against populations would be unconditionally wicked, then it would be wrong to intend to use nuclear weapons in this way under any conditions. And this is so even if the aim of forming the intention would be to make those conditions unlikely, by deterring the other side from using its weapons.

Dummett may be committed to the extreme position of opposing deterrence even if it were the only way to prevent nuclear attack, and even if it were extremely unlikely to fail. For he says that deterrence requires a conditional intention that it would be wrong to have, unless one could be *certain* that the condition would not be satisfied. So it seems that Dummett would have to reject deterrence even if the alternative would be to suffer nuclear attack. In fact, of course, the alternative could be much less serious, and there is a real possibility that deterrence will fail. But the point is that one does not have to be a utilitarian to think that deterrence might be justified if it dramatically increased our safety, and if no safer strategy were available.

Still, it is not the case that the only, or the most likely, alternative to deterrence is nuclear devastation. The worst that the United States could be forced to accept, if it abandoned its nuclear weapons, would probably be Soviet occupation. And Dummett contends that no country can justifiably threaten the obliteration of an entire population in order to avoid occupation by a foreign power.

Alan Gewirth agrees with Dummett that what is fundamentally wrong with deterrence is that it involves threatening, and so intending, to do something wrong, namely, to bomb innocent people. Of course, the underlying intention is presumably to deter nuclear attack, but the intention to deter is the intention to make a credible threat to retaliate, and this entails the intention to use nuclear weapons. Unlike Dummett, Gewirth would concede that deterrence might be defended as the lesser evil, if the threat to bomb innocent people actually prevents the bombing of innocent people, or significantly reduces the probability of nuclear war. However, Gerwirth points out that this justification would depend on assuming the effectiveness, and the unique effectiveness, of deterrence in reducing the risk of war, and both of these assumptions are doubtful. Deterrence creates the risk of war, especially in times of crisis. Moreover, there is a better alternative, namely, disarmament.

Gewirth advocates incremental reciprocal steps toward mutual disarmament. Each side must be aware of the dangers of continuing the *status quo*, and so each must be willing to take steps toward disarmament in accord with its perception of national security. Unfortunately, it is not easy to be optimistic about this strategy in view of past failures of reciprocation. For instance, in 1985, the Soviet Union announced a temporary unilateral ban on testing nuclear weapons, and it invited the United States to follow suit, but the United States did not follow. If the other side does not reciprocate, then, one must ask, is there a duty to disarm unilaterally? If not, why not, given Gewirth's objections to deterrence?

Dummett favours unilateral disarmament because he believes that threatening retaliation is wrong, even if the cost of dismantling the system of deterrence would be Soviet occupation. Gewirth, on the other hand, opposes unilateralism because he believes that it risks Soviet occupation. He believes that unilateral disarmament would jeopardize many important values that would be lost under Soviet rule. It is difficult to evaluate this dispute without knowing whether unilateral disarmament really would create a serious risk of Soviet occupation. What would be put at risk by unilateral disarmament, and how great is the risk of nuclear war under the *status quo*?

Dummett and Gewirth both assume that deterrence requires the intention to use nuclear weapons. Is this true? Deterrence clearly requires that the other side believe that nuclear retaliation is reasonably likely, and given modern methods of intelligence gathering, it requires that retaliation in fact is likely to occur. Moreover, as things now stand, it would be disingenuous for a nation with an elaborate nuclear system of the sort possessed by the United States or the Soviet Union to claim that it does not intend that there be retaliation for a nuclear attack, when it created its nuclear system precisely to make retaliation likely. However, suppose the United States had inherited its system from some other country which previously occupied central North America, and suppose the system had been designed to operate automatically. Then the Soviet Union would still be deterred from attacking, even if the United States had no intentions regarding retaliation. This seems to be a case of deterrence without the intention to retaliate. And the imagined system would still place the Soviet people at risk of nuclear retaliation. Is this not the important point? If the United States is obligated to dismantle its system of deterrence as matters now stand in fact, would it not also be obligated to dismantle the system I have imagined? If so, then the objection to nuclear deterrence cannot turn essentially on the existence of an intention to retaliate.[9]

Russell Hardin contends that the consequences of nuclear war would be so grievous that consequentialist reasoning must dominate our thinking about nuclear deterrence. He argues that the deontological reasoning of Sterba, Dummett, and Gewirth, depends on several misconceptions, and therefore, it cannot adequately deal with the issues involved in evaluating deterrence.

Hardin contends that one cannot simply transfer views about justice in war to views about the deterrence of war. Just war theory would apply to the *use* of a deterrent force, but not to the creation or maintenance of such a force. And even if one believes that it is wrong to do evil that good may come of it, one should not conclude from this that deterrence is wrong, for deterrence does not involve doing evil; it simply involves establishing and maintaining a deterrent force. Furthermore, since a credible deterrent depends on the existence of a military institution designed to retaliate, one cannot separate the evaluation of deterrence and the evaluation of retaliation. In evaluating deterrence, one must attempt to determine whether a nation would be justified in creating the institutions of deterrence. The intention relevant to assessing this choice, if intentions are relevant at all, would be the nation's intention in adopting the strategy of deterrence, viz., the intention to deter at the risk of retaliating, not the intention to retaliate. Hardin concedes that nuclear retaliation would be wrong, if it were not threatened, but

---

9 Gerald Dworkin imagines various types of deterrence with various intentions. See his 'Nuclear Intentions,' *Ethics* **95** (1985), 445-60.

he claims it does not follow that deterrence is wrong. On the contrary, deterrence may well be justified even though unthreatened retaliation would not be justified.[10]

A direct consequentialist approach would imply that nuclear retaliation would be wrong, regardless of whether it has been threatened. For if there has been a nuclear attack, nothing would be gained by nuclear retaliation, and much damage would obviously be done.[11] Therefore, Hardin's view should perhaps be that deterrence can be justified even if retaliation could not be justified. This thesis stands in stark contrast to the view of several other contributors to the volume who maintain that if it would be wrong to do something, then, with minor qualifications, it would be wrong to threaten to do it.

Now, if there is a link of this sort between the wrongness of doing and the wrongness of threatening, it cannot be a matter of logic, for the consequentialist view is not self-contradictory. Some contributors defend the link as a matter of moral principle, arguing that threatening involves intending, and it is wrong to intend to do something that it would be wrong to do. I have already argued that a threat does not require the intention to carry through. Beyond this, the complexities of the nuclear confrontation between the superpowers illustrate how different the action of threatening can be, both in its intentions and its effects, from the action of doing the threatened thing. Perhaps it is true that threatening entails the conditional intention to carry through. Even so, the intentions with which an agent would make a threat would ordinarily be different in significant ways from the intentions with which an agent would actually do a threatened thing, and the effects of threatening would ordinarily be quite different from the effects of carrying through. One would have to ignore these differences, in order to hold that

---

10 A similar thesis is quite plausible in the theory of punishment.

11 Unlike a purely retaliatory second-strike, a counter-force attack might have the advantage for a nation under attack of reducing the damage that would be caused by any subsequent attacks on it. A consequentialist would have to weigh the damage which is certain to be caused by a counter-force attack against this possible benefit.

David Copp

it would be wrong to threaten to do what it would be wrong to do (even if one admitted minor exceptions to this principle), yet these are just the kinds of difference that ordinarily lead us to evaluate actions differently, regardless of whether we are consequentialists or deontologists.

The central question still seems to be whether it can be right for a nation to establish a system of deterrence, and thereby create a threat of retaliation, given the risk that it will commit an evil act as a consequence.[12] However, one of Hardin's central points is that modern systems of deterrence largely remove retaliation from the control of political or military leaders, so that nuclear retaliation by the United States or the Soviet Union would be more in the nature of a reflex, rather than an action. Therefore, in effect, even if we believe that the wrongness of performing an action implies the wrongness of threatening to perform it, and even if we agree that an act of retaliation would be wrong, it does not follow that deterrence is wrong, for the threat created by deterrence is not the threat of an *act* of retaliation. Dummett and Gewirth would insist that a nation which created a military system designed to retaliate would be unable to deny having an intention to retaliate if attacked; but if Hardin is correct, then the intention should instead be described as an intention that there *be* retaliation for an attack, for the systems of deterrence are designed to make retaliation virtually an involuntary spasm. Perhaps then the question we should be asking is whether it can be right for a nation to establish a system of deterrence, and thereby create a threat of retaliation, given the risk of causing an unparalleled disaster?

Jan Narveson agrees with Hardin that deterrence can in principle be justified, but he argues from the right of self-defense. He claims that self-defense permits a nation which is threatened with nuclear attack to use deterrence as a defense. A nation can defend its independence, its political system, and its values, even at the cost of threatening innocent people, and even if the result is to increase the risk to innocent people. If deterrence were the only

---

12 Derek Parfit asks, 'Could it be right to cause oneself to act wrongly?' See *Reasons and Persons* (Oxford: Clarendon Press 1984), 37-40.

method by which a nation could defend itself against nuclear attack, then, he maintains, it would be absurd to ask that it not attempt to deter attack.

However, the Soviet Union and the United States both maintain that they are only interested in defense. If this were true, it would be difficult to understand why there is an arms race. For Narveson argues that a nation only interested in defense would want to stay behind in the arms race, both to avoid provoking the opponent and to make it clear that it is not trying to achieve a first strike capability.[13] If both parties were only interested in defense, the arms race should not exist, for each would seek to be behind the other; at least, they would favour weapons, such as cruise missiles, that are not suitable for a first strike, and they would disarm to the point where they have no more weapons than is strictly necessary for deterrence. Of course, Chomsky contends that the superpowers are not simply interested in defense. Rather, they have interests that make the system of nuclear deterrence and competition rational in the short run.

One might be tempted to despair of change, but Steven Patten challenges us not to do so. He argues that ordinary citizens of the democratic nuclear states have the responsibility to exercise their political power in an effort to change the politics underlying the arms race, so that arms control or disarmament will become possible. It can hardly be denied that citizens of representative democracies, such as the United States and the NATO allies which are also involved in deterrence strategy, have some power to influence their governments through the political system. Nevertheless, there is a familiar kind of 'realistic' excuse for political inaction, especially in times of war; it consists in the claim that democratic control in wartime is of limited effect, both because political power becomes more distant from ordinary citizens, and because the political leaders control and distort information to a greater degree than in peacetime.

---

13 Russell Hardin argues that a nation interested only in defense might continue to develop new systems out of fear that the other side will overtake it technologically and achieve a first strike capability.

Patten claims that an argument of this sort could not reasonably be used to excuse ordinary citizens from responsibility for their countries' involvement in deterrence strategy. It is not simply that deterrence involves a conditional intention to do something indefensible; but the strategy of deterrence is a matter of public knowledge; the citizens of democracies have the power, as individuals, to influence change; and there is the opportunity to exercise this power right now, while there will not be the opportunity once a war begins. These considerations constitute a strong case for individual responsibility. Even one who sees no reasonable alternative to deterrence, but sees the need for arms control, must accept the responsibility, Patten says, to attempt to 'influence change' by 'appropriate political means.'

It seems unlikely that serious arms control or arms reduction will become a priority for the superpowers, as long as the risk of war seems minimal to them, and as long as they continue to be able to persuade people to accept their nuclear programmes on the basis of rhetoric which associates nuclear pre-eminence with national superiority and security. Disarmament seems even less likely, unless the superpowers come to believe that they would be able to retain their pre-eminence under a non-nuclear regime, or unless the risk of war becomes intolerable, or unless there is a dramatic change in the political pressures they face. Ordinary citizens may be able to affect the political variable in all of this, so if we believe that nuclear disarmament, or arms reduction, would be better than the present balance of escalating threats, then the issue of personal responsibility raised by Steven Patten becomes central.

A great number of issues still needs to be investigated before we can be content that we fully understand the moral and strategic issues posed by the nuclear arms race and nuclear deterrence. Foremost are issues about the risks of the various strategies. Of course, we all want to know how to avoid a nuclear holocaust while at the same time serving our other values as much as possible, but every strategy is risky. On the one hand, deterrence risks nuclear disaster, for, as Bracken argues, there is a significant risk of war in times of crisis and military alert. Perhaps this danger could be reduced by arms control agreements: for example, to reduce nuclear arsenals to the minimum required for deterrence, and to outlaw weapons capable of reaching their targets from their bases in less than, say, thirty minutes. Yet even with agreement on arms control, mutual deterrence will always be accompanied by an unknown but appreciable chance of war, especially if the major powers continue to risk crises by competing for marginal advantage behind their nuclear screens. On the other hand, mutual disarmament would be unstable, unless it could be policed or supervised adequately, for there would always be the risk that one party would rearm, with a result that would be equivalent to unilateral disarmament; and we can only speculate about the risks of unilateral nuclear disarmament. What is the chance that the disarming power would lose its political institutions? What is the chance that it would be forced to pay tribute? What is the chance of foreign occupation? What is the chance of severe repression of its citizens? How can we evaluate these risks, when their magnitude is unknown, and compare them with the risk of nuclear war under a policy of deterrence, when the magnitude of this risk is also unknown?

The difficulties in estimating the hazards are partly empirical, for we need to know the likelihood of the various outcomes; but they are partly philosophical as well, for a comparison of risks requires an assessment of the relative badness of the outcomes. Just how bad would it be for a state to lose sovereignty or superiority? What is the value of having a separate state to shelter each group that would prefer a sovereign status? What is the value of national self-determination? Would it be worse to lose sovereignty to a foreign state than to an international government? If so, why? Related issues become important when we think about self-defense. Does every state have the right, or even the duty, to protect its sovereignty?

I think that issues about the risks of the various strategies are paramount, not because of a general commitment to a direct consequentialism, but because I am persuaded that nuclear war would be such a catastrophe that consequentialist considerations must dominate our thinking about nuclear war and deterrence. This is Hardin's contention, and it is one that must be evaluated quite apart from our general opinion of the dispute between consequentialism and deontology. Every plausible moral view gives some priority to the avoidance of harm and the risk of harm, and the issue raised by Hardin's contention is whether nuclear strategies are associated with risks of such serious harm that all other moral concerns are irrelevant, or at best marginal, to their evaluation.

It is true nevertheless that our beliefs about deterrence can be influenced quite powerfully by non-consequentialist considerations, and a number of these require further attention. Here is a short, and by no means exhaustive, list of outstanding problems. First, what is the relevance of just war theory to the evaluation of deterrence? Second, can well defined distinctions be drawn between choosing a strategy and choosing an action, and between choosing an action and choosing an outcome? What is the relevance of these distinctions to our evaluation of choices, and specifically to our evaluation of deterrence, if the choice of deterrence is regarded as the choice of a strategy? Third, what is the relation between a deterrence strategy and threatening, and between threatening something and intending to do it? What implication does the wrongness of doing something have for the wrongness of threatening to do it? Or, what implication does the justifiability of threatening to do something have for the justifiability of doing it?[14]

I shall conclude by mentioning issues raised by the various doctrines which contributors to this volume have called 'realistic.' On the one hand are foundational issues concerning morality and international affairs. If a Hobbesian approach can be defended, then, as we might say, the preconditions for moral judgement do not obtain in the international arena, and so there is perhaps a serious misconception involved in any moralization of debates about war and

---

14 Related questions arise in the theory of punishment. See Thomas Hurka, 'Rights and Capital Punishment,' *Dialogue* **21** (1982); and Warren Quinn, 'The Right to Threaten and the Right to Punish,' *Philosophy and Public Affairs* **14** (1985), 327-73. Quinn argues for the two part thesis that 'the right to establish a genuine threat is prior to the right to punish.' That is, first, 'the right to set up the threat can be established without first raising the question of the right to punish and, second, ... the right to the threat implies the right to punish' (360). If this were true in general, then if a system of deterrence could be justified, say on grounds of the right of self-defense, the right to nuclear retaliation would follow. Quinn tries to avoid this conclusion (366, n. 46), but his strategy for doing so commits him to giving up the second part of his thesis.

defense policy. On the other hand are issues about individual responsibility. Even if a principled opposition to the nuclear policies of our governments is justified, we still must decide what we are obligated to do as individuals, given the great number of injustices and hazards that there are in our world, and given our need to carry on with our personal lives. In what ways should our answer depend on our evaluation of the risks involved in nuclear strategies and on our assessment of the chance that our personal contribution will make a difference to the outcome? All of these issues, and many others, require further attention.[15]

Revised July, 1986

---

15 I would like to thank Gerald Dworkin, Russell Hardin and Kai Nielsen for helpful comments and criticisms.

CANADIAN JOURNAL OF PHILOSOPHY
Supplementary Volume 12

The Rationality
of Collective Suicide

NOAM CHOMSKY
Massachusetts Institute of Technology
Cambridge, MA 02139
U.S.A.

Surveying the historical record, we can find examples of societies so organized that they drifted towards catastrophe with a certain inevitability, systematically avoiding steps that could have changed this course. Our own society is an example, except that in this case the catastrophe that lies ahead involves national and perhaps global suicide. It is hardly unrealistic to surmise that we may be entering the terminal phase of history.

The course that we pursue is deeply rooted in our social institutions and relatively independent of the choice of individuals who happen to fill institutional roles in the political or economic system. Furthermore, the steps taken towards destruction have a certain short-term rationality within the framework of existing institutions and the kind of planning they engender. Such planning is largely a matter of short-term calculation of gain; this is entirely natural in competitive societies, where those who contemplate the longer term are unlikely to be in the competition when it arrives, and this natural framework of planning carries over to the political system that is, overwhelmingly, under the influence of those who own and manage the private society. The unfortunate conclusion is that while the population at large may, and certainly should do what it can to avert the most dangerous and immediate threats to survival, such efforts at best delay the inevitable as long as the institutional structures remain in place. These are facts that we must come to understand if we hope to end the arms race before it ends us.

I would like to suggest a number of theses bearing on these questions that I believe are plausible and well-substantiated in the historical and documentary record, making no attempt to establish them here,[1] but giving a few illustrations of the kind of evidence that supports them. I will concentrate on the West, specifically the United States, apart from a few remarks on the superpower enemy and the sources of its conduct, which reinforce the tendencies with which I will be concerned. This narrowing of perspective introduces certain distortions: thus, I will say nothing about the conflicts among the industrial capitalist states, which are of increasing significance in the contemporary world. Nevertheless, this focus is justified for two reasons: (1) the power of the United States since World War II, somewhat waning in relative terms (as is that of the U.S.S.R.) but nevertheless overwhelming, with few if any historical precedents: (2) the fact that it is this factor in the global complex that we may hope to influence directly and modify.

In practice, the general public has little influence on the formation of state policy through the political system. One recent illustration is the nuclear freeze campaign, which gained the support of some three-fourths of the population – a remarkably high figure

---

1 For documentation and more extensive discussion, see my *Turning the Tide* (Boston, MA: South End Press 1985) and 'The Drift Towards Global War,' *Studies in Political Economy* (Canada) 1985.

on such an issue — and certainly aimed at feasible objectives, since a nuclear freeze was advocated by the superpower enemy and endorsed overwhelmingly at the United Nations, over U.S. opposition. Furthermore, there is little doubt that a comprehensive ban on testing and development of nuclear weapons, particularly if combined with a ban on testing and development of missiles and other advanced systems of destruction, would considerably enhance the prospects for survival. Such an agreement would, for example, significantly reduce the likelihood of a first strike while retaining deterrent capacity, since a first strike requires assurance of reliability, hence regular testing, while the deterrent does not. It would therefore provide a cost-free and far more reliable alternative to current programs of extraordinary expense and scale that are allegedly directed to this end, e.g., Reagan's Strategic Defense Initiative (SDI), actually a thinly-disguised effort to develop a credible first-strike capacity.

All of this is quite irrelevant to state policy. Thus, in the 1984 presidential campaign the issue of a nuclear freeze barely arose, apart from a few meaningless rhetorical flourishes. Similarly, there was no positive response in the political system when the U.S.S.R. inaugurated a unilateral test ban on August 6, 1985, and the press was silent except to dismiss the initiative with scorn on the grounds that it 'would ring hollow even if it had not come immediately after an energetic series of Soviet test explosions' (the *New York Times*, faithfully reiterating government lies; there had been no acceleration in Soviet testing, which was lower in 1985 than in the previous year and lower than U.S. testing for 1985, while in overall tests the U.S. remains far ahead).[2] Such examples illustrate the fact that the sources of the race toward destruction are deep, sufficiently so as to render irrelevant public opinion and the feasibility of steps that would clearly enhance national security. The case is by no means unique. In the early 1950s the security of the United States had reached quite a remarkable level, by any historical measure. The U.S. had no threatening neighbors and controlled both oceans as well as large

---

2 Jeffrey S. Duncan, 'How Many Soviet Tests Make a Flurry?' *Bulletin of the Atomic Scientists*, October 1985, 8-9

parts of Eurasia and other regions. The only potential threat to its security was the development of intercontinental missiles with highly destructive (hydrogen bomb) warheads. Yet the record reveals no effort to try to impede the development of the only serious potential threat to security, though this might well have been possible at the time. Or consider the fact that in 1964 the public overwhelmingly voted against escalation of the Vietnam war, returning to power the fervent advocate of this position who was, at that very time, planning the escalation explicitly rejected at the polls. Or the fact that through the Reagan years, the public has overwhelmingly favored cuts in military spending over cuts in social programs, and indeed has expressed willingness to increase taxes to fund the latter, while Congress, responding to different voices, follows the course laid out by Administration planners under the guise of a public mood of 'conservatism' — a term which, in its contemporary Orwellian sense, refers to a form of reactionary jingoism based on commitment to increasing the power of the state and its interference in public life and overseas adventures, protecting it from scrutiny, and diminishing individual civil liberties. There are numerous other examples that illustrate the irrelevance to policy of public opinion or considerations of national security.

As every serious study shows, in the domain of international relations and security policy, the basic framework is fixed in terms of the perceived interest of groups that can mobilize the resources to shape affairs of state. In the U.S., that means an elite consisting of major corporations concerned with international business operations and advanced technology, investment banks, law firms that cater to corporate interests, and so on. They staff the executive branch of the government, produce the planning studies, and in general provide the domestic institutional basis that sets the parameters for major national policy — what they define as the 'national interest,' meaning the parochial interest of the wealthy and privileged, the owners and managers of the domestic society. Since the same groups play a dominant role in the ideological institutions — the mass media, the schools, and the universities — these topics are rarely addressed in the mainstream, and people use such terms as 'national interest' as if they were something other than a device of mystification and delusion.

One illustration of the collusion of scholarship in this system of indoctrination is that the question of corporate influence over foreign policy, which is of course extensive if not overwhelming, is under a virtual taboo in mainstream scholarship. A rare study of the topic found that within what the author calls 'the respectable literature on international relations and U.S. foreign policy,' less than 5 percent of 200 books reviewed 'granted even passing mention to the role of corporations in America foreign relations... There is virtually no acknowledgement in standard works within the field of international relations and foreign policy of the existence and influence of corporations.' The author notes that outside 'the respectable literature,' the topic is addressed; in particular, by business school professors and corporate executives, who give the topic the prominence it deserves; they are addressing the real rulers and have no need to conceal the obvious. His use of the term 'respectable literature' with reference to that part devoted to concealing the obvious (he agrees that the influence is obvious and expresses much perplexity that it is unrecognized) is not ironic, but a further reflection of the power of the system of indoctrination.[3]

Much of the population shares the insights of the business school professors and corporation executives. Thus, fully half the population believe that the government is run 'by a few big interests looking out for themselves,'[4] a view that is − quite absurdly − castigated as 'Marxist' or 'left-wing,' hardly the term that applies to half the population; the question is one of fact rather than ideology in any event. This is very likely one reason why close to half the population does not even bother to go to the polls, while for most of the rest, issues are largely irrelevant. In the 1984 presidential election, for example, Reagan obtained about 30 percent of the potential vote, voters opposed Reagan on issues by about 3 to 2, and 1 percent of

---

3 Dennis Ray, 'Corporations and American Foreign Relations,' *The Multinational Corporation, Annals of the American Academy of Political and Social Science*, Sept. 1972; for further discussion, see my *Towards a New Cold War* (New York: Pantheon Books 1982), 103f.

4 Adam Clymer, *New York Times*, November 11 1984

the electorate chose him because they considered him a 'real conservative.' This is what is called a 'landslide' in U.S. political commentary. Close investigation of American political history, the internal documentary record, and most importantly, the evolving historical record, tends to support these perceptions quite broadly. When we speak of the interests that shape security policy, we are primarily considering major business interests. This being so, it is not at all surprising that public attitudes are irrelevant, as the nuclear freeze campaign illustrates.

Assuming this to be correct, as I believe it is, is there any point even in proceeding further? That is, must we passively watch while decisions are made elsewhere? Surely not, for several reasons. First, the facts of political life are not graven in stone. It is possible that popular organizations might develop that enter the political system as competitors, though the task is far from easy. The U.S. sociopolitical system is designed to ensure that isolated individuals confront concentrated private power alone, without any 'secondary organizations' (such as politically-oriented labor unions) that would enable them to pool their limited resources to gain information, formulate ideas and plans, put them forth in the political arena, and work to implement them. The result is that the political system, particularly at the level of the national executive, is largely free of public influence or control. To counter this tendency is an extremely difficult matter, given the actual distribution of resources, but it is not an impossibility. Furthermore, there are other ways to influence policy, outside of the political system. Even a totalitarian state must ensure public acquiescence in national policy, and violence often will not suffice. In his memoirs, Albert Speer observes that Nazi Germany was never able to carry out mass mobilization for the war effort to the extent that was possible in England and the United States, because the leadership felt it necessary to conciliate the public, which they could not trust; this set back the German war effort by several years, he maintains; if he is correct, this possibly caused Germany to lose the war. In a state that is more limited in its capacity to employ violence against its own citizens, the range of measures available to influence public policy is far broader, even outside of the formal political system: a highly significant fact. And finally, there is no reason to suppose that the system of concentrated private power and the exclusion of crucial social decisions – such as investment decisions – from the arena of democratic politics represents the end of history; though it may, in my view, unless it is soon modified.

Short-term corporate planning, which sets the framework for state managers, is not concerned with long-term survival but rather with ensuring the privilege and power of those who dominate the domestic economy and the success of the institutions they control. In international affairs, the central concerns are the climate for business operations overseas and access to human and material resources. While these projects may be pursued in somewhat different ways, with varying nuances, they remain the core of the 'national interest' whoever holds political power. Matters could hardly be very different in a capitalist democracy, since satisfaction of the perceived needs of those who control investment is a prerequisite for the satisfaction, however marginally, of any other needs; this is what Cohen and Rogers call the 'demand constraint,' in a perceptive analysis.[5] It is not surprising, then, that U.S. aid to other countries correlates closely with the climate for U.S. business operations, as shown in a study by Edward S. Herman of the Wharton School.[6] This is a fact that underlies the strong secondary correlation between U.S. aid and violations of human rights observed in several studies, for obvious reasons. Such matters as these are critical for understanding the evolution of national policy.

In a major scholarly analysis of U.S. security policy based in part on recently released documents, Melvyn Leffler observes that as World War II ended, 'the American conception of national security... included a strategic sphere of influence within the Western Hemisphere [from which others, crucially Europe, were to be excluded, and where "strategic influence" includes economic control], domination of the Atlantic and Pacific oceans, an extensive system of outlying bases to enlarge the strategic frontier and project Ameri-

---

5 Joshua Cohen and Joel Rogers, *On Democracy* (New York: Penguin Books 1983)

6 See Chomsky and E.S. Herman, *Political Economy of Human Rights* (Boston, MA: South End Press 1979), I, 42f.

can power, an even more extensive system of transit rights to facilitate the conversion of commercial air bases to military use, access
to the resources and markets of most of Eurasia, denial of these
resources to a prospective enemy, and the maintenance of nuclear
superiority.' This strategic conception helps explain 'the dynamics
of the Cold War after 1948.' Leffler comments.[7]

In internal documents, planners minced no words about the imperatives of U.S. policy. George Kennan, who headed the Policy
Planning Staff of the State Department until 1950, explained in his
typically acute and forthright manner that U.S. policy must be
designed to maintain the 'disparity' between the United States,
which controlled 50 percent of the world's wealth, and other nations, which feel 'envy and resentment.' To achieve this end, we
must 'dispense with all sentimentality and day-dreaming' and such
'vague' and 'unreal objectives' as 'human rights, the raising of the
living standards, and democratization.' We can ill afford 'the luxu-
ry of altruism and world-benefaction' and will 'have to deal in
straight power concepts.' In Latin American, for example, we must
be concerned with 'the protection of our [sic] raw materials,' and
in so doing, 'we should not hesitate before police repression by the
local government' if necessary to achieve our ends.[8] This is a voice
from the humane, dovish end of the planning spectrum. The historical record shows that these precepts have been closely followed,
as they had been, in a narrower sphere, in earlier years.

The Soviet Union plainly has posed a barrier to the plans to gain
'access to the resources and markets of most of Eurasia' and to ensure 'the protection of our raw materials' in parts of the Third World.
But it is worth emphasizing that it was not considered a military
threat in the early years. U.S. planners expected that the U.S.S.R.

---

7   Melvyn Leffler, 'The American Conception of National Security and the Be-
    ginnings of the Cold War, 1945-48,' *American Historical Review* **89** (1984),
    346-400

8   PPS 23, Feb. 1948; 1950, briefing to Latin American Ambassadors. Kennan's
    remarks cited from the Top Secret PPS 23 referred specifically to Asia, but
    the U.S. is a global power, and the same conceptions apply worldwide, as
    he made clear, for example, in the cited remarks on Latin America.

would adopt a defensive stance, and that it would be many years before it could pose a military threat to Western Europe, let alone the United States. The problem facing Western Europe was not Soviet invasion, always considered a remote contingency, but rather, as the CIA concluded in 1947, 'the possibility of economic collapse in Western Europe and the consequent accession to power of Communist elements.' This was one of the reasons for the Marshall plan, also motivated by the needs of U.S. industry for export markets and overseas investment. A closely related U.S. postwar project was the destruction of the anti-fascist resistance in much of the world, often in favor of Nazi and fascist collaborators, a policy pursued quite systematically in southern Europe and much of Asia. Throughout the postwar period, the U.S. has regularly followed Kennan's early advice, supporting terrorist regimes and blocking or overturning democratic governments when this was deemed necessary to ensure the rights of U.S. investors and their local clients.

In each case, U.S. intervention was presented to the public in defensive terms, ultimately as a defense against the 'monolithic and ruthless conspiracy' (John F. Kennedy) centered in Moscow, which is determined to thwart our benevolence and take over the world (Reagan's Evil Empire). The typical event of the Cold War is intervention in this framework: Greece, Iran, Guatemala, Indochina, Cuba, the Dominican Republic, El Salvador, Nicaragua, etc. In the narrower domains of the second superpower, much the same is true. The typical event of the Cold War in the Soviet sphere is intervention in East Berlin, Hungary, Czechoslovakia, Afghanistan, always in alleged defense against American threats.

There is no doubt that each superpower would prefer that the other disappear, but each has come to realize long ago that this is impossible short of mutual annihilation, though the U.S. did adopt a 'rollback strategy' in the early years and one hears echoes of it among the more fanatic 'conservatives' today. The superpowers have therefore settled into an uneasy tacit partnership in global management, in which each appeals to the threat of the Great Satan to mobilize the domestic population (as even a totalitarian state must do) and sometimes recalcitrant allies in support of violent and destructive acts undertaken in the interests of domestic ruling groups: in the U.S., the business-based nexus that sets the basic framework for state planning; in the U.S.S.R., the military-bureaucratic elite that rules directly. This is the essence of the Cold War system, a system of confrontation and tacit cooperation, with considerable functional utility to the state managers on both sides, one reason why it persists. Of course, the system is highly unstable, and sooner or later will blow up, as has come all too close to happening many times in the past; but that is the kind of long-term consideration that rarely enters into planning decisions.

The regular need for subversion and violent intervention provides one major reason for the arms race. An intimidating posture is necessary to ensure that intervention can proceed with impunity under the 'nuclear umbrella.' As President Carter's Secretary of Defense, Howard Brown, explained to Congress: with our strategic capabilities in place, 'our other forces become meaningful instruments of military and political power.' Much earlier, Kennan's successor Paul Nitze had observed that Soviet advances in weaponry might 'impose greater caution in our cold war policies' because of fear of nuclear war (NSC-141, 1953). Nitze therefore advocated civil defense, noting that this would also facilitate a first strike. The same two arguments carry over to the current Star Wars fantasies, but more importantly, to maintenance of a sufficiently intimidating posture so that our 'cold war policies' of intervention and subversion can be carried out without undue concern. Much the same is true of our superpower rival-partner.

One might imagine that the superpowers could agree to avoid the extraordinary dangers of the arms race simply by establishing the tacit system of joint global management formally, thus avoiding the need for an ever-more intimidating posture to ensure freedom of action in their cold war policies. In fact, there have been steps in this direction: what we call 'detente' and 'arms control.' They are of very limited efficacy. As American planners correctly perceive, 'American willingness to reach a long-term accommodation during the 1970s was aborted as a consequence of the Soviets' deep-seated impulses never to flag in the quest for marginal advantages' (in particular, by offering support to victims of U.S. intervention); furthermore, 'Almost inevitably the Polands and Afghanistans lead to confrontation, even if the Angolas and Nicaraguas do not'[9] – though they may, if the U.S.S.R. seeks to impede the U.S. attack against

Nicaragua or if the U.S. undertakes direct support for the South African-backed rebels in Angola. Similarly, Soviet planners correctly recognize the deep-seated impulses of the U.S. never to flag in the quest for marginal advantages, over a much broader domain in fact, and perceive that the Vietnams, Cubas, Lebanons, Nicaraguas, etc., regularly lead to confrontation. We may put aside, as irrelevant here, the self-serving images of benevolent intent concocted on each side, e.g., Schlesinger's vision of the United States as dedicated to 'the promise of Wilsonian idealism, of the Four Freedoms, of collective security and of the peaceful resolution of disputes through new international institutions,' a picture that has as much merit as the constructions of the commissars on the other side.

Furthermore, the Cold War system demands a Great Satan. The basic point was made long ago by the American satirist H.L. Mencken, who observed that 'The whole aim of practical politics is to keep the populace alarmed (and hence clamorous to be led to safety) by menacing it with an endless series of hobgoblins, all of them imaginary,' a lesson that leaders of both superpowers, and many others, understand very well. The development of an ever-more threatening military system is in part a device of social control, in two crucial respects: (1) in mobilizing the population in support of national policy in fear of the Great Satan about to destroy us; (2) in removing the public still further from effective participation in formation of public policy, which must be designed under strict secrecy and with only narrow elite participation, given the awesome character of the weapons deployed.

As a result, detente and arms control agreements are only marginal elements of the system of global management, and will remain so. The Cold War system must be based on confrontation, intimidation, and threat.

These natural developments are further enhanced by crucial domestic factors. World War II taught the Keynesian lesson that massive state expenditures can serve to maintain the viability of the state capitalist economy, and that there is no real alternative. The lesson

---

9   James Schlesinger, 'The Eagle and the Bear,' *Foreign Affairs* **63** (1985), 937-961

was learned well by the corporate managers who flocked to Washington to run the state-controlled national economy during the war. The lesson was particularly dramatic in the light of the failure of the much more limited government intervention under the New Deal. In the early postwar period, it was recognized that similar devices would be necessary to avoid a return to serious, perhaps lethal depression. The Pentagon system quickly became the technique by which the state mobilizes popular resources to subsidize advanced sectors of industry. There are good reasons, which business elites have articulated quite clearly, why these methods are to be preferred over other devices of public subsidy for 'private' enterprise. It is not a matter of technical economics; any good economist can point to more efficient methods of state intervention. But as business circles explained, these alternatives tend to threaten established power and privilege; they create new constituencies, redistribute income, engage segments of the population in social planning, and in other ways are entirely unacceptable. In contrast, a state-guaranteed market for high technology waste production (armaments) is ideal from the point of view of the businessman. It does not interfere with management prerogatives but in fact is simply a form of forced public investment, a public subsidy to advanced sectors of industry. The beneficiaries are not only, or even primarily, military industry. Thus, the development of computers was subsidized through the military system, as are 'fifth generation' computers today, and the same is true of a wide range of other advanced technologies. SDI expenditures, for example, correspond closely to those of Japan's state-coordinated industrial system, which the U.S. is unable to duplicate directly, for a variety of social and historical reasons.

Again we can see clearly why public attitudes and feasibility of measures that would enhance the prospects for survival do not influence national security planning. They are, strictly speaking, irrelevant to its real concerns: maintaining an intimidating posture to ensure that intervention and subversion can proceed without interference, and maintaining the system of public subsidy, private profit, by which the mass of the population is compelled to invest for the benefit of the elite elements that dominate the economy and the state as well.

The very different social system of our tacit partner in global repression yields rather similar results. The rulers of the Soviet Union control the internal empire and the satellites by the threat of violence, and at least latent, sometimes actual violence is required to ensure general obedience at home more broadly. It is, therefore, entirely natural that they should assign a priority to the military and security system. Apart from that, it must be recognized that their defensive rhetoric is not wholly contrived. No Russian government, even if run by liberal democrats, would permit the East European satellites to escape their grip as long as a heavily-armed Western Germany is part of a hostile military alliance, for perfectly obvious historical and security reasons. The refusal of the U.S. even to consider Central European disengagement – e.g., Stalin's offer, how seriously intended we cannot know, to permit free elections in a unified Germany in 1952 if the state (sure to be Western-oriented) were excluded from the NATO alliance – thus has a fateful significance.

In these terms, we can come to understand what would otherwise appear a rather puzzling fact: that military systems are often devised with no military purpose. Thus, there is much concern over the fact that U.S. 'defense' spending appears to be highly inefficient from a strictly military point of view. NATO expenditures are consistently higher than those of the Warsaw Pact, even by the CIA measures that are designed to inflate Soviet spending (as is well-known), but there are constant complaints that U.S. military technology is too complicated to work, that contractors vastly overcharge, that we are 'behind' (whatever that is supposed to mean) in this and that military category. All perhaps true, but of little relevance. Or, consider the fact that Reagan's SDI was announced with no prior consultation with his Pentagon advisors: a fact revealed by knowledgeable commentators on both sides of the Atlantic.[10] This will appear entirely natural, when one understands that its purpose is not primarily military, whatever may be the private

---

10 See Wayland Kennet, spokesman on foreign affairs and defense for the Social Democrat Party in the British House of Lords, *Bulletin of the Atomic Scientists*, September 1985, 7-11; George Ball, *New York Review*, April 11 1985.

fantasies of the titular leadership assigned the task of presenting these ideas to the public. Rather, the primary purposes are to enhance the program of state subsidy to 'private' enterprise devised by the fanatic Keynesians of the Reagan Administration, and to press the highly functional arms race forward another few steps, enhancing confrontation with the Great Satan. We can also comprehend why essentially the same programs are devised at opposite ends of the political spectrum – e.g., Kennedy 'liberalism' and Reaganite 'conservatism' – when it is recognized that public resources must be mobilized through the state to 'get the country moving again' by subsidizing advanced industry, and that a new wave of foreign terror is required to ensure 'stability' and 'order' in our vast domains, with intervention and subversion (or in Kennedy's case, outright aggression, as in the bombing of South Vietnam from 1962) unchallenged under the nuclear umbrella. Much else also falls into place, when the basic principles of state policy are understood.

From these real world considerations one can understand U.S. policies on arms control and related matters. The comparative advantage of the U.S. is no longer in production, but rather, technological innovation. The U.S. will therefore welcome reduction of nuclear armaments – a matter of minor importance, since a tiny fraction of existing arsenals would cause unacceptable destruction – as long as two conditions are satisfied: an intimidating posture permitting the free exercise of subversion and intervention must remain in place, and the Pentagon system of forced investment for the benefit of high technology industry must not be challenged. Star Wars combined with build-down is a natural U.S. stance in the light of the policy imperatives. Given the character of 'strategic theory,' appropriate strategic doctrines can be designed at will, as needed. Meanwhile debates over the feasibility of missile defense, the choice of missiles, etc., will proceed along their largely irrelevant paths, while the race towards destruction goes on.

One might ask why U.S. planners do not renounce the most dangerous armaments, such as nuclear weapons, or why they do not approach the public directly and explain the exigencies of the state capitalist economy. The second question is easily answered. It is a rare politician who will approach the public with the news that the poor must bribe the rich to invest for the 'health' of the economy.

Even in a totalitarian state, such measures are typically cloaked in rhetorical poses of confrontation with Evil Empires and the need for sacrifice to survive. As for the first, the idea is impossible for both technical and political reasons. Thus, the SDI program of high technology subsidy relies crucially on advanced nuclear devices, and it would be quite a feat to convince the public that they must sacrifice in the interest of 'defense' against a mighty enemy while refraining from developing the most powerful military arsenal for protection from this threat.

The defensive rhetoric is not entirely without substance; propaganda rarely is. Each superpower is indeed threatening, and each has an ample record of atrocities and barbarism to its credit. Fear of the Great Satan is not mere paranoia, on either side. There is also no reason to suppose that the leadership generally speaks or acts out of cynicism; nor is the matter of much interest. It is not difficult to come to believe what it is convenient to believe, and history shows that leaders and educated classes generally are prone to the most astonishing fantasies, when these are beneficial to their perceived interests. It may be that Hitler and Himmler sincerely believed that Germany was under threat by a Jewish-Bolshevik conspiracy and Polish aggressors inspired by the West, so that Germany had to react in self-defense. The question may be of interest to those concerned with the psychology of a particular maniac, but it is not of great interest to students of world politics. The same is true, far more so in fact, in the case of perfectly sane people playing their institutional roles and designing plans for the short-term benefit of the groups that they represent.

The system that has evolved has deep institutional roots, is quite stable, is rational in the short-term perspective of planning, and is not difficult to 'sell' to the public. It is also a form of institutionalized lunacy. While the topics that receive most attention − e.g., the number of warheads − are of marginal concern, others are not. Continued advances in technology, as many have observed, drive the participants in the arms race towards greater reliance on automated (launch-on-warning) response systems and pre-delegation of authority, thus making war likely in times of international crisis if only by error, inadvertence, miscalculation of enemy intent, or sheer irrationality. The latter should not be discounted; recall the amaz-

Noam Chomsky

ing display of 'the best and the brightest' during the Cuban missile crisis, when they were willing to face what they regarded as a probability of one-third to one-half of nuclear war to establish the principle that we alone have a right to keep offensive missiles on the enemy's border (namely, obsolete missiles in Turkey, for which a withdrawal order had been issued but not yet implemented): surely one of the low points in human history. It is a fact of some significance that even in retrospect, this astonishing behavior is regarded as 'one of the finest examples of diplomatic prudence, and perhaps the finest hour of John F. Kennedy's presidency.'[11] Furthermore, the Cold War policies of intervention regularly bring the superpowers close to confrontation. This has been true primarily in the Middle East during the past 20 years, largely as a consequence of the U.S. refusal to tolerate a political settlement of the Arab-Israeli conflict — as has long been feasible; but the problem does not arise only there.[12]

These two issues — technical advances in weaponry, and superpower confrontation resulting from Third World intervention — are the two major problems in this domain, perhaps the major problems that should be on the international agenda. They guarantee a persistent fair probability of nuclear war. Even if one takes the probability to be low, the meaning of this fact is that a terminal conflict is highly likely; only the timing is in doubt. This consideration does not enter into planning, for the reasons already mentioned. The lu-

---

11 Graham T. Allison, *Essence of Decision* (Boston, MA: Little, Brown and Co. 1971), 39; Allison is not unmindful of the nature of the catastrophe then impending, beside which 'the natural calamities and inhumanities of earlier history would have faded into insignificance,' and notes that 'the odds on disaster' were estimated as 'between one out of three and even.'

12 See my *Fateful Triangle* (Boston, MA: South End Press 1983) for a (partial) review of the matter concerning the Middle East; other cases of confrontation have arisen since, and new evidence has emerged about earlier crises; and my 'What Directions for the Disarmament Movement?' in Michael Albert and David Dellinger, eds., *Beyond Survival* (Boston, MA: South End Press 1983) for discussion of a number of other cases. For further discussion, see *Turning the Tide* and sources cited.

nacy is institutional, not individual. It is also, unfortunately, not at all clear that the basic problems can be addressed, except in a limited and patchwork manner. It is a certainty that they cannot be addressed unless illusions are stripped away and the system is revealed for what it is.

Received November, 1985

CANADIAN JOURNAL OF PHILOSOPHY
Supplementary Volume 12

Who Can Endeavour Peace?*

ONORA O'NEILL
University of Essex
Colchester, Great Britain
C04 3SQ

I Nuclear Discourses and Nuclear Stoicism

It is even possible to write *philosophically* on ethics and nuclear issues? In spite of the growing literature which seeks to apply ethical reasoning to nuclear issues doubts run deep here. They reflect more than hesitation between consequentialist and action-based conceptions of ethical reasoning, or over paradoxes of deterrence that can

---

* I am grateful for many helpful comments on earlier versions of this paper, and especially to Charles Beitz, Robert Goodin, Peter Carruthers, Lawrence Lustgarten and Jay Bernstein.

be generated by mixing these. We may even doubt whether nuclear arms and dangers either can or should be treated as 'problems' for ethical analysis. Won't methods that pass muster for diagnosing and discussing lesser, more local crises fail here, distract from other (perhaps more 'realistic') responses, and even risk further dangers? Perhaps philosophical inquiry is not only *irrelevant*, because it cannot help *solve* nuclear 'problems,' but also *impossible* because we cannot convincingly *identify* the deepest ethical difficulties, the real constraints on their solution, or the most promising agents of change. A common theme in nuclear writings is that we lack an adequate and appropriate language in which ethical questions raised by nuclear issues can be discussed without begging vital questions: nuclear newspeaks have damaged our thinking, as nuclear weapons our safety.

Of course, we may be fortunate. Nuclear dangers may be contained or defused by policies and collaborations that need only partial, even minimal, understanding or communications. On the other hand we may not be fortunate in this way. So we have at least reason for finding out whether ethical discussion of nuclear issues can be undertaken without begging questions, and what audiences it might reach. This inquiry might be seen as one among many sorts of contingency planning, which we have reason to undertake because things may not go well. No doubt, like other contingency plans, philosophical inquiry will turn out to have been irrelevant if what happens is the best case — or the worst case. What follows is to be seen as contingency planning; it does not assume that reasoning is the only or indispensable response to nuclear dangers, but that it may be needed for some responses.

We may begin with doubts about the adequacy of nuclear reasoning and its accessibility to some apparently important audiences. Whatever categories of discourse we use will render some problems and dangers salient, and obscure others. To reach some audiences may require terms of discourse that are inaccessible to others. Yet it is obscure how one might choose among modes of discourse. Any mode of discourse excludes some categories and principles in favour of others, so may seem irrelevant to some audiences. How then can any discourse reach across national and ideological boundaries, or enable unrestricted practical discussion of global problems? Perhaps the only intellectually adequate response is silence: but silence communicates ambiguities, and may be read as collaboration with evils rather than as integrity. Perhaps engagement in specific, locally accessible modes of practical discourse is the most we can achieve. Perhaps we should not aspire to reach unrestricted, or even wide, audiences. Perhaps claims that specifically *ethical* discourse can be used to probe other types of practical judgment are groundless, and the wider ambitions of 'applied' ethics unrealizable in nuclear or other global discussions. Perhaps the only *philosophical* response must be a Derridean refusal to linger with any one mode of discourse.

Derrida's writing on nuclear issues is instructive. Many writers have *gestured* towards the instability and variety of nuclear discourses, but Derrida *displays* the cacophony. The non-nuclear exchanges of a nuclear colloquium afford no Archimedean vantage point which permits 'external' appraisal or comparison of modes of discourse or 'objective' identification of problems, policies and relevant agents. He suggests that the ensemble of nuclear discourses is 'fabulously textual,'[1] and then offers a kaleidoscope of these crazed and fractured texts. Apocalyptic visionaries and nuclear physicists, technologists and economists, scientists and science fantasists, strategists and idealists, political realists and theologians of varied persuasions talk past one another in a swirl of discourse. This rehearsal of current debates is apt enough; its practical implications do not reassure. Derrida addresses a nuclear colloquium by slipping and skipping from one mode of nuclear discourse to another. His rapid modulations refuse the commitments of each discourse, and hold up mirrors in which those who rely on some mode of discourse can glimpse themselves from new angles. The reflections are only fleetingly visible, and constitute a warning that nuclear ethics can find no uncontested vantage point above the war of nuclear discourses.

Warnings have their practical uses. Derrida's depiction of nuclear discourses allows him glancing criticisms, and distances his response

---

1 Jacques Derrida, 'No Apocalypse, Not Now,' *Diacritics* (1984), 20-31, esp. 23

from others. He offers an oblique but apt commentary on certain attempts to apply ethical theories without recognition that descriptions of problems, ethical principles themselves, and hence proposed 'solutions,' rely on categories which may be salient in some perspectives, but invisible in others. This warning is pertinent for any work in 'applied' ethics that assumes that we can uncontroversially pick out correct accounts of ethical problems, and apply ethical reasoning to them. Ethical problems of the public domain can only be described and picked out in terms of specific, complex and controversial social, political and other categories. What count as 'problems' in terms of some mode of discourse will seem so only to those who find its categories appropriate and salient, but may not ruffle or concern those whose outlook differs. (This is striking in discussions of nuclear ethics: the passions and worries of just war theorists may leave politicians unmoved; focus on a narrow conception of national interests seems axiomatic to strategists, and morally bankrupt to others.)

Those who happen to share terms of discourse may not notice these impasses. They can agree within their own circles in identifying problems, constraints on their solution, policy options and the range of agents who might implement them. The audience for a specific mode of discourse can be discerned. However, ethical discussion of nuclear issues (or other global problems) standardly aims to reach and has reason to reach a more or less unrestricted audience. This aspiration does not seem misplaced since nuclear dangers are global and the institutional bases of nuclear confrontations varied. It must then count as failure to presuppose too much shared idiom and outlook. Since nuclear dangers loom across national, ideological and professional boundaries it doesn't help to assume (falsely) that a determinate configuration of the topic is 'given' or just 'crops up' and will be accepted by those whom these boundaries separate. There is no uncontroversial or uncontroverted view of nuclear problems, of the available options or of the agents whom it may be relevant to address.

Warnings of the limitations of nuclear discourses are not of much practical use if they leave us aware that dangers are great, but uncertain how to describe or to handle them. Derrida's approach has high *practical* costs. It reveals the absence of an Archimedean vantage point of nuclear dangers, but offers no alternative terrain for practical reasoning. This may be fine for a nuclear colloquium: but if there are wider (and perhaps important) audiences for practical questions it must fail to engage them.

Silence is not an adequate alternative. In modern as in ancient empires a Stoic refusal seems to many thinkers the most they can offer in the face of power (of course, others offer the powers that be their services...). If the Stoic answer is wrong, those who overestimate their impotence and offer it may also be guilty of the *trahison des clercs*. So while we remain uncertain about Stoic views of human powers, we lack sufficient reason for silence. Even if nuclear dangers have profoundly shaken or fragmented basic understandings of human life and conflict and of their temporal horizons, there may still be practical questions. In a nuclear holocaust it wouldn't matter much that some people had kept their hands rather clean; nor that others had been mistaken in seeking audiences for practical discourse beyond the colloquia. For Pascalian reasons, if no others (there may be others), it is important to bet against Stoicism.

A decision to bet against Stoicism cannot, however, bracket disagreements about how we should discuss nuclear issues. We beg serious practical questions if we speak of events that may resemble the experience of fish being dynamited by a poacher as 'war,' and so (for example) construe nuclear issues as ones which just war theory must somehow illuminate or for which a 'war-fighting strategy' is possible. The problem may rather be that nuclear weapons 'fatally undermine the institution of war' and 'spoil war as a rational instrument of national policy.'[2] Other questions are begged by talking of a nuclear 'winter,' whose 'springtime' would come too late for most, if not all, of us; or by taking the 'options' identified by strategists as defining the scope of nuclear discussions. Such terms of discourse familiarise nuclear dangers and assimilate them misleadingly to others we have known and can grasp. So does discussion of 'rational decisions' in contexts where the speed of events

---

2 Jonathan Schell, *The Abolition* (London: Cape 1984), 25, 26, and see Richard Wasserstrom, 'War, Nuclear War and Nuclear Deterrence: Some Conceptual and Moral Issues,' *Ethics* **95** (1985), 424-44.

would outpace all the modes of investigation, deliberation and calculation that have hitherto been thought rational in public affairs.
(Here Derrida is wholly convincing.) So too does insistence on the
possibility of telling 'defensive' from 'offensive' weapons and policies in the nuclear age, and the common habit of referring to nonbelligerent targets of 'deterrence' policies as 'enemies.' Questions
are also begged by assuming that the agents to whom nuclear discussions are relevant can uncontroversially be identified with (for
example) the superpower leadership or military planners, nation-
states, alliances or the individual conscience. A bet against Stoicism
cannot be neutral about who the appropriate audiences are and
which modes of discourse can reach them.

Choices between alternative modes of discourse would be impossible if we were trapped in radical conceptual isolation. We can
choose among nuclear discourses only if we can follow and see the
point at least of a plurality of ways of describing and discussing
nuclear issues. Those who doubt that we have any such conceptual
versatility will already have rejected this discussion. Those still with
the discussion can take their own (partial) mastery of diverse discourses as some evidence for conceptual versatility. Questions about
how to choose between modes of nuclear discourse will in fact arise
for anyone who has some versatility: even for those who confidently
dismiss many forms of discourse as obscure or irrelevant.

If we can follow more than one mode of discourse, conceptual
relativism of a certain radical and isolating kind is untenable. But
this does not show that there are non-question begging ways to
choose among the nuclear discourses that we can follow. If choosing isn't merely a matter of 'picking,' but must be guided by some
principles or objectives, it may appear that no choice of idiom could
be fully justified (for reasons that parallel alleged difficulties of transcendental arguments). However, a commitment to reject Stoicism
provides one principle for choosing here, for it requires that modes
of discourse be chosen only if they permit *practical* reasoning.

A commitment to reasoning practically is a commitment to
reasoning in ways that are both *accessible* and *action guiding* for some
audience(s). *Accessible* reasoning must enable communication with
some actual audience(s). Audiences who find a mode of discourse
accessible may not find each of its uses convincing or motivational-

ly compelling, but can follow them and find its categories salient.[3] (A mode of discourse could also be chosen for theoretical elegance, for aesthetic qualities or for *in*accessibility to others: here practical concern, and so avoidance of Stoicism, are at best secondary.) *Action guiding* reasoning must be capable (to some extent) of guiding the choosing of those for whom it is accessible. Action guiding *ethical* discourse must offer at least a *rough* decision procedure for *some* ethical categories (e.g. the just, the forbidden, the permissible) for a *range* of significant situations — ethical discourse can be practical even if it offers much less than a universal ethical algorithm. Modes of discourse which are either inaccessible to an audience or incapable of guiding their actions are irrelevant to that audience's deliberations.

Anybody who aims to engage important audiences in discussion of nuclear issues must therefore adopt modes of discourse that are accessible and action guiding for those audiences *as they actually are*. This is indispensable for practical reasoning on nuclear issues. Hence the *first* step for philosophical thinking about nuclear ethics must be to identify important audiences and the modes of discourse that, as things stand, are accessible and action guiding for those audiences. Until we identify nuclear agents we canot begin to endeavour peace.

II Nuclear Audience and Abstract Agents

Agency may be fundamental to choosing among nuclear discourses, but the topic is often treated as mere background to the 'real' issues. Much of the rhetoric of peace movements and wider debates about ethics and nuclear issues assumes tacitly that individual citizens and political leaders (particularly of the 'West') are the

---

3 I have argued for this conception of practical reasoning in more detail in *Faces of Hunger: An Essay on Poverty Justice and Development* (London: George Allen and Unwin 1986), esp. ch. 3.

primary audience, and include all relevant agents. Other discussions of politics, international relations and strategy are more likely to treat nation-states or alliances as the relevant agents. In other cases accessibility is ostensibly kept very open by relying on abstract forms of (mostly) consequentialist practical reasoning, and especially on abstract models of rational choice.

One of the many attractions of consequentialist thinking for discussions of problems of the public domain, including nuclear prospects, is its apparent capacity to reach a wide range of audiences and agents by taking an abstract view of agency. Here we have ostensibly practical discourse that seems to make *no* restricting assumptions about agency. Since results may be produced by a great variety of individual and institutional action (as well as by natural processes), discourse focused on results should be widely accessible. This can seem particularly useful for discussing strategic options and nuclear possibilities and responsibilities. If consequential reasoning is not committed to a restricted account of agency, it can perhaps be accessible and action guiding for any audience, and we can avoid many hard questions about individualism and about theories of collective responsibility, while engaging all relevant audiences.[4]

As often, abstraction has its costs. Practical, including ethical, deliberation must be *accessible* to actual and not just to abstract or 'ideal' agents. The lists of options and possibilities from which accessible consequentialist reasoning begins must be options or possibilities for actual agents or agencies. Consequentialist reasoning will not be accessible, nor therefore action guiding, if it relies on an abstract view of agency and hypothetical 'options': all actual audiences, who might find *some* type of consequentialist reasoning accessible (though not necessarily motivationally compelling) use determinate categories and conceptions which bound and form their

---

4 The division between protagonists of individual and of institutional conceptions of the relevant agents in nuclear matters often coincides with divisions drawn between 'idealist' and 'realist' approaches to world affairs. The coincidence isn't complete: for some 'realists' all agents are individuals, some of whom act for states and are obliged to ignore ethical considerations – to be 'realists' – when they do so. See section IV below.

perception of problems, options and solutions. Consequentialist reasoning is only *practical* when based on a determinate and accurate view of the agents and agencies whom it addresses and their specific categories of understanding and powers of action.[5]

Many uses of consequentialist reasoning in fact draw on more determinate conceptions of their audience. For example, strategic thinkers often address major nation-states and alliances and calculate in terms of expected harms or benefits to a small range of perceived interests of those alliances or states (e.g. inhabitants killed, power limited or extended). Some of their equally consequentialist critics point out that very different conclusions could be reached by calculations which not only considered nation-states and alliances, but counted a wider range of benefits and harms to individuals.[6] Strategic thinkers who focus on the agency and interests of nations may judge a certain number of deaths on their 'own' side an acceptable (alternatively: unacceptable) cost of national survival, but will not weigh deaths in 'enemy' nations as costs at all. They count harm to an 'enemy' a *benefit*, not a further *cost*.[4] When consequentialist reasoning takes account of *all* losses and gains to *individuals*, regardless of national status, it reaches different conclusions about optimal action. Such reasoning may appear pointless to strategists (although formally similar to their own), because it addresses audiences they think powerless and irrelevant. Strategic calculation may seem irrelevant to individualist consequentialists, since it adopts a restricted view of agents, options and benefits, often without consequentialist warrant. Disagreements that consequentialists themselves may attribute to differing preferences, or 'values,' may reflect diverging conceptions of agency and engagement with different audiences.

---

5 For more extended discussion of the accessibility of consequentialist reasoning and the agents it addresses see *Faces of Hunger* chs. 4 and 5.

6 R. Goodin, 'Disarming Nuclear Apologists,' *Inquiry* **28** (1985), 153-76 and 'Nuclear Disarmament as Moral Certainty,' *Ethics* **95** (1985), 641-58

7 Why the scare quotes? To dissociate the point from the common identification of 'our side,' 'neutral' and 'hostile' nations when there is no war.

Consequentialists cannot avoid these dilemmas by sticking to an abstract account of agency. Abstraction guarantees only the widespread accessibility of the *formal structure* of consequential reasoning. It brackets widespread dissent about how to reckon determinate consequences. What agents find fully accessible – understandable and salient – is not consequential reasoning in the abstract, but the determinate types of consequential reasoning embodied in their social practices. It is these that guide their action. Consequentialists who are to reason practically about nuclear issues must argue both *for* and *from* a determinate view of the important audience(s) for practical reasoning on nuclear problems. Abstract reasoning alone is notorious for failure to engage.

Non-consequentialist reasoning runs into similar problems. If it relies on abstract conceptions of agency it may be 'abstracted from the context of the audience for which it is intended.'[8] This points to a large dilemma. Must not any practical reasoning be directed to a restricted audience, so use whatever determinate categories and principles are salient and action-guiding for that audience and the agents it includes? If so, will not all practical reasoning have restricted appeal? Won't it be mere pretence that ethical debate could have unrestricted appeal? Yet if nuclear dangers cut across all boundaries, and are affected by very diverse agents, we can hardly regard sectoral modes of nuclear discourse as a philosophically adequate contingency plan. For such discourse may fail to engage powerful and important audiences.

Our interim conclusion can only be that hypothetical abstract agents are not the relevant audience for nuclear discussion. Serious practical reasoning must engage the attention and concern of agents with power to achieve changes. In the next two sections I shall consider whether two relatively determinate conceptions of agency that are well entrenched in nuclear discussions are adequate for ethical reasoning about nuclear dangers. Section III discusses individualist conceptions of agency, section IV the agency of sovereign states. Although these two more determinate conceptions of

---

8 Ronald Beiner, *Political Judgement* (London: Methuen 1983), 85

agency are quite different, I shall suggest that *each* is committed to a certain 'thin,' but not merely abstract, view of agency which is sufficient for practical, and specifically for ethical, reasoning about nuclear dangers. If this 'thin' theory of agency is plausible, and widely accessible, action-guiding reasoning about nuclear dangers may be possible.

III Individual Agency: Echoes of Nuremberg

In the background of many discussions of nuclear dangers and prospects lie the horrors of Nazism. This is not just an historical point about the development of nuclear weapons to pre-empt the Nazis, or the emergence of the power blocs that deploy them and of doctrines of deterrence in the wake of WWII. It is also because our most compelling experience and images of conflicts between vast power and ethical discourse date from the Nazi period. We still approach questions about collaboration or resistance, about the limits of military obligation, about complicity in crimes of war and the point of keeping one's hands clean, in the idiom of the 1940s. The questions are sharpened by worse weapons (napalm, nuclear arsenals) and more pervading methods of control (more developed newspeaks, high tech totalitarianism): but the conception of the individual conscience as the crucial, but vulnerable and non-political, audience for ethical discourse still commands attention.

Ethical reasoning so construed addresses individual men and women, who can (often at great cost) *accept* or *reject* both the specific tasks and the broader roles their society offers. Their agency is manifest in abilities to *integrate* capacities to *reason* and to *act*, and to maintain some *independence* from other forces and agents. Human individuals are taken to be paradigmatic agents, for whom alone ethical deliberation, as well as other sorts of practical deliberation, are possible, salient and even required. Individualists usually hold that institutions cannot respond to ethical reasoning, but only to restricted types of practical discourse established by their constitution and charter. Individualist views of agency and responsibility are deeply entrenched in contemporary discussions of ethical dilem-

mas of war and politics. They are fundamental to the legal principles applied at Nuremberg in judging responsibility for war crimes,
and in many post WWII philosophical discussions of responsibility
for Nazi evils (e.g. Jaspers and Sartre), as well as in more recent
discussions of Nazi and other war crimes and in parts of the new
literature on Just War Theory of the 70s and 80s.

Various limitations of individualist views of agency and responsibility are well known. If the *only* agents of change for whom ethical deliberation is accessible are individual human beings, it is
impossible to give more than an *indirect* account of the ethical responsibilities of institutions. Yet institutions often harm in ways that cannot easily be ascribed to individual office holders, who can be held
responsible only for failure in their roles, and for joining or staying
in institutions which require them to do wrong. A Nuremberg view
of ethical responsibility in the public domain can be grafted onto
individualist ethical reasoning; indeed it is little more than an extension of such reasoning. That is its merit, and its defect. With
nuclear as with Nazi scenarios, this approach shows what individuals must avoid to keep their hands clean, but is silent about the actions of institutions.

Yet harms are often more plausibly attributed to institutions or
practices than to individuals. Modern institutional structures fragment information and power, and so minimise individual office
holders' grasp of the wider aims their action serves as well as their
ability to affect what is done. Bureaucracies, military services and
military-industrial complexes guarantee that individuals' understanding will be *opaque* and *fragmented* and their competence and
power *limited*. Responsibility is reduced to the small areas of *control*
that are *transparent* to specific office holders. In such institutions
keeping one's hands clean can be surprisingly easy. Even individuals with important roles in institutions that produce major harms
may not have violated ethical standards. Ignorance of the likely effects of individual action, doubts that they will have much effect
at all, pervasive powerlessness and the difficulty of allocating responsibility for systemic harm to individuals make a Nuremberg approach
to responsibility worryingly indeterminate in the face of the major
harms and dangers of modern societies. Still, if ethical reasoning
is only accessible to individual agents, we cannot do more than rely

on modes of discourse which take the point and address those agents. Such discourse may not reach or convince the powers that be: but it avoids Stoicism and may achieve 'salvation for the soul' in dark times. In the darkest times, silence may be the only power left to human individuals, but need not amount to Stoicism provided that 'I found my self respect on silence as the last power left the powerless. I show my silence so as to hurt the powerful. I hide my silence so as to plan for a restoration...'.[9]

If ethical reasoning is accessible only to individuals, its meagre help with global problems should not surprise us. Individual agents do not, after all, live up to the rational economic men, impartial moral spectators and varied ideal rational choosers who jostle in modern mythologies. Human freedom and human rationality are both limited; human agents integrate different aspects of their deliberation incompletely, and depend in varied ways on other forces and agents. This is uncontroversial. The various 'models of man' invoked in much ethical reasoning and social theory are meant as *ideals*, and what holds for 'non-ideal' conditions may be both different and underdetermined. Yet while it is acknowledged that these fictions are not the real thing, the full implications of limited capacities for agency are seldom spelled out. If we set them out it is soon apparent that the much discussed models of rational choice are not just *abstractions*, but rather misleading *idealizations* of human choosing, which is intrinsically limited by partial knowledge and restricted powers of action.[10] A cursory account of standard information about the limited understanding and powers of actual human choosers, and their incomplete integration and independence, confirms this.

Human choosing relies on concepts drawn from the variegated

---

9 Karl Jaspers, *The Question of German Guilt* (New York: Capricorn Books 1961), 112; whether silence is — vestigially — political is a recurrent theme in mid century writing on politics and responsibility, esp. in the writing of Camus and Arendt.

10 Theories are *abstract* when they *omit* (a great deal) that is true of the objects to which they apply, but *idealised* when they *add* to the properties of the objects to which they are held to apply properties which those objects lack, or have only in part.

conceptual stock in trade of a particular society at a particular time. Descriptions of situations, options and actions on which individual human choosers rely afford a selective perspective on problems and possibilities. This much is frequently acknowledged in discussions of interpretive or hermeneutic studies of society, and by theorists of ideology. It is sometimes taken to suggest that 'ethical' reasoning is confined among those who share idiom and outlook, and so is relative to specific social and ideological formations. Philosophical writing on ethics which rejects the view that ethical reasoning is relative to the determinate context in which it occurs, often offers no account of how reasoning which is *accessible* to actual audiences, with their limited capacities for agency, can avoid relativism.

Cognitive limitations restrict powers of action as well as of understanding. We can act only under descriptions that we can follow. In addition, powers of action are limited by material and institutional capacities.[11] Human freedom is therefore *doubly* restricted. It can include neither options which are incomprehensible, nor comprehensible options which agents lack power to bring about. Particular capacities for action are therefore *doubly* afffected by historical and social factors. Human cognition draws on the conceptual resources of a particular society and tradition, and human powers of action reflect both these and the material and institutional achievements of societies and traditions. The ancient Athenians were *doubly* unfree to play computer games; we are *doubly* unfree to profane their mysteries. As individuals we are surely *doubly* unfree to guarantee ourselves against nuclear catastrophe.

The integration or unity of human agency is also limited. Although some recent writing in ethics depicts human action as the systematic enactment of 'life plans,' most human choosing is less coherent and tightly structured. A partial and fragmented understanding of situations and their possibilities, guides action constrained by limited (and incompletely known) material and institutional powers.

---

11 This is not to deny that there may be legitimate uses for a purely 'negative' conception of freedom as 'non-interference'; but it is 'positive' freedom to do or forebear that constitutes the determinate limits of individuals' agency.

Nor are human agents as independent of surrounding agents and forces as idealised views of individual agency suggest. Much of the independence and coherence which human choosing displays arises from close adherence to and dependence on established and traditional categories, modes of thought and institutions. The integrity and unity that human agents achieve may reflect not so much their intrinsic unity and independence as their achieved dependence on historically determinate and coherent ways of thought and action.[12]

These limitations of human agency, in its actual and determinate forms, suggest three thoughts. The first is that it is not surprising that practical reasoning whose audience is individual human beings has had limited success, especially in complex public affairs. Rather than deploring the patchy achievements of the Nuremberg trials, or of other attempts to find who was responsible for major harms, we should be impressed by their success in adjudicating some responsibilities. (The Nuremberg trials might have been impossible but for long legal traditions, the Nazis' clear articulation of responsibilities of office and their painstaking record keeping: who expects similar trials after less orderly and documented genocides?) Analogously we should not be surprised if practical reasoning about nuclear matters addressed to individuals has scanty results. Individuals have remarkably few options to reduce nuclear dangers. For all the images we may have of non-collaboration, resistance and keeping our hands clean, there are few immediately available options amid all-volunteer military forces, Pay-As-You-Earn taxation and governments committed to varieties of 'deterrent' or 'warfighting' strategies and buttressed by huge and secretive military establishments. It should not surprise us that ethical discourse directed at evidently powerless agents has neither empowered them nor

---

12 See for example Alasdair MacIntyre, 'Corporate Modernity and Moral Judgement: are they Mutually Exclusive?' in K.E. Goodpaster and K. Sayre, eds., *Ethics and Problems of the Twenty-First Century* (Notre Dame: University of Notre Dame Press 1979), 122-35, and his *After Virtue* (London: Duckworth 1981), and Bernard Williams, *Ethics and the Limits of Philosophy* (London: Fontana 1985), as well as the very different considerations about the partial unity of human agents in Derek Parfit, *Reasons and Persons* (Oxford: Clarendon Press 1984).

achieved change and is often judged irrelevant. If it does not heed
the determinate categories and limited capacities for action of its audience it will not penetrate their deliberations.

The second thought is that if individual human beings are no
more than partially rational, free, integrated or independent of surrounding forces, and social institutions form and limit their agency, then their agency may not differ radically from some sorts of
institutional agency. The 'thin' human agency that we actually know,
unlike the idealised agency assumed in models of rational choice,
takes limited, varied and socially determinate forms. The point is
not that there is no difference between what we think of as 'natural' persons and what we think of as 'artificial' persons. Patently there
is. But 'natural' persons too are artificial in just those respects most
crucial for agency within a social context. The determinate categories
and procedures of any particular individual's agency are not naturally given, although we know of no specific type of agency which
does not depend on generic human capacities to act, and so must
regard human capacities as the natural basis for any sort of agency.
Animals, severely handicapped human beings and contemporary
artificial intelligences do not develop (much or any) capacity for agency because their capacities for cognition and action are not and cannot be extended by the complex conceptual, material and
institutional resources which structure normal human agency.

The third thought, and the most surprising, is that the fragmented and porous character of human understanding, and so of human agency, may be no disaster for ethical discourse of the sort
philosophical writing has aimed at, but rather its basis. If human
agents enjoyed a *fully* integrated, coherent and independent understanding of their situations and prospects, and comprehensive powers of action, no established mode of practical discourse could be
challenged, amended or dislodged by ethical considerations. The
challenge could not come from within, since their cognition would
(by hypothesis) be fully integrated and coherent; it could not come
from outside since their cognition would (by hypothesis) be wholly
independent and so impervious. The predicament of relativism is
unavoidable for such 'idealised' agents: each is hermetically sealed
in a determinate, coherent, unchallengeable cognitive structure; but
agents with fragmented and partially dependent cognitive capaci-

ties and powers of action can modify those very capacities. To do so they need not draw on the cognitive resources of some notional, but actually inaccessible, 'Archimedean standpoint of reason.' Rather they may gain some distance and perspective on some aspects of their understanding, by drawing on other aspects, or extend their own cognitive capacities and powers of action by learning to follow others'. Perhaps the limited and fragmented character of human agency is not only the source for the selective, perspectival and ideological character of practical reasoning (which relativists stress), but of the open-ended, critical reasoning which ethical deliberation (as often philosophically conceived) requires. It is because human cognition is standardly *opaque* and *fragmented* that human choosers can remain unaware of the further implications of beliefs that they hold, or of the likely results of actions that they undertake, and so can incorporate disparate categories and even incompatible beliefs into their thinking. Far from being hermetically sealed in closed ideological structures, between which communication is impossible, limited understanding is often shot through with diverse and even disparate sets of categories and ideological influences. Fragments of the rhetoric of the establishment drift through the discourse of the opposition. Popular contemporary ideological cocktails blend Christianity with socialism, liberalism with conservatism, material greed with a rhetoric of concern for others, and aspirations to peace with bellicose nationalism. Cognitive limitations don't guarantee that practical discourse – or even a stretch of one agent's deliberation – is tightly integrated and isolated within local conceptual boundaries, but rather allow stretches of discourse to remain open and porous even to distant and incompatible modes of discourse. Individuals' understanding of their situation and options is standardly limited, opaque and lacking in unity, and so remains revisable and open to criticism.

IV States as Agents: Reasons for Realism

When certain social and political institutions are described as 'artificial persons' this is often taken as metaphor, or as a technical term for legal realities and not as a literal claim that they are agents, let alone agents for whom ethical considerations may be accessible and action guiding. But if agency in its supposed paradigmatic, individual form is limited and 'thin' in the ways suggested, then some institutions may be agents in the literal and unmetaphorical way in which individuals are agents. If they are, there may be further, non-individual audiences for ethical discussion of nuclear dangers, including audiences with greater power to produce change than individuals have. However, the view that institutions, and in particular states, could have specifically *ethical* responsibilities, distinct from the positive responsibilities which their constitutions define, is often dismissed. Correspondingly, claims that ethical deliberation may be accessible to (some) institutions standardly meets skepticism and resistance.[13]

The argument so far has only dented this resistance by stressing the limits of individual agency. A more direct challenge to the view that agency is solely individual is made by some well-entrenched views of institutional agency. Various 'realist' modes of practical discourse, including some discussions of international relations and law, take the agency of certain institutions, in particular of nation-states, for granted. But many influential 'realists' — we may label them *strict realists* — who take such agency for granted, nevertheless deny that specifically *ethical* reasoning is relevant to states, although sometimes made accessible when introduced into affairs of state by the misguided efforts of well-meaning office holders.

'Realists,' both of stricter and of more moderate persuasion, see nation-states (and certain other institutions) as agents, for whose decisions, actions and policies reasons can be given. The vocabulary of agency indeed seems as much at home here as it is in discus-

---

13 One source of distaste is abhorrence for collective punishment. However, what offends is punishment of individuals for action by collectivities, especially when they have been marginal members. Genuinely *collective* punishment — e.g. the destruction of institutions which cause harm — does not always offend. Nothing said here depends on views about collective punishment. Non-consequentialist reasoning can separate the topics of responsibility and punishment.

sion of individual action. Human agency is often explained using political metaphors such as *sovereignty* and *autonomy*, and political agency is often explicated using anthropological metaphors such as *'body politic'* and *'political will.'* Terms such as 'action,' 'self-determination,' 'integrity,' 'freedom,' or 'rationality' fit into discussions of either type of agent. 'Strict realists,' however, claim also that states' agency is and should be limited, and in particular deaf to ethical reasoning.[14] The practical reasoning by which states decide on actions and policies should attend only to *raisons d'état*, and these refer only to national interests, however defined. The most determined 'strict realists' define them narrowly in terms of national security, assume that states are the only significant actors, that they act as units and that their principal goal is military security.[15] (Less strict realists may modify some of these assumptions or even muddy the waters by building ethical considerations into a conception of the national interest, while still maintaining that states should not attend to ethical considerations.)[16] If 'strict realists' are correct in claiming that nation-states (and presumably other institutions) *cannot* attend to ethical considerations, any specifically ethical reasoning about nuclear matters must address individuals; and while 'strict realists' do not deny individual agency, they think it irrelevant to world affairs. If individuals have scant powers to make strategic or political changes, ethical reasoning can only be marginally practical

---

14 Some 'realists' about world affairs maintain only less contentious views. Such 'pragmatic realists' may merely advocate that foreign affairs be conducted with a clear eye on the likely results of policy, or without attempts to impose contentious ethical standards in other countries. Pragmatic realism is quite compatible with the view that states may attend to ethical reasoning: indeed it is often linked with claims about 'the morality of states' such that states ought not to interfere in other states' affairs. Cf. Charles Beitz, *Political Theory and International Relations* (Princeton, N.J.: Princeton University Press 1979), part II.

15 But see Robert O. Keohane and Joseph S. Nye, *Transnational Relations and World Politics* (Cambridge, MA: Harvard University Press 1970) for discussions of the limitations of realist paradigms in international relations.

16 *Political Theory and International Relations*, Part I, Ch 4

in this area. The reasoning of churchmen, of just war theorists and of contemporary applied ethics reaches only those who can't act on it effectively. Only strategic and political discourse, which presuppose *national* interests and *national* power, count as practical nuclear discourse. In foreign and strategic affairs, 'strict realists' claim, ethical discourse is not practical. It is sentimental idealism at best, and dangerous at worst.

'Strict Realists' offer various arguments for their view of states and of the conduct of world affairs. Surprisingly, reflection on some of these casts doubt on the supposed radical difference between the agency of nation states and that of human individuals. If the two sorts of agents are more similar than 'strict realists' suppose, ethical discourse may form part, not only of the practical deliberation of individuals, but of that of a wide range of institutions, not merely national but intra-national, international and increasingly transnational.

One commonly cited reason for thinking states unreceptive to ethical reasoning is Hobbes' contention that they are in a 'state of nature,' with no common power above them, hence can have no obligations to obey the law of nature (or, by extension, other ethical principles). This argument is probably not detachable from a Hobbesian account of obligation. In any case it has recently been decisively criticised by Charles Beitz.[17] Two selections from his argument show Hobbesian foundations inadequate for 'strict realism.' First, although nation-states may not be in awe of any common power, they are not in a Hobbesian state of nature, where the weakest has power to destroy the strongest. Certain nation-states dominate others, so do not risk destruction by compliance with ethical principles. The duty of self preservation underdetermines the action of those with a large margin of safety, and so Hobbesian obligations may apply to states even in non-ideal conditions when others' compliance is not guaranteed. This, however, may not be decisive in nuclear contexts, where even the most powerful have plenty to fear. Second, Hobbesian arguments to show that individuals cannot have

---

17 *Political Theory and International Relations*, Part I, Chs. 3 to 5

obligations which endanger their lives cannot be generalised to show that states cannot have obligations which endanger their continuation. (Indeed, since efforts to preserve particular nation-states often endanger human lives, no principle of *national* self-preservation could be inviolable in a Hobbesian framework.)

A further line of thought, derived from Macchiavelli rather than from Hobbes, suggests that ethical reasoning is irrelevant for nation states because leaders and officials have no right to further their individual ethical concerns at the expense of the states they serve. Princes, or for that matter principal secretaries, must sometimes sacrifice their own principles for the sake of the state they serve: private virtues can be public vices. There is a plausible aspect to this. Office holders are often committed to acts that are optional for private citizens, and sometimes to action that is forbidden private citizens. However, the fiduciary obligations of office holders don't licence just *any* way of furthering the institutions they serve. For example, trustees may not give monies with which they are entrusted to further their favourite worthy causes; they also may not rob to enrich the trust.[18] Even when obligations of office do trump the obligations of office holders, the former may not be obligations to pursue *national* interests. The priority of national interests in practical reasoning could be established only by an argument about nation-states, and not by any general argument about obligations of office.

V A Thin Theory of Institutional Agency

There is no way to rebut all the arguments various sorts of realists might put forward to show institutions, and states in particular, deaf to ethical reasoning. To cast doubt on a wide range of realist positions, and to show ethical reasoning accessible to institutional agents, it is necessary to say something more specific about the agency of nation-states, and of some other institutions. I shall begin by com-

---

18 *Political Theory and International Relations*, Part I, Ch. 1

paring the agency of states with that of human individuals, and will then go on to argue that the two sorts of agency are similar enough to suggest that *if* ethical reasoning is accessible to individuals *then* it is not inaccessible to states. Even if these claims convince, moderate and pragmatic forms of realism would be warranted in practical, including ethical, reasoning about world affairs, but 'strict realism' would have to be rejected. (The demand that practical reasoning be *accessible* to the audience to whom it is directed may be thought a pragmatically realist requirement.)

Agency, I have suggested, is a matter of *integrating* capacities to *reason* and to *act* while retaining some *independence* from other agents and forces. Human agents, as we actually know them, are limited in each of these respects. However, these limitations do not make all ethical reasoning inaccessible to them. On the contrary, it is more plausible to think that specifically ethical reasoning would be inaccessible to 'idealised' than to human individuals.

It is uncontroversial that nation-states (and other institutions) have all four of these features, in restricted and determinate forms. Nation-states have structures which provide methods of *integrating* a large range of information in *rational* ways and *enacting* national policies, while maintaining some national *independence* from other agents (including other states) and forces. In spite of these evident similarities, a great deal of writing in ethics echoes 'strict realists' in insisting that nation-states are *not* agents for whom specifically ethical reasoning could be accessible. The main point urged is often that, in the end, talk about the agency of states is mere metaphor. Individuals have minds and states do not. The action of states may indeed be rational, but is not conscious. Does this show that states are agents for whom ethical reasoning is irrelevant?

Institutions, including states, clearly lack the forms of self awareness that human individuals have. Nothing is present to the consciousness of an institution, and in a common (if disputed) sense of the term it would be misleading to attribute intentions to institutions. But this does not settle the question of agency, because the aspects of cognition that are pertinent to agency do not hinge on self awareness. Unless we insist on a theory of action that attributes to agents only what is explicitly present to their consciousness, considerations about consciousness will not show that agency must be individual. We have already noted reasons to reject idealized pictures of cognition and action. Individual agents find only limited, often inaccurate, descriptions of their action present to consciousness. Because human cognition is both fragmented and opaque much that we do escapes our conscious attention. In extreme cases we think such absences notable and speak of self-deception or false-consciousness; but opacity and disconnectedness are features of the most mundane and uncontentious cognition and action. For this reason no plausible account of individual responsibility claims that individuals are responsible only for their actions as these are actually present to consciousness, or made present by self examination. For self-examination too is hostage to received ways of thinking, fragmented and opaque. Notoriously we excuse ourselves when accused, pointing to other less odious act descriptions; we remain oblivious of descriptions of our actions that strike others as salient. Often our pleas for excuse will be rejected because the descriptions we do not acknowledge are more significant, although neither present to consciousness, nor readily accessible using the procedures of self scrutiny actually available to us.

If presence to consciousness is not crucial for the cognitive aspects of rational agency and responsibility in individual human agents, then there may after all be no reason to reject institutional agency. Even if not conscious, some institutions may be rational in ways that bear close comparison with the limited rationality of human individuals. They may have extensive capacities to gather, process, record and integrate information. These capacities are, of course, socially formed, and deploy a restricted and determinate set of categories; so do the cognitive capacities of human individuals. If anything, the information gathering and deliberative procedures of some institutions, and especially of nation-states, may be more elaborate and systematic – more rational – than those of individuals. The bureaucracies – military and civilian – of modern states are designed to collect detailed and comprehensive information, to identify options systematically and to forecast the results of alternative scenarios with supposed precision. These cognitive capacities are indeed limited and determinate. They both guarantee that institutional deliberation will be abstract and systematic, and (where these objectives are prized) may make it superior to individual deliberation on the same topics. Like individuals, states and bureaucracies sometimes embody what we take to be distorted forms of rationality.

Even if the cognitive resources of states resemble those of individual human agents in these ways, they may seem to differ in being both less integrated and more rigid. Individual agents in the modern age live in a swirl of diverse discourses. Although this may make their thinking more fragmented and opaque than the understanding of individuals in more traditional societies may have been, it also means that they are conceptually multilingual, and can change ideological gears with disconcerting ease, and even increase and adapt their cognitive capacities. This versatility, I have suggested, may be the basis for specifically ethical discourse.

Institutions may seem more bounded by the categories of their charter and constitution, and by the flow of information and reasoning these establish. These, it is said, will mandate that information be integrated only in certain ways and guarantee that it remains fragmented in others, and will ensure that the information processing structures themselves remain intact. At the limit, if we think of ideal-typical institutions, cognitive resources are indeed rigid. Information will flow through prescribed 'channels' to be collected by specified officials under specified headings and processed, recorded and used in mandated ways. But actual agencies are not ideal-typical abstractions, any more than actual human beings are ideal rational choosers. Official modes of discourse and procedures may preclude some ways of integrating information and may resist change, but they are not impervious. Even rigid bureaucracies integrate information that is meant to be dispersed, and may change not only the unofficial ethos but bureaucratic structures themselves as new tasks are encountered and new information, techniques and modes of discourse are absorbed. Nor are all institutions designed to discipline, fragment or restrict cognition as firmly as bureaucratic structures supposedly do. Some institutions include structures for their own reform and renewal. If we compare the cognitive capacities of actual individuals with those of actual institutions, we find that both have limited and determinate but *changeable* capacities to absorb and integrate information. The cognition of institutions is not always less adaptable than that of individuals. When it is, this may be a feature of particular institutions, not of all possible institutions. If the cognition of actual institutions is or can be flexible in these ways, they need not be impervious to ethical reasoning. Institutions are not invariably confined to a rigid official idiom and deaf to considerations expressed in other terms. On the contrary, those that approach imperviousness are open to (and receive) the very sorts of criticism that individuals who have confined themselves in impervious and 'self-confirming' ideologies attract.

Perhaps the idea that institutions can have and integrate the cognitive capacities needed for agency will not now seem incredible. But institutions, including states, can only be agents if they also have the power to act in ways indicated by their cognitive capacities and some independence from other forces and agents. Institutional agency, however, does not demand unlimited powers of action or total independence, any more than individual agency does. Anybody who thinks that some human individuals have sufficient powers to act and sufficient independence to count as agents can reasonably think that *some* institutions have sufficient powers and independence to count as agents. No doubt some institutions – e.g. social practices that don't include decision procedures – have no powers to act and are not agents, while others have such circumscribed powers to act that they can hardly use ethical deliberation, or cannot count as agents because they have too little independence from surrounding forces or more clearly defined agents. (Anyone who holds 'international public opinion' responsible, or who blames 'reactionary forces' or 'the establishment' fails to pick out any agent, so uses the vocabulary of agency irresponsibly.) However, no listing of *examples* of institutions that are not agents can show that *all* institutions are deaf to ethical reasoning.

Nation-states, in fact, have more extended powers of action and greater independence from other agents and forces than other institutions. That is why we speak of *sovereign* states. They do not, of course, have unlimited powers to do anything whatsoever in complete independence from other agents. Literature on international relations is filled with discussion of the specific limits of state power, and of the variety of other institutions on which the actions even of powerful nation-states now partially depends. The powers of action of modern nation-states are limited not only by their own resources but by various international arrangements and institutions (alliances, UN organizations, the IMF), by transnational organisations of great variety, and above all by the powers of other nation states. For some Third World states the result may be a degree of dependence on richer states, transnational corporations and international agencies that makes a mockery of sovereignty; even super powers are limited powers. *Completely* sovereign states are as mythical as ideal rational choosers. Nation-states (and more limited institutional agents), like human agents, lack powers to choose all hypothetically available options, but can select from a range of actually available options. These powers are compatible with a considerable — though disputed — level of 'interdependence' even for the most powerful states.

Onc individualist rejoinder to these thoughts might be that in the end the 'decisions' of institutions are just ways of recording or amalgamating the decisions of individuals who staff them.[19] A focus on election behaviour, or corporate decision making can suggest this. But this impression may simply reflect popular individualist approaches to social 'science' which abstract a 'moment of decision,' that can be attributed to individual office holders, from the full institutional context in which decisions are embedded. Matters can be looked at differently. Decisions and policies are indeed never produced by institutional structures in the abstract: individual office holders are needed for functioning institutions. Equally, they are never produced by individuals in the abstract: an institutionally embodied context of cognitive capacities and powers of actions is needed for functioning individuals. We have reason to attribute some decisions to individuals and others to institutions, depending on their relative importance in reaching a particular decision. Decision 'makers' of both sorts can only select among actual options, *as defined in terms of the cognitive capacities and powers of action available in a given context*. Neither individuals nor institutions 'make' decisions ex nihilo; they make them from the possibilities made available by a particular range of discourses and of powers of action. If we hold

---

19 See David-Hillel Ruben, *The Metaphysics of the Social World* (London: Routledge and Kegan Paul 1985).

a 'thin' view of agency, and do not assume that consciousness is essential for agency, we will often have reason to think that institutions are agents and so can be audiences for varied sorts of practical reasoning, including ethical reasoning. Their agency will be restricted for the same reasons as individual agency is restricted: both will be deaf to reasoning that does not use accessible categories and guide choice among available actions.

VI Diffused Responsibility and Political Change

The discussion of agency in the last three sections suggests that there may be various audiences for whom specific modes of nuclear discourse can be practical, who could 'endeavour peace.' The most important points are the following: first, all effective agency is socially *determinate*; it uses the determinate categories and powers of action possessed by particular agents at a particular time. Second, all actual agents are *limited* in many respects. Their cognitive capacities are restricted, and imperfectly integrated; their powers of action are limited by these cognitive capacities, as well as by material and institutional conditions, and are never more than partially independent of other agents and forces. Third, the agents who can follow various nuclear discourses include *individuals and institutions* with varied capacities to reason and to act. Fourth, these capacities *change* and may be changed by the agents whose capacities they are. It follows that there is no single, timelessly correct, answer to the question 'who can endeavour peace?' All we can hope to discern is the relevant audience for ethical discourse about nuclear dangers at particular junctures; and we have no guarantee that there will always be an audience.

One pessimistic comment might be that this account of the limited and determinate character of agency doesn't paint a convincing picture of institutional agency, but a blurry one of individual agency. By stressing the limited unity and independence of agents, and their partial cognitive capacities and powers of action, we have ended up with an account that concedes that there is nothing sufficiently integrated or sufficiently independent of surrounding forces to count as agency. A thin theory of agency isn't enough for ethical reasoning. If the sources of action are so dispersed and fragmentary, there can be no agents who can escape the restricted idioms which ethical discourse claims to criticise. At most there may be quite limited agents with tightly integrated cognitive capacities and powers of action that permit sectoral practical discourse, but are not open enough for specifically ethical discourse about nuclear dangers. In the world as it is, we might conclude, strategic discourse is the only practical nuclear discourse. Nuclear contingency planning needs no ethical reasoning.

Even if this wholesale denial of ethical agency seems implausible, we may doubt that there are now any effective agents who can respond to ethical discourse on nuclear dangers. Maybe ethical discourse about nuclear dangers fails not because states cannot be agents, but because their agency fails in nuclear contexts. Nuclear arsenals augment destructive power but may paralyse other powers of action. Perhaps nuclear states are powerless to reduce nuclear dangers or to endeavour peace in other ways. And if this is true, then once again full nuclear contingency plans will not include ethical reasoning.

These thoughts show how hard the task of achieving *accessible* ethical discourse about nuclear matters is, and why abstracted conceptions of agency are always tempting. If ethical reasoning on nuclear issues is inaccessible to all actual agents (both individual and institutional) it may seem that nuclear contingency planning can do without philosophical components. However, there is one further, indirectly accessible possibility. Even if ethical reasoning can gain no purchase in the world as it is, it may be possible to change the world into one where it is accessible for some relevant agents by making further modes of practical discourse, and hence further possibilities of action, more widely accessible. This strategy may seem to substitute utopian rhetoric for action: surely one more clichéd call for a 'new language' or a 'common language' will not help reduce nuclear dangers.[20]

---

20 However, a *common* language may be more than we need — some quite limited access to others' modes of discourse may be enough. If solutions to global

However, if we are not certain that other approaches will end nuclear dangers, and ethical reasoning is not now accessible to any agents that can reduce nuclear dangers, a rejection of Stoicism will require moves to make additional ways of reasoning accessible. In such circumstances — they may be our circumstances — we have reason enough to make ethical reasoning accessible. This task cannot be a merely *intellectual* one of devising new modes of discourse. It must be the *practical* one of making initially alien modes of discourse more accessible to oneself, to others, or to wider institutional or collective audiences, a matter of transforming or creating agents for whom further modes of discourse are salient and some powers to reduce nuclear dangers graspable. It is not a matter of language reform but of political transformation.

What must anti-Stoics do if they seek to transform agents? Since transformation is a *practical* task they must begin with the actual, untransformed agents that contemporary individuals and institutions are. All change in agents must start from what they now are. Change must be advocated and pursued in terms of categories and powers of action already available. Discourse which is not accessible to actual agents is impractical. For example, if nation-states are among the most powerful agents of our day, and are mainly responsive to arguments conducted in terms of *national* interests and *national* sovereignty, there is little practical point in advocating nuclear policies on the basis of assuming a generally inaccessible *internationalist* standpoint.[21] In such situations the categories of nationalist and statist thinking are salient; they form what MacIntyre has called 'moral starting points.'[22]

Still, starting points are just that; they are not fixed points. Ac-

----

problems presupposed a *complete* common language, the ideological and political fragmentation which underlies those problems, and so the problems themselves, would have to fade before progress could be made.

21 Cf. John Dunn, 'Unimagined Community: the Deceptions of Socialist Internationalism,' in *Rethinking Modern Political Theory* (Cambridge: Cambridge University Press 1985), 103-118; O. O'Neill, *Faces of Hunger*, 152.

22 *After Virtue*, 205

tual conceptual schemes are fragmented and opaque, and so porous to new and even to alien material. The opacity which obstructs completeness and coherence allows for changes and so for the prospect of nuclear discourses accessible to transformed audiences, to whom some forms of ethical discourse may become salient. Reasoning which fails to secure audiences for whom ethical discourse is salient will either remain inaccessible to actual audiences, and so fail to be practical, or will achieve access at the cost of assimilation to established categories and views, which pre-empt the open-ended probing of practical discourse which philosophical ethics demands. The only (and slim) prospect for ethical reasoning about nuclear dangers must then take full account to present political structures, and then bend, break or redefine those structures and the categories of discourse that are taken as salient and so politically relevant. Since such transformations depend on the open character of practical discourse, they may begin at many points. If we do not accept the strategists' view that a few states are the only significant, but ethically incompetent, agents in these matters, or the abstract view that all agents are open to any message, then political realities will direct the first moves in ethical reasoning. For the crucial question will be 'where can which changes be best achieved now?'

This question currently receives various answers. One popular way of seeking change in existing agents and their terms of discourse is through the activities of 'peace movements.' These movements mix education, propaganda and protest politics to challenge the preeminence of establishment and strategic thinking about nuclear dangers. The results of such challenges depend greatly on media coverage. Peace protests make few inroads where media are state-controlled, and limited progress where they are not. This is not surprising. If this argument about the implications of a non-Stoic approach to nuclear dangers convinces, then the practical question to ask of peace protesting is: 'which varieties help transform the structure of agency, and which are rhetorical self-indulgence from the side lines?' Both sorts of activism may be satisfying ways to 'challenge' the status quo by expressing, indeed protesting, commitment to peace. But only the former could count as endeavouring peace. Expression has *political* point only if incidental to communication and action that has some chance of changing otherwise impervious agents. Politically effective communication is (perhaps annoyingly) only contingently connected to satisfying expression of personal commitment to an outlook. 'Peace protestors' may enjoy opportunities to express their commitment to peace which others who pursue 'normal' political and diplomatic moves or more indirect (intellectual, ideological) routes of change have to foreswear. On the other hand, established institutions and those who work through them easily lose sight of possible transformations. Often it is obscure who is more effective, or less ineffective. It may even be that the effectiveness of activities of one sort depends on the context established by activities of the other sort. It is common for proponents of 'peace activism' and of diplomatic negotiation backed by strategic planning to accuse one another of exacerbating rather than reducing nuclear dangers. Unrestricted denunciations are misplaced. In particular contexts the activities both of 'protest' and of 'normal' politics might help (or hinder) the transformation of agents who affect nuclear dangers by altering wider political and ideological settings in which nuclear options are perceived, formulated and pursued.

Often the search for transformations of the structure of agency may be rather indirectly connected with the pursuit of peace *either* by 'protest' *or* by 'normal' politics. If, for example, agents who are distant from present centres of power are to endeavour peace at all, it may be more to the point for them to put effort into criticizing and modifying the present structure of political agency and its underlying assumptions than to 'pursue peace' ineffectually by well-intentioned 'direct action' whose impact is obscure. They might, for example, achieve as much or more (though nothing that they could confidently identify and chalk up as 'their' achievement or credit) by avoiding and undermining activities which endorse or foster social or ideological forms that put national or sectoral interest ahead of the maintenance of peace.

Such activities can be practical only if aimed at changing individual and institutional capacities for action. They may begin with 'mere' rhetoric; but rhetorical change already points beyond itself, to more practical possibilities. It is easy to condemn (perhaps harder to refrain from) the more harebrained uses of the rhetoric of confrontation and national and ideological supremacy. Very few people seriously endorse the implications of 'better dead than red' (or of any counter-part to this slogan that circulates in the socialist world). They would be still less likely to do so if they saw nuclear hostilities as a real danger, or thought their own lives and their children's lives (rather than those of distant allies and 'enemies') at stake. But slightly more guarded uses of discourses of national and ideological supremacy, and the picture of the world and list of nuclear agents, options and 'enemies' that go with such views are commonplace and respecta-ble. The structure of agency would be profoundly transformed if these views were no longer respectable commonplaces. At present both individuals and institutions can *claim* to endeavour peace without dissociating their action from the rhetoric and practice of national and ideological supremacy. If peace is lost, many such agents will be in part responsible (they may not survive to be judged). Those responsible will include not only strategists and poli-ticians, but all whose discourse and activities placed the triumph of market economies or of socialist economies, of the U.S. or of the U.S.S.R., ahead of a commitment to peace. While undiluted inter-nationalism foresakes action for inaccessible rhetoric, a vast range of moves towards rejecting ideologies of national supremacy is ac-cessible for present agents.

The fundamentally *political* character of ethical discourse about nuclear dangers should now be clear. Discourse which is *accessible* to audiences with the power to seek to reduce nuclear dangers must be political: its 'moral starting point' must speak to the powers that are. The powers that are speak in many tongues. We are immedi-ately reminded of the reality which Derrida illuminates. Nuclear dis-courses are now fragmented. There is no single audience. No mode of discourse appears salient to all who might discuss or affect nuclear dangers and prospects of peace. It is not clear which audiences are important and should be addressed. The audiences that appear most powerful are often those for whom ethical discourse is least acces-sible. Hence the first task for nuclear discussions is to use modes of practical discourse which are seen by *actual* audiences not as ques-tion begging, but as salient, accessible and action guiding and which offer those agents reasons for changes and transformations which may help the emergence of audiences for whom lessening nuclear dangers is a practical prospect.

Agents who can listen to such future discourses, for whom the reduction of nuclear dangers is a practical prospect, may still be un-formed rather than fully developed, lying in wait to be galvanised when an appropriate discourse is unveiled. The emergence of an audience and of the modes of thought it finds accessible are two aspects of a single process. Stoicism can be set aside only by effort to change present agents into successors for whom various 'dis-courses of peace' are salient, accessible and practical. Individuals and institutions who do nothing to become and create such au-diences, transforming themselves and others into such agents, have not gone beyond Stoicism in the face of nuclear dangers. If they do not, at least and in the first instance, act to limit and discredit the ideologies of competitive supremacy, they risk 'a war of extermina-tion in which both parties and the right itself might all be simul-taneously annihilated [which] would allow perpetual peace only on the vast graveyard of the human race.'[23]

Received March, 1986
Revised April, 1986

---

23 Immanuel Kant, *Perpetual Peace*, 96, trans. H.B. Nisbet, in Hans Reiss, ed., *Kant's Political Writings* (Cambridge: Cambridge University Press 1970), 93-130

CANADIAN JOURNAL OF PHILOSOPHY
Supplementary Volume 12

Moral Approaches to Nuclear Strategy: A Critical Evaluation

JAMES P. STERBA
University of Notre Dame
Notre Dame, IN 46556
U.S.A.

In the current debate over nuclear strategy, various moral approaches are simply taken for granted. This is unfortunate because the particular strategic recommendations that are endorsed frequently depend upon the particular moral approach that is assumed. Obviously, if we are to rid this debate of its question-begging character, we need to evaluate critically the principal alternative moral approaches to nuclear strategy. I propose to begin this task by describing what is essential to a moral approach to nuclear strategy (Part I). I will then consider the three principal alternative moral approaches to nuclear strategy, the Utilitarian Approach, the Human Nature Approach and the Social Contract Approach (Part II), and relate them to just war theory, indicating why the Social Contract Approach should be favored over the other two (Part III). I will then conclude with some practical implications for nuclear strategy (Part IV).

I

To indicate what is essential to a moral approach to nuclear strategy is to distinguish a moral approach to nuclear strategy from various non-moral approaches. What I regard as examples of non-moral approaches to nuclear strategy are the legal approach (What nuclear strategy best accords with international law and agreements?), the national interest approach (What nuclear strategy is in the national interest of a particular nation?) and the historical or scientific approach (How can past or present nuclear strategies be best accounted for or understood?). To call these approaches non-moral, of course, does not imply that they are immoral approaches. All that is implied is that the requirements of these approaches may or may not conflict with the requirements of morality.

But what, then, essentially characterizes a moral approach to nuclear strategy? I would suggest that there are two features which essentially characterize such an approach:

(1) The approach is prescriptive, that is, it issues in prescriptions, such as 'Do this' and 'Don't do that.'

(2) The approach's prescriptions must be acceptable to all those who would be affected by them.

Feature (1) serves to distinguish a moral approach from an historical or scientific approach because an historical or scientific approach does not issue in prescriptions, although those who employ the approach are required to follow certain methodological prescriptions. Feature (2) serves to distinguish a moral approach from both a legal approach and a national interest approach because the prescriptions that accord best with international law or those that are in the national interest of a particular nation may not be acceptable to all those who would be affected by them. Here the notion of 'acceptable' means 'ought to be accepted' or 'is reasonable to accept,' not simply 'is capable of being accepted.' Accordingly, certain prescriptions may be acceptable even though they are not actually accepted by all those who would be affected by them. Likewise, certain prescriptions may be unacceptable even though they have been accepted by all those who would be affected by them.

II

Given this account of the essential features of a moral approach to nuclear strategy, there are three principal alternative moral approaches to nuclear strategy that should be considered.[1] The first is the Utilitarian Approach. Its basic principle is the following:

> Do those actions that would maximize the net satisfaction or utility of all those who would be affected by them.

The Utilitarian Approach qualifies as a moral approach because it issues in prescriptions and because it is arguable that its prescriptions are acceptable to all those who would be affected by them (since they take the utility of all those who would be affected by them equally into account).

To illustrate how this approach is supposed to apply to the question of whether nation A should adopt a particular nuclear strategy with respect to nation B, assume that nation A's choice would have the following consequences:

---

1 Obviously, there are other moral approaches to nuclear strategy that could be distinguished, but I think that the three I will be considering reflect the range of possible approaches that are relevant to the current debate over nuclear strategy.

	Adopt the strategy	Don't adopt the strategy
Net utility to A	6 1/2 trillion units	2 trillion units
Net utility to B	-2 trillion units	2 trillion units
Total utility	4 1/2 trillion units	4 trillion units

Assuming that these are all the relevant consequences, the Utilitarian Approach, by focusing on total utility, would favor the adoption of the particular nuclear strategy. Notice that in this case the choice favored by the Utilitarian Approach does not conflict with the national interest of nation A, although it does conflict with the national interest of nation B.

But are such calculations of utility possible? Admittedly, they are difficult to make. At the same time, such calculations seem to serve as a basis for public discussion. Recently, President Reagan addressing a group of black business leaders asked whether blacks were better off now because of the Great Society programs, and while many disagreed with his answer, no one appeared to find his question unanswerable.[2] Thus, faced with the difficulties of measuring utility, the Utilitarian Approach would simply counsel that we do our best to determine what maximizes net utility and then act on the result.

---

2 In fact, the debate as to whether blacks are better off now because of the Great Society programs has taken a more scholarly turn. See Charles Murray, *Losing Ground* (New York: Basic Books 1984) and Christopher Jencks, 'How Poor are the Poor?' *New York Review of Books*, May 9 1985.

The second approach to be considered is the Human Nature Approach. Its basic principle is the following:

> Do those actions that would further one's proper development as a human being.

Obviously, this approach qualifies as a moral approach because it issues in prescriptions and because it is arguable that its prescriptions are acceptable to all those who would be affected by them.

There are, however, different versions of this approach. According to some versions, one's proper development as a human being is determinable by each and every person through the use of his or her reason. This interpretation is characteristic of natural law moral theories. According to other versions, one's proper development as a human being is *not* determinable by each and every person through the use of his or her reason. For example, from a Marxist perspective, many people in capitalist societies are deluded by false consciousness and require an economic transformation of their society in order to appreciate what is congenial for their proper development as human beings. Similarly, from many religious perspectives, most people need the help of revelation to determine what is congenial for their proper development as human beings. Now while the Human Nature Approach can take various forms, I want to deal with just the form which specifies proper development in terms of virtuous activity, and, in particular, understands virtuous activity to preclude intentionally doing evil that good may come of it.[3]

The third approach to be considered is the Social Contract Approach. This approach has its origins in the social contract theories of the 17th and 18th centuries. Such theories tended to rely on actual contracts to specify moral requirements, as, for example, in John

---

3 This actually appears to be the most characteristic stance of those who endorse the Human Nature Approach in the current debate. See, for example, Germain Grisez, 'The Moral Implications of a Nuclear Deterrent,' *Center Journal* 2 (1982), 9-24; U.S. Catholic Bishops, *The Challenge of Peace* (Washington, D.C.: U.S. Catholic Conference 1983), especially the Introduction.

Locke's theory. But clearly actual contracts may or may not have been made, and, even if they have been made, they may or may not be moral or fair. This has led some philosophers to resort to hypothetical contracts to ground moral requirements. The problem has been to determine under what conditions a hypothetical contract would be fair and moral. Currently, the most favored Social Contract Approach is specified by the following basic principle:

> Do those actions that persons behind an imaginary veil of ignorance would unanimously agree should be done.[4]

This imaginary veil extends to most particular facts about oneself, anything that would bias one's choice or stand in the way of a unanimous agreement. This approach qualifies as a moral approach because it issues in prescriptions and because it is arguable that its prescriptions are acceptable to all those who would be affected by them since they would be agreed to by all those affected behind an imaginary veil of ignorance.

To illustrate the approach, let us see how it would work with respect to the example of nation A and nation B used earlier. The choice facing nation A was the following:

	Adopt the strategy	Don't adopt the strategy
Net utility to A	6 1/2 trillion units	2 trillion units
Net utility to B	-2 trillion units	2 trillion units
Total utility	4 1/2 trillion units	4 trillion units

---

4 See John Rawls, *A Theory of Justice* (Cambridge, MA: Harvard University Press 1971) and my book *The Demands of Justice* (Notre Dame: Notre Dame Univer-

Given that these are the relevant consequences, the Social Contract Approach, by focusing on the distribution of utility, would favor rejecting the particular nuclear strategy. This would conflict with the resolution of the Utilitarian Approach and the national interest of nation A, but not with the national interest of nation B.

So far, I have suggested that prescriptivity and acceptability of the prescriptions to all those who would be affected by them are the two essential features of a moral approach to nuclear strategy. I have also sketched three principal alternative approaches which qualify as moral approaches to nuclear strategy. What I haven't done is given any reasons why a moral approach to nuclear strategy should be given precedence over any non-moral approach with which it conflicts. Thus, before I attempt to critically evaluate these three approaches with an aim to determining particular requirements for nuclear strategy, I propose to address briefly the question of the justification for following a moral approach to nuclear strategy.

Now it seems to me that the most serious challenge to a moral approach to nuclear strategy is what Michael Walzer calls the Realist Position, and what I would like to call the Realist Approach.[5] Walzer characterizes this approach in the words of Thucydides: 'they that have odds of power exact as much as they can, and the weak yield to such conditions as they can get.' But to best see this approach as a challenge to a moral approach, it needs to be interpreted prescriptively as follows:

> The powerful ought to exact as much as they can and the weak ought to yield to the best conditions they can get.

---

sity Press 1980), especially Chapter 2. To guarantee unanimity, it is necessary to assume that persons behind a veil of ignorance will be motivated only by information they are permitted to take into account. This means they cannot have any free-floating motivations or interests. It is also necessary to assume that persons behind a veil of ignorance are not committed to an all-or-nothing fanatical conception of the good because such a conception would rule out the possibility of reasonable compromise as the basis for agreement.

5 Michael Walzer, *Just and Unjust Wars* (New York, N.Y.:Basic Books 1971), Chapter 1

What is Walzer's response to the Realist Approach? Walzer claims that the powerful and the weak share a moral vocabulary, that is, they hold common moral values, that condemn unrestricted use of power.[6] Thus, according to Walzer, the powerful are bound by a moral approach to nuclear strategy because they are committed to morality in related contexts, and therefore, it would be fundamentally inconsistent or irrational for them to reject morality in the context of nuclear strategy.

How good is this defense? For those who share common moral values that condemn the unrestricted use of power, this defense can be quite effective. But what about those who renounce our moral vocabulary and our shared values? Although some philosophers think that nothing more can be said to such people in defense of a moral approach, that would mean that it could be equally rational for some people to follow a moral approach to nuclear strategy and for others to follow a non-moral approach which radically conflicts with it. No wonder then that some philosophers have tried to show that morality is not only consistent with but also required by reason.[7] And while I think that a defense of this sort can be successful, here I will just assume that either Walzer's defense or some stronger defense can serve to justify adopting a moral approach to nuclear strategy.[8]

Now in order to determine which of these three moral approaches to nuclear strategy is preferable, I will first set out a fairly traditional just war theory, and then show how these three moral approaches support particular versions of that theory.

---

6 Ibid.

7 For example, Kurt Baier, *The Moral Point of View* (Ithaca, N.Y.: Cornell University Press 1958); Alan Gewirth, *Reason and Morality* (Chicago: University of Chicago Press 1977).

8 For what that stronger defense of morality would be like, see my 'Justifying Morality: the Right and the Wrong Ways,' *Synthese* (Kurt Baier Festschrift) forthcoming.

III

In a traditional just war theory there are two basic elements: an account of just cause and an account of just means.[9] Just cause is usually specified as follows:

> There must be substantial aggression and nonbelligerent correctives must be hopeless or too costly.

Needless to say, the notion of substantial aggression is a bit fuzzy, but it is generally understood to be the type of aggression that violates people's most fundamental rights. To suggest some specific examples of what is and what is not substantial aggression, usually nationalization of particular firms owned by foreigners is not regarded as substantial aggression while the taking of hostages is so regarded. But even when substantial aggression occurs, frequently nonbelligerent correctives are neither hopeless nor too costly.

Of course, pacifists would maintain that nonbelligerent correctives, or at least nonlethal correctives, are never hopeless or too costly. Thus, for pacifists there aren't any just causes. But let us set the pacifist issue aside for the moment and go on to specify just means. Just means incorporates a number of conditions:

(1) The harm resulting from the belligerent means employed should not be disproportionate to the military objective to be attained.

(2) Harm to innocents should not be directly intended as an end or a means.

(3) Harm to innocents should be minimized by accepting risks (costs) to oneself that would not render it impossible to attain the military objective.

---

9 For example, see Thomas Aquinas *Summa Theologica* II II Q 64 A7 and II II Q40 A1.

James P. Sterba

Obviously, the notion of what is disproportionate is a bit fuzzy in (1), but the underlying idea is that the harm resulting from the belligerent corrective should not outweigh the benefit to be achieved from attaining the military objective. By contrast, (2) is a relatively precise requirement. Where it was obviously violated was in the antimorale terror bombing of Dresden and Hamburg and in the use of atomic bombs against Hiroshima and Nagasaki in World War II.[10]

Some people think that (1) and (2) capture the essential requirements of just means. Others maintain that something like (3) is also required. Michael Walzer provides an example from Frank Richard's memoir of World War I which shows the attractiveness of (3).

> When bombing dug-outs or cellars, it was always wise to throw the bombs into them first and have a look around after. But we had to be very careful in this village as there were civilians in some of the cellars. We shouted down to them to make sure. Another man and I shouted down one cellar twice and receiving no reply were just about to pull the pins out of our bomb when we heard a woman's voice and a young lady came up the cellar steps .... She and the members of her family ... had not left [the cellar] for some days. They guessed an attack was being made and when we first shouted down had been too frightened to answer. if the young lady had not cried out when she did we would have innocently murdered them all.[11]

Many restrictions on the operation of police forces also seem to derive from a requirement like (3).

Now to better understand our three alternative moral approaches to nuclear strategy, we need to determine to what degree this just war theory would be supported by each of these moral approaches. Of course, one or more of these approaches may ultimately favor the pacifist position, but assuming that these approaches were to favor some version of a just war theory, which version would that be? Later we will take up the pacifist position.

Obviously, the Utilitarian Approach would have little difficulty

---

10 Even if these bombings did help shorten World War II, and there is considerable evidence that they did not, they would have still been in violation of requirement (2) on just means.

11 See Walzer, 152.

accepting the requirement of just cause and requirement (1) on just means because these requirements can be interpreted as having a utilitarian backing. However, this approach would only accept requirements (2) and (3) on just means conditionally since occasions would surely arise when violations of these requirements would maximize net utility.

Unlike the Utilitarian Approach, the Human Nature Approach is relatively indeterminate in its requirements. All that is certain, as I have interpreted the approach, is that it would be absolutely committed to requirement (2) on just means. Of course, the other requirements on just cause and just means would be required by particular versions of this approach.

What is distinctive about the Social Contract Approach is that it seeks to combine and compromise both the concern of the Utilitarian Approach for maximal net utility and the concern of the Human Nature Approach for the proper development of each individual. In its hypothetical choice situation, persons would clearly favor the requirement of just cause and requirement (1) on just means although they would not interpret them in a strictly utilitarian fashion.

Yet what about the requirements (2) and (3) on just means? Since persons behind a veil of ignorance would not be committed simply to whatever maximizes net utility, they would want to put a stricter limit upon the harm that could be inflicted on innocents in defense of a just cause than could be justified on utilitarian grounds alone. This is because persons behind a veil of ignorance would be concerned not only with what maximizes net utility but also with the distribution of utility to particular individuals. Persons imagining themselves to be ignorant of what position they are in would be particularly concerned that they might turn out to be in the position of those who are innocent, and consequently, they would want strong safeguards against harming those who are innocent, like requirements (2) and (3) on just means.

But would persons behind a veil of ignorance want to distinguish, as requirement (2) on just means does, between harm intentionally inflicted upon innocents and harm whose infliction upon innocents is merely foreseen? On the one hand, they could adopt a uniform restriction upon the infliction of harm upon innocents that ignores the intended/foreseen distinction. On the other hand, they could adopt a differential restriction which is more severe than the uniform restriction against the intentional infliction of harm upon innocents but is less severe than the uniform restriction against the infliction of harm that is merely foreseen. What needs to be determined, therefore, is whether there is any rationale for favoring a differential restriction on harm over the uniform restriction.

Certainly, from the perspective of those suffering the harm, it appears to matter little whether the harm would be intended or just foreseen by those who cause it. From the perspective of those suffering harm, what matters most is simply that the overall amount of harm be restricted irrespective of whether it is foreseen or intended.

Nevertheless, from the perspective of those causing harm, one's interest in doing good is limited more by a restriction against foreseen harm than by a comparable restriction against intended harm. This is because a restriction against foreseen harm limits one's actions when one's ends and means are *good* whereas a restriction against intended harm limits one's actions when one's ends or means are *evil* or *harmful*. Accordingly, one's interest in doing good is better served by a differential restriction that is weaker against causing foreseen harm and stronger against causing intended harm. Furthermore, provided that the differential restriction is designed so that its overall effect is to exclude roughly the same amount of harm to innocents as would be excluded by the uniform restriction, there should be no objection to such a restriction from the perspective of those who are suffering harm.

There are, however, two objections to this use of the foreseen/intended distinction that should be considered. The first is that we cannot in practice distinguish between what is foreseen and what is intended. The second is that the grounds for introducing this distinction are question-begging against a utilitarian perspective.

Now the practical test that is frequently used to distinguish between foreseen and intended elements of an action is the Counterfactual Test. According to this test, two questions are relevant:

(1) Would you have performed the action if only the good consequences would have resulted and not the evil consequences?

(2) Would you have performed the action if only the evil consequences resulted and not the good consequences?

If an agent answers 'Yes' to the first question and 'No' to the second then some would conclude that (1) the action is an intended means to the good consequences, (2) the good consequences are an intended end, and (3) the evil consequences are merely foreseen.

But does this test work in practice? Douglas Lackey has argued that the test gives the wrong result in any case where the 'act that produces an evil effect produces a larger good effect.'[12] Lackey cites the bombing of Hiroshima as an example. That bombing had two effects: the killing of Japanese civilians and the shortening of the war. Now suppose we were to ask:

(1) Would Truman have dropped the bomb if only the shortening of the war would have resulted but not the killing of the Japanese civilians?

(2) Would Truman have dropped the bomb if only the Japanese civilians would have been killed and the war not shortened?

And suppose the answers to these questions are respectively 'Yes' and 'No.' Lackey concludes from this that the killing of civilians at Hiroshima, self-evidently a means for shortening the war, is by the Counterfactual Test classified not as a means but as a mere foreseen consequence. On these grounds, Lackey rejects the Counterfactual Test as a practical device for distinguishing between the foreseen and the intended elements of an action.

Unfortunately, Lackey rejects the Counterfactual Test only because he expects too much from it. Lackey expects the test to determine all of the following:

---

12 Douglas P. Lackey, 'The Moral Irrelevance of the Counterforce/Countervalue Distinction,' *The Monist*, forthcoming in 1987. For a similar view, see Susan Levine, 'Does the "Counterfactual Test" Work for Distinguishing a Means from a Foreseen Concomitant,' *Journal of Value Inquiry* 18 (1984), 155-7.

(1) Whether the action is an intended means to the good consequences;

(2) Whether the good consequences are an intended end of the action;

(3) Whether the evil consequences are simply foreseen consequences.

In fact, this test is only capable of determining (1) and (2). And the test clearly succeeds in doing this for Lackey's own example, where the test shows the bombing of Hiroshima to be an intended means to shortening the war, and shortening the war an intended consequence of the action.

To determine (3) an additional test is needed, which I shall call the Nonexplanation Test. According to this test, the relevant question is:

> Does the bringing about of the evil consequences help explain why the agent undertook the action as a means to the good consequences?

If the answer is 'No,' that is, if the bringing about of the evil consequences does not help explain why the agent undertook the action as a means to the good consequences, then the evil consequences are merely foreseen. But if the answer is 'Yes,' then the evil consequences are an intended means to the good consequences.

Of course, there is no guaranteed procedure for arriving at an answer to the relevant question of the Nonexplanation Test. Nevertheless, when we are in doubt concerning (3), seeking an answer to this question will tend to be the best way of reasonably resolving that doubt. For example, applied to Lackey's example, the Nonexplanation Test comes up with a 'Yes,' since the evil consequences in this example do help explain why the bombing was undertaken to shorten the war. For Truman ordered the bombing to bring about the civilian deaths which by their impact upon Japanese morale were expected to shorten the war. So, by the Nonexplanation Test, the civilian deaths were an intended means to the good consequences of shortening the war.[13]

The second objection to the use of the forseen/intended distinction is that the ground for introducing this distinction is question-begging against a utilitarian perspective. That ground, you will recall, is one's interest in doing good. What this objection denies is that any non-question-begging reason can be given for prefering one's interest in doing good over one's interest in bringing about good consequences.

Notice, however, that one's interest in bringing about good consequences is not in direct conflict with one's interest in doing good. Rather it directly conflicts with one's interest in limiting the amount of harm to innocents that can be done in the pursuit of good consequences. And this latter interest is one that persons behind a veil of ignorance would strongly want to protect. Moreover, once the degree of protection for this interest has been determined, there is little reason to think that one's interest in bringing about good con-

---

13 This Nonexplanation Test also solves a related problem of distinguishing foreseen from intended consequences noted by Charles Fried. (Charles Fried, *Right and Wrong* [Cambridge, MA: Harvard University Press 1978], 23-4.) Fried was concerned with the following example, first discussed by Philippa Foot (Philippa Foot, 'The Problem of Abortion and the Doctrine of Double Effect,' *Oxford Review* 5 [1967], 5-15): 'Imagine that a fat person who is leading a party of spelunkers gets herself stuck in the mouth of a cave in which flood waters are rising. The trapped party of spelunkers just happens to have a stick of dynamite with which they can blast the fat person out of the mouth of the case; either they use the dynamite or they all drown, the fat person with them.' Now suppose someone would claim that using the dynamite was simply a means of freeing the party of spelunkers and that the death of the fat person was just a forseen side-effect. Fried's problem was that while he rejected this account of the action, he could find no way of successfully challenging it. What he clearly needed was the Nonexplanation Test. For suppose we employ the test and ask whether the death of the fat person helps explain why the dynamite was used to free the spelunkers from the cave, the answer we get is clearly 'Yes.' For how else could the use of the dynamite free the party of spelunkers from the case except by removing the fat person from the mouth of the cave in such a way as to cause her death? It follows, according to the Nonexplanation Test, that the death of the fat person was a means intended for freeing the party of spelunkers and not merely a foreseen consequence of the use of the dynamite.

sequences would be better served by a uniform than by a differential restriction on such harm.[14]

The opposite is true, of course, for one's interest in doing good. That interest, as we have seen, favors a differential restriction (with its foreseen/intended distinction) over a uniform restriction. And it is for this reason that persons behind a veil of ignorance would want to adopt such a restriction.

Yet even though persons behind a veil of ignorance would favor a differential restriction on harm to innocents, they would not favor an absolute restriction upon intentional harm to innocents. They would recognize as exceptions to such a restriction cases where intentional harm to innocents is either

(1) trivial (e.g. as in the case of stepping on someone's foot to get out of a crowded subway),

(2) easily reparable (e.g., as in the case of lying to a temporarily depressed friend to keep her from committing suicide) or

(3) sufficiently outweighed by the consequences of the action (e.g., as in the case of shooting one of two hundred civilian hostages to prevent in the only way possible the execution of all two hundred).

Accordingly, while persons behind a veil of ignorance would favor requirement (2) on just means, their commitment to this requirement would also have to incorporate the above exceptions. Even so, these exceptions are far more limited than those that would be tolerated by the Utilitarian Approach.

In sum, the Social Contract Approach would strongly endorse the requirement of just cause and requirements (1), (2) and (3) on just means. Yet its commitment to requirement (2) on just means would fall short of the absolute commitment that is characteristic of the Human Nature Approach to nuclear strategy.

---

14 It may even be the case that a weaker restriction on the foreseen harm allows more good consequences to be achieved than a stronger restriction on intended harm rules out.

It is clear, therefore, that our three moral approaches to nuclear strategy differ significantly with respect to their requirements for a just war theory. The Utilitarian Approach strongly endorses the requirement of just cause and requirement (1) on just means but only conditionally endorses requirements (2) and (3) on just means. The Human Nature Approach endorses requirement (2) on just means as an absolute requirement, but is indeterminate with respect to the other requirements of just war theory. Only the Social Contract Approach strongly endorses all of the basic requirements of a traditional just war theory, although it does not regard requirement (2) on just means as an absolute requirement. Fortunately for traditional just war theory, there are good reasons for favoring the Social Contract Approach over each of the other two moral approaches to nuclear strategy.

One reason for favoring the Social Contract Approach over the Utilitarian Approach is that its requirements are derived from a veil of ignorance decision-procedure that utilitarians and contractarians alike recognize to be fair. It is not surprising, therefore, to find utilitarians, like John Harsanyi and R.M. Hare, simply endorsing this decision-procedure and then trying to show that the requirements that result from it are actually those that would maximize utility.[15] Yet we have just seen how the concern of persons behind a veil of ignorance with the distribution of utility would lead them to impose a stricter limit upon the harm that could be inflicted upon innocents in defense of a just cause than could be justified on grounds of maximizing utility alone. At least with respect to just war theory, therefore, the Utilitarian Approach and the Social Contract Approach differ significantly in their practical requirements.[16]

Obviously, then, utilitarians who endorse this decision-procedure

---

15 See John Harsanyi, *Rational Behavior and Bargaining Equilibrium in Games and Social Situations* (Cambridge, MA: Cambridge University Press 1977) and R.M. Hare, 'Justice and Equality,' in James P. Sterba, ed., *Justice: Alternative Political Perspectives* (Belmont, CA: Wadsworth 1980), 105-19.

16 The two approaches also differ in their requirements for distributive justice (see Rawls, *A Theory of Justice*) and retributive justice (see my *The Demands*

are faced with a difficult choice: either give up their commitment to this decision-procedure or modify their commitment to utilitarian goals. Nor can utilitarians easily choose to give up their commitment to this decision-procedure because the acceptability of utilitarianism as traditionally conceived has always depended on showing that fairness and utility rarely conflict, and that when they do, it is always plausible to think that the requirements of utility are morally overriding. Consequently, when a fair decision-procedure shows a significant conflict with utility − which it is not plausible to think can always be morally overridden by the requirements of utility − that procedure succeeds in exposing the inadequacy of the Utilitarian Approach to nuclear strategy.

Needless to say, it is possible to modify this veil of ignorance decision-procedure so as to bring the choices of persons using it in line with the Utilitarian Approach to nuclear strategy. One way to achieve this is to reconstitute the persons using this decision-procedure so that they would no longer take seriously the distribution of utility to particular individuals. This could be done by conceiving of persons using this decision procedure as living seriatim the lives or, better, integral parts of the lives of many randomly selected individuals from among those who would be affected by the decision. In this way, each person using this decision-procedure would be able to realize, at least approximately, the average utility of all those affected by the decision. Consequently, each person would no longer have any reason to take seriously into account the distribution of utility to individuals when using this decision-procedure.

Yet this proposal for modifying the veil of ignorance decision-procedure simply exposes the inadequacy of the conception of the nature of persons implicit in the Utilitarian Approach. For in order to choose to maximize average utility, persons using this decision procedure would have to think of themselves as living seriatim integral parts of the lives of many randomly selected individuals. To

---

of Justice [Notre Dame, IN: University of Notre Dame Press 1981], Chapter 3 and 'Is There a Rationale for Punishment?' *American Journal of Jurisprudence* 29 [1984], 29-43).

make such a choice, therefore, would require that, at least for moral purposes, persons begin to think of themselves in a radically different way. In this connection, John Rawls has argued that choosing to maximize total utility also implies an inadequate conception of persons because such a choice would only be made by a sympathetic spectator who regards everyone's desires and satisfactions as if they were the desires and satisfactions of just one person.[17] It could be argued, therefore, that both of these choices fail to pay sufficient attention to the distinction between persons – the choice of the highest total utility requiring that persons think of themselves as parts of one 'total person,' and the choice of the highest average utility requiring that persons think of themselves as parts of what could be called 'average persons.' This failure to pay sufficient attention to the distinction between persons, a failure resulting in the Utilitarian Approach's conditional endorsement of requirements (2) and (3) on just means, provides yet another good reason for favoring the Social Contract Approach over the Utilitarian Approach to nuclear strategy.

Now these reasons for favoring the Social Constract Approach over the Utilitarian Approach to nuclear strategy are also reasons for favoring the Human Nature Approach because the Human Nature Approach is also concerned with fairness and the distribution of utility to particular individuals. Nevertheless, there are other reasons for favoring the Social Contract Approach over the Human Nature Approach.

One reason is that the Social Contract Approach does not endorse any absolute requirements. In particular, the Social Contract Approach does not endorse an absolute requirement not to intentionally harm innocents. The Social Contract Approach recognizes that if the harm is trivial, easily reparable or sufficiently outweighed by the consequences, there can be an adequate moral justification for permitting such a harm.

Of course, some might regard the fact that the Social Contract Approach does not endorse any absolute moral requirements as a liability rather than as an asset of the approach. Yet when defenders

---

17 Rawls, *A Theory of Justice*, 22-7

of absolute requirements are asked to support their views in just the kind of cases in which the Social Contract Approach would permit exceptions to its requirements, they usually appeal to divine command theory.[18] Unfortunately, when divine command theory is used to decide morally difficult cases, it embraces an anything-could-be-right-if-God-command-it view with all the absurdities that are traditionally associated with the view.[19] Consequently, there just does not appear to be any reasonable alternative to a moral approach like the Social Contract Approach which allows its moral requirements to bend but not break in morally difficult cases.

Another reason for favoring the Social Contract Approach over the Human Nature Approach is that the Social Contract Approach is determinate in its requirements; it actually leads to a wide range of practical recommendations. By contrast, the Human Nature Approach lacks a deliberative procedure that is capable of producing agreement with respect to practical requirements. This is evident from the fact that supporters of this approach tend to endorse radically different practical requirements. In this regard, the veil of ignorance decision-procedure employed by the Social Contract Approach appears to be just the sort of morally defensible device that is needed to achieve determinate requirements.

Finally, the particular requirements of just war theory endorsed by the Social Contract Approach are further supported by the presence of analogous requirements for related areas of conduct. Thus, the strong legal prohibitions that exist against punishing the innocent provide support for the strong prohibition against harming innocents expressed by requirements (2) and (3) on just means. This is just the type of correspondence we would expect from an adequate moral theory: requirements in one area of conduct would be analogous to requirements in related areas of conduct.

Yet even assuming that the Social Contract Apporoach is morally superior to the other two approaches for just the reasons given,

---

18 See, for example, John Finnis, *Natural Law and Natural Rights* (Oxford: Oxford University Press 1980), especially Part 3.

19 See John Chandler, 'Divine Command Theories and the Appeal to Love,' *American Philosophical Quarterly* 22 (1985) 231-9.

there remains the question of whether this approach might ultimately favor a form of pacifism over its preferred version of just war theory.

Now it is sometimes claimed that pacifism is an incoherent view. In a well-known article, Jan Narveson rejects pacifism as incoherent because it recognizes a right to life yet rules out any use of force in defense of that right.[20] The view is incoherent, Narveson claims, because having a right entails the legitimacy of using force in defense of that right at least on some occasions. But as Cheyney Ryan has pointed out, Narveson's argument only works against the following extreme form of pacifism:

> Pacifism I
> Any use of force is morally prohibited.[21]

It doesn't touch the form of pacifism that Ryan thinks is most defensible, which is the following:

> Pacifism II
> Any lethal use of force is morally prohibited.

This form of pacifism only prohibits the use of lethal force in defense of people's rights.

Ryan goes on to argue that there is a substantial issue between the pacifist and the nonpacifist concerning whether we can or should create the necessary distance between ourselves and other human beings in order to make the act of killing possible. To illustrate, Ryan cites George Orwell's reluctance to shoot at any enemy soldier who jumped out of a trench and ran along the top of a parapet half-dressed and holding up his trousers with both hands. Ryan contends that what kept Orwell from shooting was that he couldn't think of the soldier as a thing rather than a fellow human being.

But do we have to objectify other human beings in order to kill them? If we do, this would seem to tell in favor of the form of

---

20 Jan Narveson, 'Pacifism: A Philosophical Analysis,' *Ethics* 75 (1965), 259-71

21 Cheyney Ryan, 'Self-Defense and Pacifism,' in James P. Sterba, ed., *The Ethics of War and Nuclear Deterrence* (Belmost, CA: Wadsworth 1985), 45-9

pacifism Ryan defends. However, it is not clear that Orwell's encounter supports such a view. For it may be what kept Orwell from shooting the enemy soldier was not his inability to think of the soldier as a thing rather than a fellow human being but rather his inability to think of the soldier who was holding up his trousers with both hands as a threat or a combatant. Under this interpretation, Orwell's decision not to shoot would accord well with the requirements of just war theory.

Let us suppose, however, that someone is attempting to take your life. Why does that permit you, the pacifist might ask, to kill the person making the attempt? Isn't such killing prohibited by the principle that one should never intentionally do evil that good may come of it? Of course, the Social Contract Approach would not endorse this principle as an absolute requirement, but surely it cannot be reasonable to regard all cases of justified killing in self-defense as exceptions to this principle.

One response to this pacifist objection is to allow that killing in self-defense can be morally justified provided that the killing is the foreseen consequence of an action whose intended consequence is the stopping of the attempt upon one's life. Another response is to allow that intentional killing in self-defense can be morally justified provided that you are reasonably certain that your attacker is wrongfully engaged in an attempt upon your life. It is claimed that in such a case the intentional killing is not evil, or at least not morally evil, because anyone who is wrongfully engaged in an attempt upon your life has already forfeited her or his right to life by engaging in such aggression.

Taken together, these two responses are an adequate reply to the pacifist objection. The first response is theoretically closer to the pacifist's own position since it rules out all intentional killing. But suppose we apply the Nonexplanation Test to the case at hand, and ask: Does the bringing about of the evil consequence (the killing) help explain why you undertook your particular act of self-defense as a means of stopping the attempt upon your life? To answer this question with the 'No' that is required if the evil consequence is merely foreseen, it must be the case, other things being equal, that the particular act of self-defense was chosen because it was less likely to produce the evil consequence (the killing). For only then would

the evil consequence (the killing) not help explain why you undertook this particular act of self-defense to put a stop to the attempt
upon your life. Nevertheless, since it is not clear that such options
will always be available in paradigm cases of self-defense, it is important to have the second response to the pacifist objection, which
permits intentional killing, to fall back on.

IV

The requirements for just war theory that have been defended so
far are directly applicable to the question of the morality of nuclear
war. In particular, requirements (2) and (3) on just means would
prohibit any counter-city or counter-population use of nuclear
weapons. While this prohibition is not absolute, it is simply not foreseeable that any use of nuclear weapons could ever be a morally
justified exception to this prohibition.

But what about a counter-force use of nuclear weapons? Consider the massive use of nuclear weapons by the United States or
the Soviet Union against industrial and economic centers. Such a
strike, involving three to five thousand warheads, could destroy between 70-80 percent of each nation's industry and result in the immediate death of as many as 165 million American and 100 million
Russians respectively, in addition to running a considerable risk of
a retaliatory nuclear strike by the opposing superpower.[22] It has also
been estimated by Carl Sagan and others that such a strike is very
likely to generate firestorms which would cover much of the earth
with sooty smoke for months, creating a 'nuclear winter' that would
threaten the very survival of the human species.[23] Applying require-

---

22 *The Effects of Nuclear War* (Office of Technology Assessment, Washington,
   DC: US Government Printing Office 1979), 94, 100; Nigel Calder, *Nuclear
   Nightmares* (New York: Viking 1979), 150; Sidney Lens, *The Day Before Dooms-
   day* (Boston: Beacon Press 1977), 102

23 Carl Sagan, 'Nuclear War and Climate Catastrophe: Some Policy Implications,' *Foreign Affairs* 62 (1983), 257-92

ment (1) on just means, there simply is no foreseeable military objective which could justify such morally horrendous consequences.

The same holds true for a massive use of nuclear weapons against tactical and strategic targets. Such a strike, involving two to three thousand warheads, directed against only ICBMs, submarine and bomber bases could wipe out as many as 20 million Americans and 28 million Russians respectively, in addition to running a considerable risk of a retaliatory nuclear strike by the opposing superpower.[24] Here too there is a considerable risk of a 'nuclear winter' occurring. This being the case what military objective might foreseeably justify such a use of nuclear weapons?

Of course, it should be pointed out that the above argument does not rule out a limited use of nuclear weapons at least against tactical and strategic targets. Such a use is still possible. Yet practically it would be quite difficult for either superpower to distinguish between a limited and a massive use of nuclear weapons, especially if a full-scale conventional war is raging. In such circumstances, any use of nuclear weapons is likely to be viewed as part of a massive use of such weapons, thus increasing the risk of a massive nuclear retaliatory strike.[25] In addition, war games have shown that if enough tactical nuclear weapons are employed over time in a limited area, such as Germany, the effect on noncombatants in that area would be much the same as in a massive nuclear attack.[26] As Bundy, Kennan, McNamara and Smith put the point in their recent endorsement of a doctrine of no first use of nuclear weapons:

> Every serious analysis and every military exercise, for over 25 years, has demonstrated that even the most restrained battlefield use would be enormously destructive to civilian life and property. There is no way for any-

---

24 *The Effects of Nuclear War*, 83, 91; Jerome Kahan, *Security in the Nuclear Age* (Washington, DC: The Brookings Institution 1975), 202; Sidney Lens, 98, 99, 102

25 Sidney Lens, 78-9; Spurgeon Keeny and Wolfgang Panofsky, 'MAD versus NUTS,' *Foreign Affairs* 60 (1981-82), 297-8; Ian Clark, *Limited Nuclear War* (Princeton: Princeton University Press 1982), 242

26 Sidney Lens, 73

one to have any confidence that such a nuclear action will not lead to further and more devastating exchanges. Any use of nuclear weapons in Europe, by the Alliance or against it, carries with it a high and inescapable risk of escalation into the general nuclear war which would bring ruin to all and victory to none.[27]

For these reasons, even a limited use of nuclear weapons generally would not meet requirement (1) on just means.

Nevertheless, there are some circumstances in which a limited use of nuclear weapons would meet all the requirements on just means. For example, suppose that a nation was attacked with a massive nuclear counter-force strike and it was likely that, if the nation did not retaliate with a limited nuclear strike on tactical and strategic targets, a massive attack on its industrial and population centers would follow. Under such circumstances, it can be argued, a limited nuclear retaliatory strike would satisfy all the requirements of just means. Of course, the justification for such a strike would depend on what foreseen effect the strike would have on innocent lives and how likely it was that the strike would succeed in deterring a massive attack on the nation's industrial and population centers. But assuming a limited nuclear retaliatory strike on tactical and strategic targets was the best way of avoiding a significantly greater evil, it would be morally justified according to the requirements of just means.

Yet what about the morality of threatening to use nuclear weapons to achieve nuclear deterrence? Obviously, the basic requirements of just war theory are not applicable to threats to use nuclear weapons. Nevertheless, it seems clear that the Social Contract Ap-

---

27 McGeorge Bundy, George F. Kennan, Robert S. McNamara and Gerald Smith, 'Nuclear Weapons and the Atlantic Alliance,' *Foreign Affairs* 61 (1982), 757; it should be noted that Bundy, Kennan, McNamara and Smith believed that their endorsement of a doctrine of no first use of nuclear weapons *may* involve increased spending for conventional forces in Europe. Others, however, have found NATO's existing conventional strength to be adequate to meet a Soviet attack. See David Barash and Judith Lipton, *Stop Nuclear War* (New York: Grove Press 1982), 138-40; Harold Brown, U.S. *Department of Defense Annual Report* (1981).

proach would favor the following analogous requirements of what we could call 'a just threat theory.'

> Just Cause
>
> There must be a substantial threat or the likelihood of such a threat and nonthreatening correctives must be hopeless or too costly.
>
> Just Means
>
> (1) The risk of harm resulting from the use of threats (or bluffs) should not be disproportionate to the military objective to be attained.
>
> (2) Actions that are prohibited by just war theory cannot be threatened as an end or a means.
>
> (3) The risk of harm to innocents from the use of threats (bluffs) should be minimized by accepting risks (costs) to oneself that would not render it impossible to attain the military objective.

Now if we assume for the moment that the requirement of just cause is met, the crucial restriction of just threat theory is requirement (2) on just means. This requirement puts a severe restriction on what we can legitimately threaten to do, assuming, that is, that threatening implies an intention to carry out under appropriate conditions what one has threatened to do. In fact, since, as we have seen, only a limited use of nuclear weapons could ever foreseeably be morally justified, it follows from requirement (2) that only such a use can be legitimately threatened. Obviously, this constitutes a severe limit on the use of threats to achieve nuclear deterrence.

Nevertheless, it may be possible to achieve nuclear deterrence by other means; for example, by bluffing. This possibility has not been sufficiently explored because it is generally not thought to be possible to institutionalize bluffing. But suppose we imagine bluffing to include deploying a survivable nuclear force and preparing that force for possible use in such a way that leaders who are bluffing a morally prohibited form of nuclear retalization need outwardly distinguish themselves from those who are threatening such retaliation only in their strong moral condemnation of this use of nuclear weapons. Surely this form of bluffing is capable of being institutionalized.

This form of bluffing can also be effective in achieving deterrence because it is subject to at least two interpretations. One interpretation is that the leaders of a nation are actually bluffing because while the leaders do deploy nuclear weapons and do appear to threaten to use them in certain ways, they also morally condemn those uses of nuclear weapons, so they can't really be intending to so use them. The other interpretation is that the leaders are not bluffing but are in fact immoral agents intentionally committed to doing what they regard as a grossly immoral course of action. But since the leaders of other nations can never be reasonably sure which interpretation is correct, a nation's leaders can effectively bluff under these conditions.

Moreover, citizens who think that only a bluffing strategy with respect to certain forms of nuclear retaliation can ever be morally justified would look for leaders who express their own views on this issue in just this ambiguous manner. It is also appropriate for those who are in places of high command within a nation's nuclear forces to express the same ambiguous views; only those low in the command structure of a nation's nuclear forces need not express the same ambiguous views about the course of action they would be carrying out, assuming they can see themselves as carrying out only (part of) a limited nuclear retaliatory strike. This is because, as we noted earlier, such a strike would be morally justified under certain conceivable but unlikely conditions.

Yet even granting that a threat of limited nuclear retaliation and a bluff of massive nuclear retaliation can be justified by the requirements of just means, it would not follow that we are presently justified in so threatening or bluffing unless there presently exists a just cause for threatening or bluffing. Of course, it is generally assumed that such a cause does presently exist. That is, it is generally assumed that both superpowers have a just cause to maintain a state of nuclear deterrence vis-à-vis each other by means of threats and bluffs of nuclear retaliation.

But to determine whether this assumption is correct, let us consider two possible stances a nation's leaders might take with respect to nuclear weapons:

(1) A nation's leaders might be willing to carry out a nuclear strike *only* in response to either a nuclear first strike or a massive conventional first strike on itself or its principal allies.

(2) A nation's leaders might be willing to carry out a massive conventional strike *only* in response to either a nuclear first strike or a massive conventional first strike on itself or its principal allies.

Now assuming that a nation's leaders were to adopt (1) and (2), then threats or bluffs of nuclear retaliation could not in fact be made against them! For a threat or bluff must render less eligible something an agent might otherwise want to do, and leaders of nations who adopt (1) and (2) have a preference structure that would not be affected by any attempt to threaten or bluff nuclear retaliation. Hence, such threats or bluffs could not be made against them either explicitly or implicitly.

Of course, a nation's leaders could try to threaten or bluff nuclear retaliation against another nation but if the intentions of the leaders of that other nation are purely defensive then although they may succeed in restricting the liberty of the leaders of that other nation by denying them a possible option, they would not have succeeded in threatening them, for that would require that they render less eligible something those leaders might otherwise want to do.[28]

---

28 On my view, to succeed in threatening two conditions must be met:

(1) One must have the intention to carry out the action one is purporting to threaten under the stated conditions; that is, one must expect that if the stated conditions do obtain then one will carry out that action.

(2) The preference structure of the party that one is trying to threaten must be so affected that something the party might otherwise have wanted to do is rendered less eligible.

Now if we take them at their word, the leaders of both super-powers seem to have adopted (1) and (2). As Casper Weinberger recently characterized U.S. policy: 'Our strategy is a defensive one, designed to prevent attack, particularly nuclear attack, against us or our allies.'[29] And a similar statement of Soviet policy can be found in Mikhail Gorbachev's recent appeal for a return to a new era of detente.[30] Moreover, since 1982 Soviet leaders appear to have gone beyond simply endorsing (1) and (2) and have ruled out the use of a nuclear first strike under any circumstances.[31]

Assuming the truth of these statements, it follows that the present leaders of the U.S. and the Soviet Union could not be threatening or bluffing each other with nuclear retaliation despite their apparent attempts to do so. This is because a commitment to (1) and (2) rules out the necessary aggressive intentions that it is the purpose of such threats or bluffs to deter. Leaders of nations whose strategy is a purely defensive one would be immune from threats or bluffs of nuclear retaliation. In fact, leaders of nations who claim their strategy is purely defensive yet who persist in attempting to threaten or bluff nuclear retaliation against nations whose proclaimed strategy is also purely defensive eventually throw into doubt their own commitment to a purely defensive strategy. It is for these reasons that a just cause for threatening or bluffing nuclear retaliation would be not available under present conditions.

Of course, the leaders of a superpower might claim that threatening or bluffing nuclear retaliation would be morally justified under present conditions on the grounds that the proclaimed defensive strategy of the other superpower is not believable. Surely this stance would be reasonable if the other superpower had launched an aggressive attack against the superpower or its principal allies. But neither U.S. intervention in Nicaragua nor Soviet intervention in Afghanistan nor other military actions taken by either superpower

---

29 Caspar Weinberger, 'Why We Must Have Nuclear Deterrence,' *Defense* (March, 1983), 3

30 *The New York Times*, May 9 1985

31 See Leonid Brezhnev's message to the U.N. General Assembly on June 2 1982.

are directed against even a principal ally of the other superpower. Consequently, in the absence of an aggressive attack of the appropriate sort and in the absence of an opposing military force that could be used without risking unacceptable losses from retaliatory strikes, each superpower is required to provisionally place some trust in the proclaimed defensive strategy of the other superpower because it is morally objectionable to multiply one's 'enemies' without reason.

Nevertheless, it would still be morally legitimate for both superpowers to retain a retaliatory nuclear force so as to be able to threaten or bluff nuclear retaliation in the future should conditions change for the worse. For as long as nations possess nuclear weapons, such a change could occur simply with a chance of leaders coming to power who can only be deterred by a threat or bluff of nuclear retaliation.

For example, suppose a nation possesses a survivable nuclear force capable of inflicting unacceptable damage upon its adversary; yet possession of such a force alone would not suffice to deter an adversary from carrying out a nuclear first strike unless that possession were combined with a threat of limited nuclear retaliation or a bluff of massive nuclear retaliation. (With respect to massive nuclear retaliation, bluffing would be required here since leaders who recognize and respect the above just war constraints on the use of nuclear weapons could not in fact threaten such retaliation.) Under these circumstances, I think the required threat or bluff would be morally justified. But I also think that there is ample evidence today to indicate that neither the leadership of the United States nor that of the Soviet Union requires such a threat or bluff to deter them from carrying out a nuclear first strike.[32] Consequently, un-

---

32 See Kahan, *Security in the Nuclear Age*; Lens, *The Day Before Doomsday*; Henry Kendall and others, *Beyond the Freeze* (Boston: Beacon Press 1982); George Kistiakowsky, 'False Alarm: The Story Behind SALT II,' *The New York Review of Books*, April 2 1979; Les Aspin, 'How to Look at the Soviet-American Balance,' *Foreign Policy* 22 (1976), 96-106; Gordon Adams, 'The Iron Triangle,' *The Nation* 116 (October 1981), 425, 441-4. Much of this evidence is reviewed in my paper, 'How to Achieve Nuclear Deterrence Without Threatening Nuclear Destruction,' included in *The Ethics of War and Nuclear Deterrence*, 155-68.

der present conditions, such a threat or bluff would not be morally justified.

Nevertheless, under present conditions it would be legitimate for a nation to maintain a survivable nuclear force in order to be able to deal effectively with a change of policy in the future. Moreover, if either superpower does in fact harbor any undetected aggressive intentions against the other, the possession of a survivable nuclear force by the other superpower should suffice to deter a first strike since neither superpower could be sure whether in response to such strike the other superpower would follow its moral principles or its national interest.[33]

Of course, if nuclear forces were only used to retain the capacity for threatening or bluffing in the future should conditions change for the worse, then surely at some point this use of nuclear weapons could also be eliminated. But its elimination would require the establishment of extensive political, economic and cultural ties between the superpowers so as to reduce the present uncertainty about the future direction of policy, and obviously the establishment of such ties, even when it is given the highest priority, which it frequently is not, requires time to develop.

In the meantime a nuclear force deployed for the purpose of being capable of threatening or bluffing in the future should conditions change for the worse, should be capable of surviving a first

---

33 It might be objected that this proposed policy is hypocritical because it allows a nation following it to benefit from an adversary's uncertainty as to whether that nation would follow its moral principles or its national interest. But it seems odd to deny a nation such a benefit. For we all know that moral people can lose out in many ways to those who are immoral. Occasionally, however, being immoral does have its liabilities and one such liability is that it is hard for immoral people to believe that others will not act in just the way they themselves do, especially when the benefits from doing so are quite substantial. Why then should not moral people be allowed to extract some benefit from the inability of immoral people to believe that moral people are as good as they say they are? After all, it is not the fault of moral people that immoral people are blinded in their judgment in this regard. Consequently, I see no reason to allow a nation to benefit from its adversary's uncertainty as to whether it will follow the requirements of morality or those of national interest.

James P. Sterba

strike and then inflicting either limited or massive nuclear retaliation on an aggressor. During the Kennedy-Johnson years, Robert McNamara estimated that massive nuclear retaliation required a nuclear force capable of destroying one-half of a nation's industrial capacity along with one-quarter of its population, and comparable figures have been suggested by others. Clearly, ensuring a loss of this magnitude should consitute unacceptable damage from the perspective of any would-be aggressor.

Notice, however, that in order for a nation to maintain a nuclear force capable of inflicting such damage, it is not necessary that components of its land-, its air- and its sea-based strategic forces all be survivable. Accordingly, even if all of the land-based ICBMs in the United States were totally destroyed in a first strike, surviving elements of the U.S. air and submarine forces could easily inflict the required degree of damage and more. In fact, any one of the 37 nuclear submarines maintained by the United States, each with up to 192 warheads, could almost single-handedly inflict the required degree of damage. Consequently, the U.S. submarine force alone should suffice as a force capable of massive nuclear retaliation.

But what about a nuclear force capable of limited nuclear retaliation? At least with respect to U.S. nuclear forces, it would seem that as Trident I missiles replace less accurate Poseidon missiles, and especially when Trident II missiles come on line in the next few years, the U.S. submarine force will have the capacity for both limited and massive nuclear retaliation. However, until this modernization is complete, the U.S. will still have to rely, in part, on survivable elements of its air- and land-based strategic forces for its capacity to inflict limited nuclear retaliation. And it would seem that the Soviet Union is also in a comparable situation.[34]

To sum up, I have argued for the following practical implications for nuclear strategy:

---

34 *Soviet Military Power* (U.S. Department of Defense, Washington, DC: U.S. Government Printing Office 1983); David Holloway, *The Soviet Union and the Arms Race* (New Haven, CT: Yale University Press 1983); Andrew Cockburn, *The Threat* (New York: Random House 1983), Chapter 12

106

(1) Under present conditions, it is morally justified to possess a survivable nuclear force in order to be able to quickly threaten or bluff nuclear retaliation should conditions change for the worse.

(2) If conditions do change for the worse, it would be morally justified at some point to threaten a form of limited nuclear retaliation.

(3) If conditions worsen further so that a massive nuclear first strike can only be deterred by the bluff or threat of a massive nuclear retaliation, it would be morally justified to bluff but not threaten massive nuclear retaliation.

(4) Under certain conceivable but unlikely conditions, a limited retaliatory use of nuclear weapons against tactical and strategic targets would be morally justified in order to restore deterrence.

These are the practical implications for nuclear strategy that have emerged from a critical evaluation of the Utilitarian, Human Nature and Social Contract Moral Approaches to nuclear strategy and from a rejection of the pacifist challenge to just war theory.[35]

Yet isn't there something better than the practical implications that I have just proposed? What about President Reagan's Strategic Defense Initiative or 'Star Wars' defense? Admittedly, this strategy is presently only at the research and development state, but couldn't

---

35 Now it might be objected that these same practical implications could be derived from a Utilitarian Approach to nuclear strategy. This is certainly a possibility although defenders of the Utilitarian Approach have not claimed to have derived such implications. Yet given that the utility calculations are so complex in the case of nuclear strategy, it seems preferable to establish the theoretical superiority of the Social Contract Approach and then use that approach to derive practical implications for nuclear strategy rather than to try to establish a practical reconciliation between these approaches to nuclear strategy.

such a strategy turn out to be morally preferable to the one I have proposed? Not as far as I can tell, for the following reasons.

Strategic Defense Initiative or SDI is sometimes represented as an umbrella defense and sometimes as a point or limited defense. As an umbrella defense, SDI is pure fantasy. Given the variety of countermeasures either superpower might employ, such as shortening the booster phase of their rockets so as to make them less of a target for lasers and dispersing various types of decoys, no defensive system could track and destroy all the land- and sea-based warheads either superpower could use in an all-out attack.[36] Estimates by supporters of SDI have put the effectiveness of such a defensive system at 30 percent.[37] This means that SDI could reduce by 30 percent the effective nuclear force either superpower might use against the other.

But a similar or greater reduction of nuclear forces could more easily be achieved by bilateral negotiations if a reduction of nuclear forces is what both superpowers want. Moreover, a unilateral attempt to get such a reduction though SDI is not likely to succeed. Either superpower only needs to increase its nuclear forces by 30 percent to offset the effect of SDI. And this is what either superpower might do if it thought that an SDI program was part of a general defensive and offensive nuclear buildup.

In addition, the cost of SDI is astronomical. President Reagan wants a research and development budget for SDI of over 30 billion dollars for the next five years. For comparison, that is more than the total research and development and *production* costs for the B1 bomber or for the MX missile system. And estimates for the total cost of SDI are in the neighborhood of 1 trillion dollars.[38] In com-

---

36 U.S. Office of Technology Assessment, *Ballistic Missile Defense Technologies* (Washington, D.C.: U.S. Government Printing House 1985); Union of Concerned Scientists, 'Ballistic Missile Defense: A Dangerous Dream,' in *Braking Point* 2 (1984), 1-2

37 See Colin Campbell, 'At Columbia, 3 Days of Arms Talks,' *New York Times*, February 11 1985 and 'Star Wars Chief Takes Aim at Critics,' *Science*, August 10 1984.

38 Union of Concerned Scientists, 'Boosting Stars Wars,' *Nucleus* 6(1985), 2, 4

parison, the total federal budget for 1985 was only 1.8 trillion dollars. Now what kind of a nation would spend 1 trillion dollars for an SDI that gave it a 30 percent reduction of the nuclear forces that could be used against it — a reduction that could have been achieved by bilateral negotiations and would most likely be negated in the absence of such negotiations? Certainly not a nation that is known for the wisdom of its leaders or its citizenry. For these and other reasons, I think that SDI is certainly not morally preferable to those practical implications for nuclear strategy that I have been defending.[39]

Received January, 1986
Revised April, 1986

---

39 I wish to thank Michael Walzer, Edmund Pincoffs, and Andrew Oldenquist for their comments on an earlier version of this paper which was presented at a Conference on Just and Unjust Wars held at Pace University. I also wish to especially thank David Copp for his very helpful comments on a penultimate version of this paper.

CANADIAN JOURNAL OF PHILOSOPHY
Supplementary Volume 12

The Morality of Deterrence

MICHAEL DUMMETT
New College
Oxford University
Oxford, Great Britain
0X1 3BN

One of the most outstanding characteristics of human beings is their adaptability. As we readily learn to take new conditions of life for granted, so we have learned to live with the bomb. For nearly forty years we have lived in the shadow of possible cataclysmic disaster brought about by human action; and we treat this unprecedented danger simply as a background, on which we focus only occasionally, to the common business of living. What else is possible, save persistent hysteria? But, as part of a mechanism for avoiding hysteria, we are in danger of rendering the topic unreal to ourselves even when we are explicitly considering it, by treating it as an *abstract* question. We use the concepts of first strike, retaliation, megadeaths, and so forth, which we apply in just the spirit of those discussing strategy for a board game, while averting our minds from what it is that we are actually talking about. Indeed, if our concern is purely strategic, this does no harm, since the question then involves something isomorphic to a problem in a conceivable board game. When our concern is a moral one, however, or, more generally, when it has to do with what is actually to happen to mankind, it is fatal to treat the question as an abstract one, for it is in just these respects that the isomorphism fails.

The idea that war can be permissible, if it is fought according to rules, is common both to chivalry and to the doctrine of the just war. This idea implies that though warfare is often wrong, it is not unconditionally wrong. Chivalry and the just war doctrine both prohibit the killing of those who are not attempting to kill you. Traditionally, the term 'murder' has not been understood so broadly as to include every act of killing a human being, but as comprising any act of killing the innocent; so understood, murder is conceived as falling under an absolute prohibition. 'Innocent' is here opposed, not to 'guilty,' but to 'harmful': you are required to refrain from killing, not those whose actions are inculpable, but those who are not willingly harming or attempting to harm you or those you are obliged to protect. According to this principle, you have the right to kill someone if that is the only feasible way of preventing him from killing you, and need not first enquire whether he is suffering from some insane delusion or rational misapprehension that renders his conduct free from blame; but you do not have the right to kill someone solely because he is doing or has done something wicked, if you do not need to do so to stop him or if what he is doing is not proportionately grave. A natural misunderstanding of the term 'innocent' as used here has played its part in breaking down our inhibitions against the killing of civilians in war. We think, with justice, that the enemy conscript is hardly to blame for what he is doing; the terrorist justifies his actions by saying, falsely, 'All are guilty'; but in neither case is innocence, in the sense of inculpability, the relevant consideration.

The rules of chivalry have as their purpose to render human what is intrinsically an inhuman way of acting towards others; the simple idea that lies behind its prohibition of killing unarmed people, as well as its code for combat between those who are armed, is that killer and killed must have been given an equal chance of coming out of the combat alive. The just war doctrine is a much more systematic attempt to answer moral questions; and we must first frame these questions aright. To ask after the grounds for pacifism is obviously a legitimate enquiry; but to embark on it risks putting the onus of proof in the wrong place. For any given action, the first question is whether one may legitimately justify it on the ground that no sufficient reason appears for prohibiting it, or whether, conversely, one must refrain from it unless there is sufficient positive justification for it. Since moral issues are usually far from clear, the correct placing of the onus of proof is of particular importance: the notion of the onus of proof comprises the core of truth in the theory of prima facie right propounded by Ross.

If we ask after the grounds for pacifism, we dispose ourselves to put the onus of proof on the pacifist; we are challenging him to produce sufficient grounds for not taking part in war. To him, this seems unfair; he sees it as both rational and morally necessary to refrain from war in the absence of any sufficient justification for taking part in it: a justification he has been unable to find. One does not have to be a pacifist to see the matter in this light; that is how the proponents of the just war doctrine saw it, too. They were not trying to answer the question: in what circumstances does waging war become morally unlawful? Their question was, rather: what could possibly justify conduct so contrary to what is ordinarily acceptable?

I think it possible to discuss the morality of nuclear deterrence without first opting for any of the variant ethical theories on offer, and, in particular, without rejecting consequentialism, even in its more radical, act-consequentialist, version. It was from a deontological and absolutist base that the moral theologians and jurists developed the doctrine of the just war; but it is not because of this base that they saw the onus of justification as lying on the one who would wage war rather than on the one who would refrain from it. Given that one may justly fight if certain conditions are satisfied,

113

it may also become one's duty to do so in some cases; but the moral principles on which such a judgement rests have still to be arrived at by answering the question, 'What could justify actions on the face of them so horrible?', and not the question, 'What positive reason could be found for refusing to act in this way?'

Subtle argument is an important ingredient in ethical enquiries; but an ability to recognise when it is out of place is of equal importance. It needs no argument, for example, to show that it is monstrously wicked to exterminate millions of people in gas chambers. If someone says that it is monstrously wicked, you do not have to ask on what ethical theory he bases his conclusion, or to examine the steps by which he arrived at it. No ethical theory can stand in judgement upon so fundamental a delivery of moral intuition; it stands in judgement upon the theory, for any theory that renders such as assessment doubtful is thereby shown to be erroneous.

To recognise that nuclear warfare is unconditionally wrong, we need to know only two things: that the same moral principles that govern the lives of all of us apply to governments and to what is done at the command of governments; and that moral principles are universal. If a moral principle is valid at all, it is valid for everyone, in all places, in all circumstances and at all times; war cannot suspend moral principles, though it provokes their violation. If the obliteration of whole cities, or whole populations, is not murder, there is no such thing as murder; if it is not wrong, then nothing is wrong.

Am I saying any more than that, if nuclear attacks can be reconciled with the moral law, then no type of action is *absolutely* wrong, that is, such that no conceivable instance of it could ever be justified? Must not a consequentialist, at least an act rather than a rule consequentialist, deny that any type of action is absolutely wrong in this sense, although he will recognise many individual acts as wrong? And am I not, therefore, merely presuming the falsity of act consequentialism, without having taken the trouble to argue it? So long as act consequentialism has not been ruled out as a possible basis for moral principles, my claim assumes that there could be no evil greater than nuclear warfare that engaging in nuclear warfare could conceivably avert: and how can I assume that without enquiry?

Well, what sort of evil might one seek in this manner to avert? What candidate have you for a greater evil? That seems easy to say: nothing could be much worse than many of the things that constantly happen and that we do nothing to avert. What could be more horrible than the mass public beatings and killings that followed the overthrow of Allende in Chile, succeeded by the tortures and the 'disappearances,' events paralleled in Argentina and other Latin American countries? What greater evil could exist than a regime under which the so-called security forces could torture a woman in the course of giving birth, as was reported to have happened in Argentina, or a man be systematically tortured for over a year as an experiment to see if his personality could be changed, as was reported in Chile? You may not believe these stories, though in my opinion you are deluding yourself if you do not. Their actual truth does not affect the present argument, however: just suppose them to be true for the sake of the example. And now suppose that these things could have been permanently ended by dropping nuclear bombs on New York and destroying it with all its inhabitants; suppose that, by doing so, one could be sure — at least surer than one can ever be about the result of victory in war — that the whole of Latin American would enjoy humane, pacific, law-abiding government. Or suppose that the long agony of the Lebanon, from the beginning of the civil war until now, could have been averted by wiping out Tel Aviv. You may object that I am assuming that the United States is wholly responsible for what has happened in Latin America, or Israel for what has happened in the Lebanon. Not at all: you cannot appeal to consequentialism one moment, and repudiate it the next. I am, for these examples, arguing on consequentialist principles, to meet a consequentialist challenge: from a consequentialist standpoint, the responsibility for a given evil of those killed in order to avert that evil, though possibly relevant, cannot be a necessary part of a justification for killing them. Or choose some other horror of our time, say the malnutrition to which the world economic system condemns millions and from which millions die, and suppose it eliminable by the destruction of any major city of your choice. Would anyone seriously suppose the obliteration of the city, in any of these cases, to be a justifiable act? You may explain this by saying that no one, in his heart, is a true consequentialist; or you may explain it by saying that even consequentialism must distinguish between the evil of destruction by act of God — that of a city by an earthquake, say — and that of destruction by deliberate human agency. Consequentialism, if it remained true to its principles, could not make such a distinction merely by saying that something worse had happened in the one case than in the other, for then it would indeed be judging good and evil by the intrinsic nature of human acts, and would have surrendered to deontologism. It would have to say, rather, that the one was worse than the other because of further effects brought about, not by the deaths of millions and the obliteration of their habitation, but by the knowledge, concerning certain people, that they had done these things. I do not stop to discuss whether an adequate consequentialist explanation could be given of our certainty that those ends would not justify those means; it is enough for my purpose that we are certain of this. If there is any case about which we might become uncertain, it would be one in which the evil to be averted was one that was otherwise to come upon *us*; for instance, if it was *our* country that was to suffer the fate of Chile or of Cambodia, or to be reduced to the destitution of the poorest third world countries. That exactly proves my point. If you think that the aversion of such an evil from ourselves might justify the mass annihilation of others, though you would not think that the liberation of those who in fact suffer from it could sanction similar means, then you have indeed repudiated morality as such; you think that there is nothing one may not lawfully do in order to avert a sufficiently grave ill from oneself, though one would not do it, and should, or at least need, not do it to avert the same evil from others.

The world is as it now is precisely because the only time a nation has had an opportunity to use nuclear weapons against an enemy that could not retaliate, it did so. If it had refrained, all our expectations would be different. I do not think that, in such a case, the nuclear arms race would have started. Surely Soviet Russia would have been as anxious to obtain the secret, and would have done so, one way or the other; but we should surely also have had an anti-nuclear treaty, and probably, though suspicious of each other, would have observed it. Not only people died at Hiroshima and Nagasaki; hope and trust died, too, and we live in a world in which they have died. We live, as no one has ever lived before, with the consciousness that it is quite possible that, in the comparatively near future, we shall wipe out our entire species, and possibly much other life as well; if those who first obtained the atomic bomb had been able to refrain from using it, we should not entertain that possibility. So far from refraining, they used it without a qualm. A distinguished and highly respected physicist who worked on the Manhattan project reported in a television interview that, when they heard of the obliteration of Hiroshima, they broke out the champagne. He also told us that, many years later, he was struck by the contrast between what he and his colleagues were doing that evening and what was happening at the same time in Hiroshima. He said this, not in a tone of remorse, but with the quiet pride of one claiming admiration for his sensitivity in ever having such a thought. It is our knowledge that such callousness is not only characteristic of those who run the world, but that it does not need to be concealed, because it does not produce universal disgust, but instead in no way weakens the respect in which they are held, that underlies the despair that lies deepest in the feelings of all of us.

The justification now offered for possessing nuclear weapons is, of course, that it serves to deter others from using them against us. To consider whether this justification is sound, one must first ask, as I have done, whether it would ever be right to use nuclear weapons; that is, to do what one is attempting to deter others from doing by threatening to do it oneself. If there would be nothing wrong in doing something in certain circumstances, there can be nothing wrong in threatening to do it in those circumstances; the argument about deterrence then simply does not arise. That is why I have so far discussed only the use of such weapons, not the threat to use them. When the morality of the deterrent is under discussion, however, it is well to know where the participants in the discussion stand on the morality of use. In the aftermath of the second world war, there was some debate — not lively, because there were few to take the unofficial side — about the morality of dropping atomic bombs in Hiroshima and Nagasaki. The debate has now moved on to more topical questions; but, as far as I have noticed, those who defend possession of the deterrent are just those who once defended the wiping out of the two Japanese cities. Yet, if I am right about that, Professor Anscombe, one of a tiny handful who opposed the granting by Oxford University of an honorary degree to President Truman, was fully justified in asking, in the pamphlet she wrote on the occasion, 'If you honour this man, what Cesare Borgia, what Genghis Khan, will you not honour?' The apologists of deterrence hasten to explain that they are not defending the *use* of nuclear weapons; they are defending only the possession of them to prevent their use. I notice, however, that they very seldom, if ever, pronounce on the rightness or wrongness of the only two actual uses of them that have so far been made in war, though this is crucial to the argument. If their opinion on this matter is what used to be the received opinion about it, namely that it was justified to drop the bombs on those two cities, then their disclaimer is hypocritical; they are not really arguing on the basis that it would be wicked for us to do what we threaten to do. There may, of course, be some who believe that the destruction of Hiroshima and of Nagasaki were terrible crimes, but yet think the deterrent justified; one who shares the former belief, but disputes the latter, can argue with such people on a common basis. He is strongly advised, however, first to ascertain that such a common basis exists, by challenging the others to declare their views on Hiroshima and Nagasaki, the present silence about which strikes me as ominous.

The opponent of nuclear weapons may be invited to say what differentiates them from other weapons. Obviously there is no moral difference between the destruction of a city by a nuclear bomb and by obliteration bombing with ordinary high explosives, as Dresden was destroyed, or by the creation of a fire storm by means of incendiaries, as in the notorious fire raid on Tokyo; if one is wicked, the other is wicked, as I believe both to have been. Some would see the possibility of catastrophic long-term effects extending far beyond the country attacked as making a crucial moral difference between nuclear and 'conventional' weapons; but, in my view, it can affect only the degree of wickedness in using them, not whether it would be wicked or not, although, of course, it is an important cause of the terror that lurks deep within us all. Non-nuclear but unconventional means of warfare, such as biological ones, merit equal condemnation, though they receive far less publicity; I know no one who takes the position that every means of killing members of an enemy population is justified, save the use of nuclear weapons.

Some urge that there are nuclear weapons, such as depth-charges, that could be used against strictly military targets without even side-effects on civilians. The correct response to this is to deploy the notion of a 'fire-break.' The line between nuclear and conventional weapons is clearly marked and perceived; once any nuclear weapons have been used, there is no saying where either side will draw the line. In any case, the point, though important in itself, is inessential to the present argument; we are discussing, not nuclear weapons as such, but the nuclear deterrent, and the deterrent does not consist of depth-charges. In the repulsive jargon proper to this subject, the strategy of deterrence cannot be limited to counter-force, but must include 'counter-value' also, that is, the annihilation of civilian populations on a massive scale.

Given, then, that the use of nuclear weapons would constitute an appalling crime – at least, that use of them which is threatened on the strategy followed by the American and British governments and other members of the NATO alliance, and must be threatened on any deterrent strategy – the question becomes whether it can be right to threaten what it would be wrong to do. When this question is applied to individuals, the answer must be a cautious 'Yes'. Schoolmasters do it all the time, though they risk having their bluff called; in an extreme case, I might threaten to shoot someone who was making off with some treasured possession of mine, even though I should not be justified in shooting anybody just to protect my property. If a scrupulous moralist objected to this, he would have to do so on the ground of dishonesty, which would apply equally if I had a right to do what I threatened; in itself, my making the threat in no way partakes of the moral evil of what I am threatening to do. There are two conditions, however. The first is that I should have a firm intention not to act as I threaten, if my bluff is called; and the second is that I am, with good reason, certain that I shall not in fact so act in response to a sudden action by the person at whom my threat is directed. I shall have the best ground for such certainty if I know that I cannot carry out my threat; for instance, if I am pointing an unloaded revolver. I may also be certain if I know myself well enough, and know how I behave in a crisis; if I lose my head and fire, killing the thief, I show myself to have done wrong in ever attempting the threat.

The argument cannot be transferred from individuals to governments. An individual may know that his threat is idle; a government cannot make idle threats, both because the actual orders will soon be known to the other side's intelligence services and because no government will remain indefinitely in office. It may be said that the orders require an explicit command from the supreme authority — Prime Minister or President — before they can be implemented, and that that authority may have no intention of ever issuing that command. He, or she, might not have; but that is not enough. The individual in supreme authority has, first, to be sure how he will react in crisis; if, like the present President of the United States, he is disposed to talk of revenge when some 120 soldiers are killed in a terrorist attack, how he will react when millions of citizens are suddenly and horribly botted out? He must, secondly, make arrangements for the contingency of his being killed himself, in an attack on the capital or by a co-ordinated shot from an assassin; indeed, for the death of his Cabinet ministers and other colleagues as well. There must therefore be an entire chain of succession. If the strategy of deterrence is to be justified on the ground that it is a threat that will never be executed, whoever is in supreme command must be sure that all those in the chain share his negative intentions. If this were done by estimation of personalities, it would be utterly fallible; if it were done by explicit instruction, it would still be fallible, and the likelihood of the secret's leaking would vitiate the entire bluff. The decisive point is, however, that no President and no Prime Minister remains in office for more than a few years. No such individual could therefore justify setting up a complex and murderous engine for massacring millions of people on the ground that he sincerely intended never to use it; he would be bequeathing it to his successors, whose identity he would not know, and of whose intentions he could not be sure if he did. By constructing the engine, he would be offering his successors the possibility of using it; by committing his country to the policy of deterrence, he would be making it hard for them to back away from it. A government with a nuclear deterrent is nothing like a householder with even a loaded revolver in his hand.

Thus even the supreme political authority could not justify pursuing a policy of deterrence on the ground that it was no more than a bluff. Indeed, I think that it could not be a bluff, if it was to be expected to work; the policy demands an actual intention to retaliate by a nuclear attack to whatever action by the other side you are trying to deter them from, which, of course, in our case, need not itself be a nuclear attack. However this may be, the matter stands much worse with those who will have no power to make the vital decision, but have the option of supporting or opposing the policy of deterrence. These − the ordinary voters − cannot know what is in the mind of the Prime Minister or President; all they know is what the government says, which is of course that the deterrent will be used once it has failed to deter. To rely on its having a secret intention not to use it, whatever happens, is therefore to make an act of blind faith. What is needed to justify a threat to do something immoral is not blind faith but certainty; blind faith cannot come near to sufficing for a justification, at least in any grave matter; and what could be graver than this? This faith is utterly blind; everything tells against it. One thing I have already mentioned: the danger, of which the politicians will be aware, that, by forming the intention not to carry out the threat, they will make it ineffective. What sense does it make to trust politicians − any politicians − not to do what they say they will do? Politicians, in power or out of it, lie as a matter of course, a fact to which there are countless attestations. They cannot be trusted to do what they say they *will* do; how can they be trusted in this instance *not* to do what they say they will do? Someone may have the thought: *our* politicians would never do anything so appallingly wicked. If so, he is deluding himself. The only thing we can say for certain is that American and British politicians had no scruples, forty-one years ago, against dropping nuclear bombs on defenceless cities; and there is not the ghost of a reason to suppose any moral improvement in them in the interim. There is no ground whatever for believing that our deterrence policy is a bluff, or would remain one if it were now. Someone who would refuse to support such a policy unless it were a bluff should also refuse to support it if he thought there to be any genuine possibility, however small, that it was not a bluff. Having no ground whatever to believe it to be a bluff, he cannot support it. Advancing this argument for supporting it seems to me no more than self-deception. It is an attractive form of self-deception, for someone with decent feelings, because it allows him to cling to the supposed security of the deterrent without in any degree compromising his conviction that murdering people by the million is morally abhorrent. But I think that it involves a denial of reality; and, if I may so put it, I do not think that on Judgement Day it will sound a very convincing plea to say, 'I never thought they really meant to.'

We have, therefore, to enquire, not about idle threats, but about conditional intentions. If doing something is wrong, is forming a conditional intention to do it – in circumstances in which it would still be wrong – itself wrong? Professor Bernard Williams has argued, in precisely the present connection, for a negative answer; but I find his argument amazingly weak. His argument was that such a conditional intention would not necessarily be wrong in a case in which one was certain that the condition would not be fulfilled.[1] This of course reflects the paradox of the strategy of deterrence; namely, that its purpose is, by forming and announcing a conditional intention to resort to a nuclear attack, to render the fulfillment of the condition highly unlikely. The argument succeeds, however, only if one is literally *certain* that the condition will remain unfulfilled. Just as a threat to do something wrong remains uninfected by the immorality of what is threatened if, but only if, the person who makes the threat is certain that he will not carry it out, so the formation of a conditional intention to do something wrong remains uninfected if, but only if, the person forming it is certain that the condition will never be satisfied. Whereas, however, it is easy to threaten to do what you know you will not do, it is dubious if you *can* form an intention to do something in circumstances which you are certain will never arise. Mrs. Thatcher might, for example, idly speculate on what she would do if she were Pope; but she can hardly form an intention to do it if she is elected Pope. If it be supposed that it is possible to be certain that the condition under which we are threatening a nuclear attack will not be realised, what we shall have is not a conditional intention at all, but a threat known

---

1 Bernard Williams, 'Morality, Scepticism and the Nuclear Arms Race,' in Nigel Blake and Kay Pole, eds., *Objections to Nuclear Defence: Philosophers on Deterrence* (London: Routledge and Kegan Paul 1984), 99-114

to be idle; the only slightly bizarre circumstance is that it is the very making of the threat which renders it idle.

As we have seen, a genuinely idle threat to do something wrong may be excusable; but the person making it had better *know* that it is idle, rather than merely thinking so, let alone falsely thinking so. Professor Williams has himself written on the subject of moral luck: if I shoot someone by accident and he dies, I have done something much worse, not just in its effects, but morally, than if he sustains only a minor wound, even though my action, and the circumstances in which I did it, were the same in both cases. So here: someone who wrongly believed the deterrent to be an idle threat is to be judged, in respect of his responsibility for a consequent holocaust, not on the basis of his belief, but on that of what in fact resulted. In any case, Williams does not have a genuine case of a permissible conditional intention to do something wrong. Even if he had, he would seem, in so criticising those who have said you ought not to intend anything immoral, even conditionally, to have confused moral philosophy with mathematics; the point is not to point out some limiting case in which an alleged theorem fails, but to discuss the realities of our existence from a moral standpoint. The supposition that we would be *certain* that nuclear hostilities will not result from the present confrontation of two camps armed as heavily as they can afford is no less than preposterous. Apart from all the possibilities of accident that have been surveyed in great detail, a nuclear war needs only one false guess by one side about the other's intentions; one mistaken attempt to call what is wrongly thought to be bluff; one threat, made in the conviction that it would work, from which the side that made it cannot then climb down. Could one have been certain that there would be no nuclear war during the Cuban missile crisis, when the Soviet warships in fact turned back at the last moment? Can one be certain now that there will never be a renewed American attempt to invade Cuba, or that a retaliatory American strike against Syria will not bring Russia and the United States face to face in the Middle East, and that, if either of these things happens, it will not, by miscalculation, provoke a nuclear war? The United States is already paranoid about Russia; and the propaganda that justifies the expenditure on nuclear weaponry inflames that paranoia. The Soviet Union, constantly reviled by Western politicians, openly spoken of as the enemy in strategic discussions, and forced for years to endure a ring of nuclear weapons in that proximity to its territory that Kennedy declared the United States unable to tolerate, would appear to have more reason for paranoia, although, as far as I can see, in fact is less subject to it. So we have two massive states, with their attendant satellites, armed with a vast arsenal, and each consumed by fear and loathing of each other; granted that neither wants to destroy the other if the price is its own destruction, who in his right mind can claim to be certain that they will not do so?

If it is wrong to do something, it must necessarily also be wrong to form the intention of doing it. If someone tells you what he intends to do, your saying, 'But that would be morally wrong,' is an objection to his having that intention; it does not admit the response, 'It will be time to tell me that only when I do it; at the moment I merely *intend* to do it, and there can be nothing wrong with an intention.' This is not a mere special case of the principle that one must not do anything that makes it significantly more likely that one will do something wrong. If I know that I am liable to lose my temper with someone, I ought to try to keep out of his way; but this obligation may be overridden by some strong reason to see him or to go where he is likely to be. The formation of an intention has, however, a more intimate connection with the act intended than that of rendering the performance of the act more probable; and it is important to state the relevant connection correctly. It is not merely that the point of forming the intention can only be whatever point there is in performing the act; it is, rather, that, by forming the intention, I give my will to the act. It is a universally acknowledged principle that no one is culpable for an act, however wrong objectively, to which he in no degree gave his will, and that the degreee of his guilt depends jointly on the degree of the objective wrongness of the act and on the degree to which he gave his will to it; that is why premeditated murder is held to be worse than murder committed in unreflective response to provocation. Now the point of forming a conditional intention may well differ from that of performing the act conditionally intended; and that is illustrated by the strategy of deterrence. Here the point of forming and announcing the conditional intention is to prevent the condition from arising; if it does arise, there will then be no point in performing the act (save to preserve one's credibility, if that were still of any importance). It is just this to which people appeal when they defend deterrence; they are forming the conditional intention with an eye, not to realising the consequent, but to falsifying the antecedent; and so there can be nothing wrong with it. This is, however, to seize on the wrong point. In forming a conditional intention, I am giving my will to the act intended just as in forming a categorical intention; the only difference in this respect is that I am giving my will to it only under the condition in question. If something would be wrong in all circumstances whatever, as indiscriminately obliterating vast numbers of people is wrong in all circumstances whatever, then it is wrong to form the intention to do it in any circumstances whatever, even if the aim is to render those circumstances unlikely, and however laudable such an aim.

I think that the only reason people shy away from the conclusion that I am urging is fear; they cannot see how we dare back down from the position we have assumed. It is not quite clear what it is that they fear: a Soviet occupation or a nuclear war. If the whole of the West renounced nuclear weapons, the use of nuclear weapons by the Soviet Union would become most unlikely; but their renunciation by the allies of the United States, but not by the United States itself, is thought to increase the chances of a nuclear war. Because nothing more hideous than a nuclear war can easily be conceived, people slip into thinking that anything is justified which might prevent it; but I should like to express, in secular terms, my agreement with the American Catholic bishop who said, like Tolstoy, that we should not regard the survival of the human race as an end to which everything should be subordinated: still less, I should add, some particular branch of it. I saw a fragment of a television broadcast about civil defense plans in Cornwall being made by some local committee. They may well have been deluding themselves about the conditions with which Cornish survivors of a nuclear war would have to cope; but there was general agreement that it would be necessary to 'cull' the old, the sick and the mentally abnormal, and I switched off in the middle of a wrangle about whether the doctor or someone else should decide who had to be killed for the sake of the rest. From where have we acquired the assumption that it is better for some to survive, presumably to procreate further generations, even at the cost of doing violence to every decent human feeling, than for all to die with dignity and as much comfort as they can afford to give each other in the process? Why is it supposed to be of supreme importance that the human race itself, let alone a bunch of Cornishmen, should survive, if it has made itself utterly unlovely, and must make itself more unlovely still as the price of survival?

As a means of preventing a nuclear war, the policy of deterrence makes little sense, and can be explained only by saying that we are on a tightrope, and do not know how to get off: better an unstable equilibrium than no equilibrium at all. It is normally explained differently: as a way of preventing a conventional war which we should lose, or a Soviet threat to which we should be forced to surrender. It seems to me unlikely that the Soviet Union would want to add to its troubles by extending its domination to western Europe, even if we include Greece; they never attempted to bring Yugoslavia to heel, even though we should have treated it as being, like Hungary and Czechoslovakia, within their sphere of influence. I should think the greater danger would lie in American attempts to destabilise or wreck the economies of neutralist Western countries; but I do not pretend to know what would happen. Nor, I think, does anyone else, which reduces to futility justifications of deterrence by appeal to its consequences and the consequences of abandoning it. My argument is to the effect that the obliteration of whole cities or of an entire population is unconditionally wicked, and therefore not to be contemplated as a possible course of action, even only as a threat to deter others from doing what we do not want them to do. Suppose, however, that we were convinced that, if we were to abandon the deterrent, the Soviet Union would take over our country; could that be a sufficient reason for maintaining it? I have argued that it would not be, even if it were the worst thing in the world; but how can it be the worst thing in the world? What, in other words, makes *us* so special? We have in no case any right to seek to preserve *our own* liberties by threatening to bring about the deaths of millions.

Those who dare not abandon the policy of deterrence can do no more than hope that it will stave off a nuclear holocaust for − well, for how long? For another few decades? Do they dare to hope, for as long as a century? What is supposed to happen then? We *have* to find a way of making war of any kind impossible: otherwise mankind either has very little future or will deserve none. Moral considerations aside, to continue as at present makes no sense save in the hope of quickly finding some other way to make at least nuclear war impossible. This is the way out proposed by the multilateralists, those who recognise that the balance of terror is not stable in more than the relatively short term, but who trust in a negotiated escape from it. How much longer will the present impasse continue before they recognise that to be impossible? The only course of action that either holds out any hope or accords with the most insistent demands of the moral law is to try to prevent our country from continuing to have anything to do with nuclear weapons.

Received March, 1986
Revised May, 1986

CANADIAN JOURNAL OF PHILOSOPHY
Supplementary Volume 12

Reason and Nuclear Deterrence

ALAN GEWIRTH
University of Chicago
Chicago, IL 60637
U.S.A.

The nuclear arms race between the United States and the Soviet Union has reached a stage of unparalleled destructive potential. Fueling the race are not only an immense series of mighty technological developments but also each side's unremitting quest for both security and power. Thus, each side is animated by intense competitiveness with and deep distrust of the other.

I Rationality and Reasonableness

My primary purpose in this essay is not to examine the historical background or the current status of this murderous competition but rather to inquire into what can and should be done to avoid its dangers. For this purpose, we must make the most intensive possible use of reason. For reason gives us the surest way to attain truth, including practical truth about what ought to be done in the various predicaments that confront human beings.

Now there are two main different concepts of practical reason: namely, *rationality* and *reasonableness*. Rationality consists in calculation of the most efficient means to one's ends. Since these ends are usually even if not always self-interested, rationality is a feature of efficient, self-interested action. And since, to be efficient, such calculation must take veridical account of relevant facts, rationality includes this empirical element also. Thus a person or group is rational if he, she, or it operates efficiently in this way.

The other main concept of practical reason is reasonableness. This consists in impartial, favorable consideration of the rights and other interests of all the persons affected by a given action or policy. It requires mutual positive concern for the rights of other persons as well as of oneself. Thus reasonableness is dedicated to a broad common or general interest, as opposed to the self-interest of the agent alone, and it is directly a moral quality of equitableness, as against the moral neutrality of rationality.

These two concepts of practical reason are directly derivative from the two most widely recognized kinds of reasoning or inference. Rationality is an application of inductive inference; for the calculation of means to ends is a species of inferring from causes to effects, which involves probabilistic generalizing from past experienced sequences to necessary causal connections. Reasonableness, on the other hand, is an application of deductive inference, for it involves an appeal to the principle of non-contradiction when it holds that what is right in one case must be right in any relevantly similar case, or that the rules one applies to oneself must also apply to all the other persons who fall under them. More specifically, it can be shown that every agent, on pain of self-contradiction, must accept the moral principle of reasonableness which I have elsewhere called the Principle of Generic Consistency. This principle requires of every actual or prospective agent that he act in accord with the generic rights of his recipients as well as of himself. Social policies and institutions must also reflect this logically necessary principle of reasonableness if they are to be morally justified.[1]

In the earlier history of modern moral philosophy, rationality is most directly associated with Hobbes and Hume, while the logical appeal to reasonableness in ethics is most directly associated with Kant. Both these branches of practical reason have in common a concern for the conditions of the ascertainment of truth, and both set criteria, although of two different sorts, for the evaluation of actions and institutions.

We must also note two further points about these concepts of practical reason. When it is said that the criterion of rationality is concerned with the pursuit of *self*-interest, the scope of these 'selves' may vary from individual persons to states or nations. The concept of the state, in turn, may range from the ruling group in each nation to its whole population at large. Within the context of the nuclear arms problem, however, the self-interest with which rationality is primarily concerned is the national interest, and this in turn consists primarily in security from external attack. But for the United States the national interest also includes the central value of freedom, both personal and political. It is this component of our national interest that constitutes the most basic moral difference between the United States and the Soviet Union.

A second point concerns motivation. Since persons and groups are usually even if not always motivated by self-interest, and since rationality is the efficient calculation of the means to one's self-interested ends, it follows that motivation is directly built into the use of or appeal to rationality. On the other hand, motivation is not similarly built into the very concept of reasonableness. It is true that many persons and groups may and do have moral motivations and that these can have a strong influence on policy. But in pursuing their own interests, persons and groups need not be, and often are not, motivated to give any direct consideration to the interests of

---

1 See Alan Gewirth, *Reason and Morality* (Chicago: University of Chicago Press 1978), chs. 2-5; 'The Rationality of Reasonableness,' *Synthese* 57 (1983), 225-47; 'The Epistemology of Human Rights,' *Social Philosophy and Policy* 1,2 (1984), 1-24.

other persons and groups, especially when these are in conflict with their own perceived interests and they think they can get away with such disregard of others' interests.

This contrast between the fully motivational character of rationality and the incompletely or negatively motivational character of reasonableness has an important implication for the critical problem of the nuclear confrontation between the United States and the Soviet Union. The solution to this problem might seem obvious: stop the arms race, destroy all nuclear weapons, and enter into serious and sincere negotiations with a view to setting up a lasting peace wherein disagreements are handled not by force of arms but by impartial consideration of each case on its merits, and with due concern for the rights and interests of each side. This reasonable solution has not been adopted, even to the extent permitted by the conflicting values and power-drives, because the perceived and effective motivation for its adoption has been lacking. In other words, partly because of their mutual distrust, it has not been sufficiently noted by each side that such a reasonable solution is also rational for itself, and that the whole nuclear arms race, involving as it does preparation for waging nuclear war, is basically irrational.

This situation is a version of the 'Prisoner's Dilemma,' where the rationally best solution for each side is to cooperate with the other in reducing tensions and weapons, but, because of their mutual distrust and failure to communicate adequately, the two sides follow instead a policy of non-cooperation and attempted self-aggrandizement which turns out to be rationally worse for each side.

If, then, the nuclear confrontation is to receive a solution which is both practically effective and morally reasonable, the solution must both begin from and take full account of the perceived motivations of each side; that is, it must show how the solution is rational for each side in terms of its own self-interest. This is one of the main things I shall try to establish in this paper.

In pursuit of this objective, we must begin from the present situation. Each side engages in the nuclear arms race with a view to what it calls *deterrence*. According to the policy of nuclear deterrence, the United States credibly threatens to subject the Soviet Union's military forces, and with them sizeable parts of its population, to nuclear bombing if the Soviet Union attacks the United States or its allies. And the Soviet Union addresses a similar threat of nuclear retaliation to the United States.

We must now consider three central questions about this policy: First, is the policy of nuclear deterrence rational for either side? Second, is the policy of nuclear deterrence reasonable for either side? Third, are there any preferable alternatives to the policy of nuclear deterrence that are both rational and reasonable for each side?

II Is Nuclear Deterrence Rational?

Let us now take up the first question: whether the policy of nuclear deterrence is rational for either side. In dealing with this question, we must keep in mind the probabilistic character of rationality. Since rationality involves calculation of the most efficient means to one's self-interested ends, its inferences cannot be logically necessary; they can achieve at most only varying degrees of probability as we try to predict future efficiencies or other consequences on the basis of past observed connections.

I shall now present an argument that is designed to show that the policy of nuclear deterrence is indeed rational for each side, in that it is an efficient means of protecting the national interest in security from nuclear attack. The focus of the argument is on the idea of rationally grounded trust. It holds that when parties equipped with nuclear weapons are rational, this can serve to ground a certain trust of each toward the other and a corresponding mutual abstention from the use of nuclear weapons.

The Deterrence Argument

The argument is in five steps, as follows: (1) The Soviet Union can be trusted to act, so far as it can, for what it considers to be its own best interests. (2) Such action by the Soviet Union surely includes its acting in such a way that it is not subjected to nuclear bombing by the United States. (3) If, however, the Soviet Union were to attack the United states or its allies, then, according to the policy of nuclear deterrence, with its credible threat of nuclear retaliation, the

133

Soviet Union *would* be subjected to nuclear bombing by the United States. (4) Hence, because of this policy, the United States can trust the Soviet Union not to attack the United States or its allies. By parity of reasoning, the converse also holds: the Soviet Union can trust the United States not to attack the Soviet Union or its allies. (5) Therefore, because of its invaluable contribution to the avoidance of a nuclear holocaust, the policy of nuclear deterrence is rational for each side.

I shall call this the *deterrence argument*. Each of its steps can be criticized on various grounds. But first I want to consider certain positive aspects of the argument. One of its implications is that, because of the deterrence policy, the two adversary nations' paramount but distinct interests in security become a kind of *common interest*, in a stronger sense than the merely distributive one that the Soviet Union and the United States each has its own national interest in not being bombed or attacked by the other. In this stronger sense of common interest, the objects of their respective interests are the same both extensionally and intensionally. Just as the Soviet Union has an interest in not being bombed by the United States, so too the United States has that very same interest: that the Soviet Union not be bombed by the United States. The converse also holds; just as the United States has an interest in not being bombed by the Soviet Union, so too the Soviet Union has the same interest: that the United States not be bombed by the Soviet Union.

Entirely apart from moral or humanitarian considerations of reasonableness, which as we have seen do not have the requisite motivational force, the deterrence argument holds that it is primarily the policy of nuclear deterrence that generates this strong community of interest. The United States has an interest in not bombing the Soviet Union because it is aware that this bombing will result in the United States' being bombed in turn by the Soviet Union, and conversely. Thus the community of interest arises from the fact that each side's self-interest in not being attacked has been made to coincide with an other-benefiting interest in not attacking the other side. But, without the policy of deterrence, there would not be this coincidence of interests because there would not be such mutually assured devastation or destruction.

Because of this mutuality and community of interest, the policy of nuclear deterrence, according to the deterrence argument, is not only rational but also reasonable in its effects even if not in its primary motivation. For it involves that the United States acts with due regard for the Soviet citizens' basic rights to life and physical integrity as well as for American citizens' rights; and similarly for the Soviet Union.

We may elucidate this point more graphically by referring to the assumptions of the familiar Prisoner's Dilemma. Viewed purely from the standpoint of rational self-interest, the primary interest of each state may be said to consist in bombing the other without being bombed in return, because in this way the inimical rival state will be disarmed. From the same motivational perspective, mutual abstention from bombing is only second best, mutual bombing is third best, and being bombed without bombing is fourth best.

Soviet Union

		Bomb	Don't Bomb
United States	Bomb	3,3	1,4
	Don't Bomb	4,1	2,2

On this model, the United States is supposed to reason as follows: either the Soviet Union will bomb us or it will not. If it does bomb us, then our bombing them in retaliation is better than our not bombing them, because otherwise not only will they get away with an unpunished atrocity but they may think they can continue bombing or otherwise attacking us with impunity. If, on the other hand, the Soviet Union does not bomb us, then again our bombing them is better than our not bombing them, because in this way we can do away with their nuclear threat once and for all without suffering retaliation. Hence, on either alternative, it is better for us to bomb the Soviets than to refrain from bombing them. And the Soviet Union, according to this model, will reason in the same way, so that its primary interest is likewise to bomb rather than to refrain from bombing the United States. Hence, each state, following its own narrow self-interest, bombs the other, even though it is far more in each side's self-interest, and hence far more rational, to cooperate by neither's bombing the other. So we get the famous paradox of the Prisoner's Dilemma: each side, by following its own narrow self-interest, does less well for its self-interest than if it were to cooperate for mutual interest.

Now, according to the deterrence argument, it is the policy of nuclear deterrence that, in final analysis, prevents the realization of this abominable scenario of each side's bombing the other. For that policy seves to guarantee that the upper right and lower left boxes of the above Prisoner's Dilemma will not be effective, because each side knows that it cannot bomb the other without being bombed in return. It is ultimately for this reason that the two states have a *common interest* in not bombing one another, so that the lower right box, mutual abstention from bombing, remains effective. Thus the deterrence policy is indeed rational for each side.

This argument need not incur the charge that it commits the fallacy of *post hoc ergo propter hoc*. It does not say that the *only* thing that has actually kept the Soviets from bombing or otherwise attacking the United States or its allies is the fear of being bombed in return. We cannot know with any assurance whether or not this is so. It is sufficient to hold that this threat is the ultimate or culminating reason in the Soviets' rational strategic thinking; and similarly for the United States. This is the reason that establishes that each state has a common, motivationally effective interest in not bombing the other. And it is for this reason, in final analysis, that each state can *trust* the other not to bomb it, so that the policy of nuclear deterrence is rational for each side.

Means-End Paradoxes

An important objection against this attribution of rationality, however, is that the deterrence policy seems to be self-contradictory.

For the policy says, in effect: 'If you want to prevent the use of nuclear weapons, then you should credibly threaten to use them,' Here the end − *prevention* of use − seems to be opposed by the advocated means − *credible threat* of use. For if the threat is to be credible, then one must seriously be prepared and intend to do the very thing one is trying to prevent being done, namely, use nuclear weapons.

This is perhaps the most basic of the many paradoxes that have been found in the deterrence policy. It has not hitherto been noted, however, that this paradox is a species of a more general kind of paradox that also characterizes many other forms of practical rationality. The genus of these rationality paradoxes I have called *means-end paradoxes*. Their general form is this: if you want to achieve a certain end, then you should use means that are contrary to that end. Put schematically, the paradoxes are of the form: if you want E, then you must do non-E. The paradox consists in the fact that it seems to be both counterintuitive and counterproductive, and thus irrational, to hold that the way to get some E is to act in a way that is opposed to E.

It may help to grasp the rationale of this seeming irrationality if we note some other examples of means-end paradoxes. One is the famous paradox of freedom: if you want to promote freedom, then you must restrict freedom. For if you do not restrict freedom, then some persons will be left free to coerce other persons, thereby removing or restricting the latter's freedom, so that if you want to promote freedom overall, then you must restrict the freedom to interfere with freedom. Another means-end paradox is the paradox of power: if you want to curb power, then you must use power. For the act or process of curbing power requires the occurrent or dispositional use of power. This paradox and the paradox of freedom provide prime arguments against pacifism and anarchism, respectively.

Other examples of means-end paradoxes are the two opposite paradoxes of private and public interests. One is Adam Smith's famous paradox: if you want to promote the common interest, then you should not aim at that but instead you should pursue your own private interest. The other is the Prisoner's Dilemma paradox, which in one form or another is found in many philosophers going back

Alan Gewirth

to Plato: if you want to promote your own private interest, then you should pursue the common interest. A related example of this last paradox is Jesus' dictum: if you want to save your own life, then you should lose it.

Despite their apparently inconsistent form, none of these paradoxes is a genuine contradiction. For different qualifications attach to the antecedent end and the consequent means. Thus in the paradox of nuclear deterrence, which says that if you want to prevent the use of nuclear weapons then you should credibly threaten to use them, the end is *prevention* of use and the use in question is that of *one's adversary*, while the means is the *credible threat* of use and the threatened use in question is that of *the agent himself*. Now while prevention of use is partially antithetical to credible threat of use, because the former tends to reject use while the latter tends to accept use, the two are not so completely opposed to one another that they canot coexist, and even coexist simultaneously. For the credible threat to use nuclear weapons may be the means to prevent their actual use; but the threat to use them is not itself their actual use.

All the means-end paradoxes are modes of rationality because, while the means contain components that are conceptually opposed to the end, they also are causally effective in promoting or achieving the end. The reason for this causal effectiveness amid conceptual contrariety is that the contrariety is limited in at least two ways. First, the contrariety leaves sufficient conceptual space, so to speak, for the end to arise despite the partial conceptual contrariety of the means. Thus, as we saw in the nuclear deterrence paradox, prevention of use is only partially opposed to credible threat of use. Second, in the case of the means that are conceptually opposed to their respective ends — such means as restricting freedom, exerting power, pursuing one's private interest, threatening to use nuclear weapons, and so forth — the means have causal characteristics that enable them to surmount their partial conceptual opposition to the respective ends by bringing other forces to bear that serve to promote the ends. Thus, according to the deterrence argument, when A addresses to B the credible threat that A will use nuclear weapons if attacked by B, this threat arouses fear in B that causes B to desist from attacking A.

138

For these and other reasons, the means-end paradoxes are different from George Orwell's famous *1984* slogans, such as 'War is peace' and 'Truth is falsehood,' despite certain superficial similarities of form. The Orwellian falsisms do not state means to ends, and they provide no differentiating qualifications for their subjects and predicates that serve to limit the extent of their conceptual opposition. In addition, of course, their intention is simply to obfuscate, so that they lack the rational basis on which each of the means-end paradoxes has been seen to rest.

Irrationality of the Deterrence Policy

Despite its paradoxical character, then, the policy of nuclear deterrence has important elements of rationality. Nevertheless, this rationality is severely limited, for at least two reasons. First, the deterrence argument assumes that the leaders on each side can always be trusted to be rational or that they will always operate with a degree of rationality that is sufficient to prevent their ever getting into a situation where they feel they must make good on their threats to launch a nuclear attack. But these leaders are only human; they may miscalculate about what their opponents will do, or they may be driven to unreasoning fury by what they perceive as insults, challenges, or other grievances. In addition, accidents may occur. As a result, a nuclear attack may be launched even though it is irrational.[2]

It is indeed true that all national policies may be adversely affected by the irrationality of the leaders. But because no policy involves lethal dangers comparable to those of the nuclear confrontation, it is in the highest degree irrational to put one's permanent trust in the continuing rationality of political leaders when a lapse from rationality on their part can have such fatal consequences.

---

2 See Daniel Frei, *Risks of Unintentional Nuclear War* (Totowa, N.J.: Allanheld, Osmun & Co. 1983), esp. ch. 4.

Alan Gewirth

A second reason for the very limited character of the deterrence policy's rationality bears on the relation between threat and execution. As we have seen, according to this policy the United States credibly threatens to subject the Soviet Union to nuclear bombing if the Soviet Union attacks the United States or its allies. But, if this threat were actually to be executed, the result would be suicidal for the United States. For the Soviet Union has an extensive second-strike capacity whereby it can retaliate for any nuclear attack on itself with a devastating counter-attack that could destroy all or most of the population centers in the United States. The United States has no realistic way either to defend itself against such destruction or to destroy a sufficient number of the Soviet Union's weapons to prevent such retaliation. Hence, ultimately, the United States' threat of nuclear retaliation for an attack of itself is not credible, because the Soviet Union knows that the United States knows that it would be devastated or destroyed if it were to make good on its threat.

All these considerations also apply, of course, in reverse, i.e. for the Soviets' policy of deterrence whereby they credibly threaten to retaliate against the United States for any nuclear attack. Hence, the policy of nuclear deterrence is irrational for each side, for it would lead to their mutual assured destruction, i.e. to their mutual suicide.

It may be replied that the objection I have just presented is unsound because it confuses threat with execution. The policy of nuclear deterrence is one of *threatening* nuclear retaliation, not one of *executing* the threat. To put it in other terms, in the deterrence policy the use of nuclear weapons is only dispositional or hypothetical, not occurrent or categorical. Nevertheless, there still remains the question of what will happen if deterrence fails, i.e. if the threat at some point fails to deter.

It must also be kept in mind that the distinction between deterrent threats and their execution is greatly narrowed because of the requirement of credibility. For nuclear deterrence to work, its threat of retaliation must be *credible* to the other side. Such credibility rules out mere bluffing, and while it may coexist with a certain amount of mixed signals, deception, ambiguity, uncertainty, and so forth on both sides, this itself may create a dangerous instability.

The conclusion that emerges from these considerations is that, while the policy of nuclear deterrence may be rational in the short

140

run, to rely on it for the long run would be irrational. Other, alternative policies must be devised in order to lessen and ultimately to remove the mortal danger that is implicit in the policy of nuclear deterrence.

III Is Nuclear Deterrence Reasonable?

Let us now turn to our second central question: whether the policy of nuclear deterrence is morally reasonable for either side. Whereas the criterion of rationality is concerned with the security interests of one country alone (in our sense, of course, the United States), the criterion of reasonableness in the present context concerns the mutual interests of the United States and other countries, especially where basic rights are at stake. More generally, the political applications of the criterion of reasonableness require certain kinds of mutuality of consideration in the relations of governments to one another, of governments to their citizens, and of governments to the inhabitants of other countries.

Let us first dispose of a spurious argument for the reasonableness of the policy of nuclear deterrence. The argument is that, because it is a policy of *mutual* assured destruction, it fulfills the reasonableness requirement of mutuality of consideration. This argument is spurious because the mutuality and impartiality required by reasonableness is not merely a formal relation of equality, for it this were the case it could be satisfied by universal death. On the contrary, reasonableness also has an essential substantive component: mutuality of consideration must also include a positive, favorable concern for the rights of other persons as well as of oneself.

This point also serves sharply to limit the degree of reasonableness incorporated in the common interest which we saw above is fostered by the deterrence policy. For that community of interest, important though it is, is also based on the threat of mutual destruction.

The strongest moral objection against the policy of nuclear deterrence is that it threatens the lives, and hence the most basic rights, of millions of innocent persons in other countries as well as the United States. Here, the requirement of reasonableness bears directly on the relation of governments to the inhabitants of other countries, although it also bears consequentially on the inhabitants of the home country as well. For if it is morally wrong to bomb innocent people, then it is also morally wrong to intend or threaten to bomb them. But the policy of nuclear deterrence entails just such as murderous intention or threat, whether directly, as in counterpopulation deterrence, or indirectly, as in counterforce deterrence. Hence, the policy cannot be morally justified: far from being reasonable, it is simply a policy of indiscriminate murder.

Suggested Distinctions Between Right and Wrong

Many attempts have been made to avoid this condemnatory conclusion. The attempts have all proceeded by drawing distinctions between various aspects of the policy of nuclear deterrence, such that, even if on one pole of the distinction the policy is morally wrong, on the other pole the policy is not morally wrong.

One distinction that has been offered is between merely possessing nuclear weapons and intending to use them. The contention is that the former is morally permissible while the latter is not.[3] This, however, is a distinction without a difference, at least in the context of nuclear deterrence. For if there is no even conditional intention to use nuclear weapons, then it is pointless to possess them with a view to deterring a nuclear or other attack.

A second, equally pointless distinction is between threatening and deterring. It has been contended that one can have nuclear weapons for deterrence without threatening other persons with their use. Thus, by this distinction, deterrence by itself would be morally permissible.[4] But this suggestion is conceptually incoherent. For

---

3 This distinction has been upheld by John Cardinal Krol and John R. Connery, as reported by Richard A. McCormick, 'Nuclear Deterrence and the Problem of Intention: A Review of the Positions,' in Philip J. Murnion, ed., *Catholics and Nuclear War* (New York: Crossroads 1983), 173, 174.

4 For this distinction, see Bernard Brodie, *War and Politics* (New York: Mac-

what deterrence *means* is threatening to retaliate for some offense. Hence, to deter without threatening is as conceptually impossible as is to run without moving one's legs, or to eat without ingesting.

Let us now consider a third suggested distinction which is much more plausible and important. This is the distinction between the intention to *use* nuclear weapons and the intention to *deter* their use.[5] It is maintained that the policy of nuclear deterrence is morally acceptable despite the lethal threat it poses to millions of innocent persons, because the intention behind the threat is precisely to prevent the threat from being executed or realized. This point is thus closely related to the distinction between threat and execution that I considered in connection with the question of rationality.

Despite its plausibility, this distinction does not establish the reasonableness of the deterrence policy, for reasons similar to those that bear on rationality. For the intention to *deter* the use of nuclear weapons is the intention to make a *credible threat* to use the weapons, since deterrence involves precisely such a threat. Hence, the immorality of threatening innocent persons with death applies also to the intention to practice deterrence, that is, the intention to engage in a deterrence policy which threatens millions of innocent persons with death.

Let us see if we can avoid this difficulty of the suggested distinction by dropping its focus on intention and focusing instead on the *likely consequences* of the deterrence policy. Intention will still be present, since any overt policy involves actions and hence intentions. But the emphasis, so far as concerns the criterion of reasonableness, will be not on the intentions themselves but rather on the likely effects of the actions that embody them.

From this point of view, let us ask the following question: Is it still wrong to *threaten* to kill millions of innocent persons if this is

---

millan 1973), 404 (quoted in Michael Walzer, *Just and Unjust Wars* [New York: Basic Books 1977], 281) and James P. Sterba, 'How to Achieve Nuclear Deterrence Without Threatening Nuclear Destruction,' in James P. Sterba, ed., *The Ethics of War and Nuclear Deterrence* (Belmont, CA: Wadsworth 1985), 155-68.

5 See David Hollenback, *Nuclear Ethics* (New York: Paulist Press 1983), 73, 83.

the only practically effective way of assuring both that they as well as other millions will not *actually* be killed and that other basic rights of our society will not be destroyed? This question incorporates, of course, some very strong factual assumptions about the probable effects of the policy of deterrence and about the unavailability of alternatives. But one assumption of the question seems difficult to dispute: that *if* a choice must be made between the *threat* of death and the *actual infliction* of death, then the former is rationally to be preferred.

The thesis underlying this argument is not the principle of double effect.[6] If this principle were being applied here, it would involve that the deterrence policy has two effects, one which is good (preventing the actual killing of the innocent) and the other which is evil (threatening such killing). According to the principle of double effect, for the deterrence policy to be morally permissible, the threat would have to be only the foreseen but unintended effect of the policy. But this provision does not apply to the policy of nuclear deterrence, because in that policy the threat is made intentionally; the evil threat is given as an intended means to the good effect.

The argument I have presented is also not a form of 'consequentialism' in the utilitarian sense that any right, no matter how basic, may be overridden when the beneficial consequences of so doing are sufficiently extensive to outweigh the costs. For the concern here is not to maximize goods or utilities but rather to avoid greater evils for all the threatened victims of a nuclear holocaust. Hence, the consequentialism of this argument is distributive and negative, not aggregative and positive: the envisaged consequence or aim is to prevent violation of the basic rights of every person, not to maximize goods overall without regard for their distribution.[7]

---

6 On this principle, see Alan Donagan, *The Theory of Morality* (Chicago: University of Chicago Press 1977), 158-164.

7 On the distinction between distributive and aggregative consequentialism, see Alan Gewirth, *Human Rights: Essays on Justification and Applications* (Chicago: University of Chicago Press 1982), 251-3, 335; also *Reason and Morality*, 215-16, 296, 325, 327.

The Lesser-Evil Argument

The principle underlying my above argument for the moral reasonableness of the deterrence policy can be put more plausibly as the
thesis that, when a choice must be made between evils, the lesser
evil should be chosen over the greater, especially if this is the only
or main way of preventing the greater evil. Or, in another formulation, when two moral rights are in conflict − here, the right to life
and the right to be free from threats of death − that right must be
given precedence whose object is more necessary for action.[8] One
can act under threat of death, but not with actual death. Hence, if
it can plausibly be maintained that innocent persons' rights *to life*
can be protected *only* by infringing the rights of those or of other
innocent persons *to be free from threats of death*, then the former rights
must take precedence over the latter.

Moral criticisms of the deterrence policy, weighty as they are,
sometimes overlook that moral choices are often not between good
and evil but rather between degrees of evil. In cases of moral conflict, a possible course of action must be evaluated not only in itself
but also by comparison with its alternatives. Thus even if it is true
that 'whatever is wrong to do is wrong to threaten,'[9] this still leaves
it also true that actually to do a wrong is worse than merely to threat-
en to do that same wrong. And when the threat is given for the
sake of preventing the actual doing and when it makes this prevention more likely, the threat receives a moral justification which the
quoted dictum obscures. In this way, the principle that the lesser
evil must be chosen over the greater serves to justify the deterrence
policy whereby the *threat* to kill innocent persons serves as a means
of preventing their *actual* killing.

Among the crucial factual assumptions of this argument are that
the two evils it sets out are both exclusive and exhaustive, i.e. that
the deterrence policy's threats of death will not lead to actual inflictions of death, and that there are no alternative ways of preventing

---

8 See *Reason and Morality*, 343-4.

9 Paul Ramsey, as quoted in Walzer, *Just and Unjust Wars*, 272

the actual inflictions *except* the threats. I have already expressed my doubts about the former assumption above, and will examine the latter assumption below.

But there are also serious moral difficulties with lesser-evil arguments themselves, including the present one. For such arguments to be morally sound, the two alternatives between which a choice is to be made must not be gratuitiously imposed by the agent, as in the gunman's 'Your money or your life.' This involves the question of whether the recipient, the person on whom the evils impend, has done anything to deserve them. In the gunman case, the answer is, of course, negative. In the deterrence situation, however, a distinction must be recognized between governments and peoples. The governments of the United States and the Soviet Union have indeed engaged in hostile policies which have operated to generate, even if not to justify, the threats each addresses to the other. This antecedent context, with its crimes on each side, imposes drastic limitations on the degree of reasonableness that can be achieved by any solution to the nuclear problem.

On the other hand, the peoples of the respective countries, the millions of innocent civilians whose lives are threatened by the deterrence policy, have not themselves done anything to merit such a threat. In this regard, nuclear deterrence is different from ordinary penal deterrence, whose threats are directly addressed only to persons who actually commit or contemplate committing crimes, and who can therefore avoid the execution of the threats on themselves by refraining from committing crimes. Hence, the two alternative evils with which the deterrence policy confronts the millions of innocent civilians are indeed imposed gratuitously on them, since they have done nothing to deserve this predicament. This point indicates a very serious limitation on the moral reasonableness both of the deterrence policy and of the lesser-evil argument that was invoked to justify it.

The most serious moral difficulty of lesser-evil arguments is that they may involve the violation of important rights. In the deterrence situation, as we have seen, the right in question is that of innocent persons to be free from threats of death. Here, however, it must also be noted that in the background of the deterrence policy's pair of alternatives – the threat of death as against the actual infliction of death – there is another pair of alternatives, one of which does not involve any violation of rights. For, in effect, the United States is saying to the Soviet Union, 'Do not attack us, or we will attack you.' Here, the former alternative is itself morally justified, so that, behind the lesser-evil situation and conditioning it, there is a further possibility which is not itself evil. The threat of death is set forth only conditionally, and the condition – that the other side refrain from attacking – is itself morally justified. This, again, marks a considerable moral difference from the gunman situation.

The lesser-evil argument for the moral reasonableness of the deterrence policy, then, is unsound insofar as each of its alternatives involves the violation of basic rights. But it is sound in two respects: first, insofar as the lesser violation serves to prevent the greater one; and second, insofar as the greater violation – the actual killing of the innocent – can also be prevented by a line of conduct – refraining from attack – which is itself reasonable. The crucial moral difficulty here, however, is that the persons whose lives are threatened are for the most part not the same as those who will determine whether the lethal, bomb-precipating attacks will occur. As I shall emphasize below, this difficulty requires that the criterion of reasonableness be extended to the relation of governments to their peoples, so that democratic control of policy can be more fully assured.

My conclusion on this question of the reasonableness of the nuclear deterrence policy, then, is similar to that on the question of rationality. The policy is morally reasonable as a temporary device insofar as the threat to bomb serves to prevent actual bombing; but the policy must be followed only as a means to establishing and stabilizing further alternatives that do not involve the threat of murder and other violations of important rights against millions of innocent persons.

IV Beyond Nuclear Deterrence

I turn, finally, to our third question: How, then, can the severe shortcomings of the nuclear deterrence policy be avoided? Are there any alternatives that are both more rational and more reasonable?

In considering alternatives to nuclear deterrence, we must recall what was said earlier about motivation. Because self-interest is directly motivational, and because rationality is concerned with the most efficient means in pursuit of self-interest, motivation is directly built into the criterion of rationality. This does not mean that persons or groups always act rationally. But when they do not, this is not because of lack of motivation but usually either because of intellectual failure to calculate correctly or because of non-moral emotional factors that deflect them from what they regard as their long-range self-interest. Hence, if proposed alternatives are to have genuine chances of being acceptable to individuals and governments as they actually are, the alternatives must appear to each side to be efficient means to their respective self-interest, and especially their basic interests in survival and national security.

We may divide proposed alternatives to the deterrence policy into three broad categories. The first I shall call *realistic*. I use this word with considerable reluctance, but I adopt it here because it has become the accepted term in political science for the thesis that power is the only or the dominant concern of political actors. The realist view pushes to an exclusivist extreme the motivational concern with national egoism or self-interest that we have seen to supply the dominant end of rationality. Its alternatives to the deterrence policy, however, are hardly rational, for they involve relentless pursuit of hope-for weapons superiority in preparation for a protracted nuclear war in which the United States is to 'prevail.'[10] The lunacy of this proposal should be evident to anyone who knows the power of nuclear arms, their possession by each side for purposes of second-strike retaliation, and the unavailability or great porousness of possible defenses. Hence, despite its concern with power, this realist view can be dismissed as a plausible alternative to nuclear deterrence not only on grounds of its extreme moral unreasonableness but also because it ignores the realities of the power of nuclear weapons.

---

10 For relevant quotations from National Security Council documents, see Theodore Draper, *Present History* (New York: Vintage Books 1984), 36 ff.

A second version of a realist position is a certain quasi-Marxist view. It holds that the present nuclear crisis derives from systems of national power that rest on the economic interests of dominant classes; hence, it advocates revolutions that would overthrow those systems. The difficulties of this view derive not only from the power question of whether such revolutions could be successful but also from the further moral question of whether the subsequent regimes would be any better. Surely distinctions must be drawn between types of regime; revolutions are much harder to justify against regimes that make available civil-libertarian methods of protest and social change. Hence, this view's blanket advocacy of revolution is hardly acceptable.

Let us now consider a second group of alternatives, which I shall call *idealistic*. These go to the opposite extreme from the realist view. Instead of focusing, as does the first realist position, on exclusive considerations of power and national egoism or self-interest, the idealist alternatives emphasize kinds of altruism that push to an extreme the other-regarding aspects of reasonableness. Hence, they also fall outside the range of plausible alternatives because they do not take sufficient account of existing power relationships and motivational considerations, including pertinent facts that bear crucially on important values held by one side or the other.

One example of an idealist proposal is found in Jonathan Schell's assertion that the nuclear problem can be resolved only by total disarmament, both conventional and nuclear, by all nations, and by a complete surrender of all types of national sovereignty. Thus he speaks of 'revolutionizing the politics of the earth ... In sum, the task is nothing less than to reinvent politics: to reinvent the world.'[11] This sweeping vision is a counsel of despair because it provides no way, based on existing motivations, of moving from our present situation to the goal it upholds. If we must 'reinvent politics,' what is there in our *present* politics that will enable us to do so?

Another example of an idealist proposal is unilateral nuclear dis-

---

11 Jonathan Schell, *The Fate of the Earth* (New York: Avon Books 1982), 226

Alan Gewirth

armament: that the United States should give up all its nuclear weapons regardless of whether the Soviet Union agrees to reciprocate in any way.[12] Such disarmament would indeed remove the risk of nuclear war, since one of the two main potential participants would no longer be in a position to participate. Thereby, too, the United States would disavow the potential murderousness that the policy of nuclear retaliation entails, although it would still maintain its conventional forces.

A main, apparently plausible premise of the proposal for unilateral nuclear disarmament may be put in the following equivalent ways: we must avoid nuclear war at all costs; the supreme value is the avoidance of nuclear war; any policy that serves to remove the danger of nuclear war ought to be followed. The trouble with these premises is that, if they are taken literally, they would commit us to possibly surrendering vitally important phases both of our rational means of ensuring national security and of our moral rights of reasonableness. For example, one sure way to avoid nuclear war would be to put all NATO military forces, including those of the United States, under the command of the Soviet Defense Ministry. But this would impose on the United States and Western Europe a totalitarian regime similar to that found in Czechoslovakia, Poland, and other East European countries.

There are various confusions in the underlying premises of the proposal for unilateral nuclear disarmament. To say that we must avoid nuclear war at all costs is like saying that we must avoid death at all costs. One confusion is between necessary and sufficient conditions. Life, i.e. the avoidance of death, is indeed the necessary condition of the attainment of all other values. But it is not the sufficient condition of that attainment. There are many values besides life, which in fact make life worth living. Similarly, the avoidance of nuclear war is indeed a necessary condition of the attainment of all other values, but it is not a sufficient condition. There are many other vitally important values besides nuclear peace. Thus, even if

---

12 See Douglas Lackey, 'Missiles and Morals: A Utilitarian Look at Nuclear Deterrence,' *Philosophy and Public Affairs* 11 (1982), 189-231.

it is true that without nuclear peace we shall all be dead, and even if it is also true that it is better to be Red than dead, it still remains the case that it is possible to avoid both being Red and being dead. The rights and other values involved in the latter, more extensive avoidance deserve the fullest possible protection. But such protection would be severely jeopardized if not entirely surrendered by a policy of unilateral nuclear disarmament.

The Pragmatic Alternative

I turn now to a third group of alternatives to the policy of nuclear deterrence, which I shall call *pragmatic*. In contrast to the snyoptic visions of the realist and idealist positions, the pragmatic view emphasizes incremental, reciprocal steps toward the goal of mutual nuclear disarmament. If one step works, it can lead to another in a gradual, experimental process. The emphasis on such incrementalism is found both in the social engineering ideas of John Dewey and in what Karl Popper has called 'piecemeal' methods of social change,[13] and in specific application to the nuclear problem it has been espoused in positions that range from the GRIT ('Graduated Reciprocation in Tension-reduction') put forth by Charles Osgood a quarter-century ago,[14] to the 'Tit-for-Tat' and 'live and let live' strategies presented by Robert Axelrod and Freeman Dyson in 1984.[15] As Russell Hardin and others have pointed out, the nuclear test ban treaty of 1963 was engendered by such a small-step process

---

13 See John Dewey, *Reconstruction in Philosophy* (Boston: Beacon Press 1948), chs. 7-8; *The Public and Its Problems* (New York: Henry Holt and Co. 1927), 84 ff. See also Karl Popper, *The Poverty of Historicism* (London: Routledge and Kegan Paul 1957). For an extensive discussion of the 'strategy of disjointed incrementalism,' see David Braybrooke and Charles E. Lindblom, *A Strategy of Decision* (New York: Free Press 1963), chs. 5-6.

14 Charles E. Osgood, *An Alternative to War or Surrender* (Urbana, IL: University of Illinois Press 1962), ch. 5

15 Robert Axelrod, *The Evolution of Cooperation* (New York: Basic Books 1984),

that was initiated unilaterally by President Kennedy and then reciprocated and advanced by Premier Khrushchev.[16]

In addition to its incremental emphasis, the pragmatic alternative also differs from the realist and idealist positions in its emphasis on mutuality, as opposed to both egoism and altruism. This mutuality reflects the self-interested motivations of each party for its own national security and thus is more likely to win their adherence. The mutuality in question refers both to ends and to means. It aims at the goal of mutual nuclear disarmament and it uses reciprocally acceptable steps to attain this goal. In this way, the pragmatic alternative is reasonable as well as rational.

It is also important to note, however, that the pragmatic position as here understood also involves a broader moral conception. A strategy like Axelrod's 'Tit-for-Tat,' even with its combined incrementalist and mutualist emphases, could characterize the cooperative bargaining procedures of gangster individuals or states if it were not guided by an egalitarian-universalist moral principle of reasonableness like the Principle of Generic Consistency to which I referred above. Such a principle emphasizes not only the interests of the particular bargainers but also the rights of all persons. Hence, it serves to restrict the spheres within which games-players or bargainers may legitimately seek one another's cooperation, by assuring that the rights of other persons and groups are also respected. In this way the pragmatic position can serve as a guide to that more general justice which has often been rightly held to be a necessary condition of a truly stable and genuine peace.

My present direct concern, however, is with the nuclear problem. The pragmatic approach rests on the view that each side is rationally aware of the dangers both of the nuclear deterrence policy and of the arms race and that each would be willing to take reciprocal steps that reduce the tensions generating these dangers if the steps

---

chs. 2-3; Freeman Dyson, *Weapons and Hope* (New York: Harper and Row 1984), 274 ff.

16 See Russell Hardin, *Collective Action* (Baltimore, MD: Johns Hopkins University Press 1982), 210.

were in accord with their respective conceptions of national security and political values. If one such rationally based step on one side were reciprocated by the other side, mutual trust could gradually be developed and increased.

To have a schematic idea of how this tit-for-tat process might work, suppose the United States were to announce that it was going to remove – or, better yet, destroy – fifty of its intermediate range warhead-carrying missiles stationed in West Germany. The Soviet Union would be invited to send observers to verify that this was being done, and would also be invited to reciprocate by removing or destroying fifty of its SS-20 missiles, or comparable weapons, aimed at Western Europe. If the Soviet Union were to reciprocate in this way, the United States would then take further disarming steps and would invite further reciprocation from the Soviet Union. In this way, important steps would be taken toward nuclear disarmament or at least toward drastic reductions in the respective nuclear arsenals.

But what if the Soviet Union, instead of cooperating, were to defect, i.e. were to denounce the whole thing as an imperialist plot and install more missiles? In this case, the United States, in game-theory parlance, would have been played for a 'sucker.'[17] But, following the tit-for-tat strategy, it would thereupon match the Soviet Union's increase, while at the same time calling attention to its irrationality. Then it would try once again to set the reducing process in motion.

Three Conditions of Rational Competition

An important ground for thinking that the Soviet Union would cooperate in this general mutual reduction process is that the nuclear arms competition really is irrational. Hence, if the United States were to take steps to stop and reverse the competition, the Soviet Union,

---

17 See Axelrod, *The Evolution of Cooperation*, 8-10.

insofar as its leaders are also rational, would seize the opportunity to act accordingly.

This crucial point about the irrationality of the nuclear arms competition can be established more explicitly as follows. In order to be rational, any competition must fulfill three conditions: a *cardinal* condition, an *ordinal* condition, and a *proportionality* condition. The cardinal condition is that a maximum relevant to the competition has not yet been reached; for if it has been reached, then further competition is pointless. For example, if a baseball pitcher is on the way to a no-hitter, then it is rational for him to continue pitching in the hope of achieving the no-hit maximum. But if, at the end of nine innings, he has already achieved this goal while his own side has scored several runs, then he, as a pitcher, cannot do any better in that game. Hence, for him to continue the competition would be irrational, since he has already achieved the relevant maximum.

The ordinal condition for the rationality of a competition is that one of the competitors must be in a position to outstrip or win over the other. For example, if two baseball teams are in a scoreless tie after nine innings, it makes sense to continue the competition. But suppose 35 innings have gone by and neither team has scored. Then it seems pointless to continue trying to defeat the other; the game should be halted and declared a tie.

The proportionality condition, finally, is that continuing the competition must not lead to results that are far worse than the avowed purpose of the competition. At the extreme, these results would include death or severe injury either for the victor alone or for victor and vanquished together. Apart from obvious examples of this in the sometimes crippling physical injuries suffered in various athletic contests, the grim trench warfare of World War I provided a graphic instance of the violation of this condition. The few yards 'gained' each week by one side or the other did not begin to compensate for the hundreds of thousands of deaths on each side. Another, less lethal example is where a man works ceaselessly to bankrupt his competitors or at least to make more money than all of them, only to suffer deep remorse later and to conclude that his whole life has been wasted because dedicated to a worthless competitiveness.

Now the nuclear arms race fails to satisfy each of these three conditions. Hence, it is irrational. To show this in sufficient detail would require, of course, a host of factual considerations. Here I must be brief.

First, the nuclear arms race fails to satisfy the cardinal condition, because each side has long since gone beyond the maximum of armaments needed to destroy the whole human race many times over. Hence, it is a case of pointless overkill to continue producing nuclear weapons.[18]

Second, the nuclear arms race fails to satisfy the ordinal condition. For at least the past three decades the race has been fueled by the aim on one side or the other of first catching up with and then getting ahead of the other side either offensively or defensively or both, and qualitatively as well as quantitatively. And at each turn where one side has gotten ahead of the other, the latter has more than compensated for the gap. This has been the case with the first developments of the hydrogen bomb, with the intercontinental ballistic missile, and with the MIRV (i.e. the multiple independently targetable reentry vehicle), and similar parity has now been attained with the cruise missiles.[19] Hence, given the resources on each side and the determination to use them to make up any gaps, the attempt to attain a permanent superiority in nuclear arms over the other side is futile; neither side will acquiesce in the other's superiority. Moreover, each side's steps to increase its security by getting ahead of the other side serve only to increase the latter's feelings of insecurity and thereby exacerbate the very problem they are designed to solve. It must hence be rationally recognized that there is a general, enduring nuclear equilibrium between the two superpowers, so that it is irrational to continue to seek superiority. Therefore, the ordinal condition for a rational nuclear arms competition also cannot be satisfied.

---

18 See Richard Smoke, *National Security and the Nuclear Dilemma* (Reading, MA: Addison-Wesley Publishing Co. 1984), 243 ff.

19 See Smoke, *National Security and the Nuclear Dilemma*, 152, 161, 175 ff. See also Lawrence Freedman, *The Evolution of Nuclear Strategy* (New York: St. Martin's Press 1981), ch. 24.

Alan Gewirth

Finally, the nuclear arms race fails to satisfy the proportionality condition. There are strong grounds for believing that a nuclear explosion of 100 megatons over major urban centers would cause a 'nuclear winter' in which most of human and other life would be extinguished.[20] Even if further research should indicate that the effects would be less catastrophic, there is still the strong probability not only that a nuclear war cannot be won but that even to engage in it is suicidal. Hence, continuing the nuclear arms race is self-defeating: its potential results threaten to destroy the very national security which constitutes the avowed purpose for engaging in the race.

It is such considerations that provide grounds for holding both that the nuclear arms competition is irrational and that if the leaders on one side were to initiate the process of winding the competition down, the other side would reciprocate.

Reciprocative Trust

This process can also lead to an important degree of trust on each side. We saw at the outset that a crucial part of the nuclear problem derives from the deep distrust that each side has toward the other. This distrust is not, indeed, total; it is mitigated by the trust we have seen that each side has in the other's rationally refraining from nuclear attack because of the threat of retaliation inherent in the deterrence policy. This trust, however, is *minatory*, based on threat and hence on fear. It is thus quite distinct from the *amicable* trust that we have, for example, with Canada or Britain, based negatively on entire lack of fear about the other's intentions toward us and based positively on genuine mutual friendship. The question is whether we can move from the present wary relationship of minatory trust with the Soviet Union to a more extensive trust that will genuinely

---

20 See R. P. Turco, et al., 'Nuclear Winter: Global Consequences of Multiple Nuclear Explosions,' *Science* 222 (23 December 1982), 1283-92. See also Paul R. Ehrlich, Carl Sagan, et. al., *The Cold and the Dark: The World After Nuclear War* (New York: W.W. Norton & Co. 1984).

enable us to avoid the dangers of the present policy of nuclear deterrence and its accompanying arms race.

The pragmatic policy I have outlined does, I think, have a good chance of generating such further trust. I shall call it *reciprocative trust*. It would be based on palpable awareness on each side of the matching verified steps they have taken to reduce their nuclear threats against one another. Such reciprocative trust would also have the important merit of fostering practically effective communication between the two sides on the vital issues that are of joint concern to them. An elemental example of such communication based on reciprocative trust already exists in the 'hot line' that connects the White House and the Kremlin by a telecommunications link. A valuable addition to this is the proposal made by Senators Nunn and Warner that separate but jointly manned 'national nuclear crisis reduction centers' be established in the respective capitals in order to reduce the risk of nuclear incidents.[21] An appropriate extension of such communication centers might have helped to avoid the tragic disaster of the Korean airliner that flew over the Soviet Union in 1983.

The rational outcome of the pragmatic policy with its reciprocative trust would be for the two sides to engage in negotiations aiming to ban the nuclear weapons stockpile altogether, because of its potentiality for leading to mutual suicide and the destruction of the human race. It has been alleged that nuclear arms cannot be 'disinvented,' that 'The atomic fire cannot be extinguished. The fear of its use will remain a part of the human psyche for the rest of human history.'[22] To this the appropriate reply is that just as nuclear weapons were invented by humans, so they can also be controlled by humans. The latter would, of course, demand far more extensive forms of cooperation than the former. For while the invention of nuclear weapons was accomplished by the work of only a rela-

---

21 Sam Nunn and John W. Warner, 'Reducing the Risk of Nuclear War,' *The Washington Quarterly* 7 (1984), 3-7

22 Harvard Nuclear Study Group, *Living with Nuclear Weapons* (New York: Bantam Books 1983), 5

tively small number of humans, the abolition of those weapons would require control of a much larger number of humans, including, but not limited to, their governments. Nevertheless, the difference here is one of degree, not of kind, and the needed control can be achieved by extending the reciprocative trust I am here advocating so that the fullest possible means of verification are available to each side. Conventional arms would remain, with increased notification being required concerning troop movements, maneuvers, and other related matters.

The Normative Primacy of Morality

My argument in this section has focused on the requirements of rationality, with their concentration on the protection of national self-interest. We have also seen, however, that the reciprocative trust based on rationality incorporates important elements of mutuality of consideration and hence moral reasonableness. The structure of my argument, then, has involved that reasonableness is here maintained as an effect of rationality rather than on its own grounds. But how is this relation consistent with the categoricalness and normative primacy of morality?

Two points must be stressed in reply. First, there is a distinction between the order of justification and the order of motivation. In the order of justification, moral reasonableness is indeed categorical and overriding: it sets requirements for actions and institutions that are normatively necessary, so that they take precedence over all other practical criteria. But in the order of motivation, as we have seen, moral requirements are often ineffective, especially when opposed by direct self-interest. The structure of my argument, then, has been that the motivational force of rationally-based national self-interest, effective as it can be in its own terms, can also supply the needed motivation for a morally reasonable, just solution to the nuclear problem. But this motivational sequence does not remove the justificatory primacy of morality; it seves rather to give effect to that primacy, just as, in municipal contexts, the force of legal sanctions gives effect to the requirements of morality.

A second point bears on the application of the reasonableness requirement within each state. As consisting in mutuality of consideration, reasonableness includes the right to equal freedom, and this in turn requires that all persons be free to participate on equal terms in the decision-making process concerning matters that vitally affect them. Thus the problems of nuclear policy must not be reserved for governments alone, let alone their operating in secrecy. On the contrary, the pragmatic method of reciprocative trust should be open to the advocacy of all persons and groups in the respective countries. In this regard, of course, the civil liberties available in the United States give it a pronounced moral advantage over the Soviet Union.

My whole argument for the irrationality of the nuclear arms race has been based on the assumption that each side engages in the race for the purpose of bolstering its own security. If, however, there are groups in each country that desire continued expansion of weapons production for other reasons, such as the 'military-industrial complex' about which President Eisenhower warned in his farewell address, then here too there is a further ground for increased democratic control.

What I have tried to show in this paper is that the present posture of nuclear deterrence has important elements of both irrationality and unreasonableness that make it impossible to accept as an adequate long-range policy. Established as a means of coping with the mortal danger of the nuclear hostility between the two superpowers, the policy itself contributes to that very danger. I have also tried to show that there are alternatives that should be rationally acceptable to each side because they are in accord with each side's own basic motivations toward its respective interests in national security. And because these alternatives involve the cessation of a gigantically murderous threat, and promote the mutual consideration of interests, the alternatives also move in the direction of fulfilling the requirements of moral reasonableness.

Received September, 1985

CANADIAN JOURNAL OF PHILOSOPHY
Supplementary Volume 12

Deterrence and Moral Theory*

RUSSELL HARDIN
University of Chicago
Chicago, IL 60637
U.S.A.

Introduction

Issues in public policy have been challenging and remaking moral theory for two centuries. Such issues force us to question fundamen-

---

* I wish to thank David Copp, Thomas Donaldson, J.L.A. Garcia, Richard Miller, Christopher W. Morris, Joseph S. Nye, Jr., Susan Moller Okin, Charles Silver, Steven Walt, students and faculty at the weekly lunch of the Divinity School of the University of Chicago in November 1984, and participants

tal principles of ethics while they cast doubt on our ability to generalize from traditional intuitions. No issue poses more remarkable difficulties for moral theory than nuclear weapons policy. Because the consequences of their deployment and therefore possible use could be grievous beyond those of any previously conceivable human action, these weapons frame the conflict between outcome-based, especially utilitarian, and action-based deontological moral theories more acutely than perhaps any other we have faced. Just because nuclear weapons may bring about the most grievous outcome imaginable, they elevate concern with outcomes over concern with actions. More generally, they wreak havoc with the focus on the morality of individual choices and actions, set limits to the notion of intention and the doctrine of double effect, call into question the so-called just-war theory, and overwhelm the intuitionist basis of much of ethical reasoning.

Of course, utilitarians have their own severe difficulties with deterrence, as they do with any major policy issue, because their moral assessment of the policy requires objective assessments of the likelihood that deterrence will fail and that the weapons will be used and of the scale of damage the weapons will cause. The only progress that has been made toward providing credible assessments of these is the dismal progress of coming to recognize that the scale of damage that would result from a serious nuclear war has become so awesome as possibly even to obliterate humanity.

I do not think a utilitarian can confidently assert what is the morally best policy on nuclear weapons, but I will not pursue such calculations here.[1] Rather, I wish to discuss several problems that nuclear deterrence poses for action-based deontological moral theories. In all of these problems, it is remarkable how radically the

---

in the seminar on Practical Reason at the University of Chicago and in the 1984 Amintaphil conference at Notre Dame University for comments on an earlier draft of this paper.

1 Russell Hardin, 'Unilateral Versus Mutual Disarmament,' *Philosophy and Public Affairs* **12** (1983), 236-54; and 'Risking Armageddon,' in Avner Cohen and Steven Lee, eds., *Nuclear Weapons and the Future of Humanity* (Totowa, NJ: Rowman and Allanheld 1985 [forthcoming])

utilitarian and the deontological perspective come into conflict; the usual trick of showing how deontological rules for action are really utilitarian does not work. Despite apparent differences, the problems I wish to discuss — in intention, the doctrine of double effect, just-war theory, and intuitionist reasoning — are not entirely separable. Their chief points of commonality here are that they all involve relationships between actions and consequences and that they all are complicated by the institutional nature of the system of nuclear deterrence.

While there is virtually unanimous agreement in the writings of moral theorists on nuclear weapons that the weapons should not be deliberately used, there is widespread disagreement over whether their use may meaningfully be threatened in order to deter awful actions by another state. I wish here not to argue for or against deterrence but only against certain kinds of argument about it. Even more than did Nazi genocide for an earlier generation, deterrence poses for us a unique moral problem. Against Nazi genocide the only moral dilemma was not whether it was right or wrong but what to do about it. Nuclear deterrence, however, belies the commonplace claim that all moral theorists generally agree on what is right or wrong, that they merely have different bases for making their judgments.

Consequences are so grievous in this context that consequentialist considerations should dominate all others in anyone's reasoning about the morality of nuclear-weapons policies. At the very least, consideration of consequences should be given some force even in the most action-based or deontological of arguments about nuclear weapons. A purely principled argument made without consideration of whether it implies the likelihood of the destruction of a large part of humanity cannot plausibly count as a moral argument, no matter where the principles come from.

My purpose here, however, is not to defend this view, which I will assume is accepted, but to show how it, the strategic nature of actions, and the institutional nature of nuclear policies and actions complicate reasoning about nuclear weapons from moral theories that are largely action-based. It is plausible that the current revival of philosophical interest in nuclear-arms policies will stimulate reconsideration of meta-ethical issues simply because the possibility of nuclear war is so stark and because the choice of policies to prevent it shows up central difficulties in the two major traditions in western moral philosophy.

Deterrence

It is not surprising that action-based theorists should have difficulty with deterrence, which is inherently a consequentialist program. But there is another problem with nuclear deterrrence that may more perversely confuse action-based deontological reasoning: it is inherently an institutional, not a personal program. If deterrence is to work it must be made credible. Hence, retaliation must be massively organized in advance; it cannot be left wholly to the discretion of a moral chooser who may or may not be available to act when the time comes. What we must judge is not actions taken when the time comes so much as the policy taken in advance.

Oddly, this point in another context has been the focus of a commonplace critique of utilitarianism. It is said to be a problem with utilitarianism, at least with Act-utilitarianism, that it always leaves it up to individuals to choose on the ground of the best outcome on the whole. But this undercuts the whole point of such institutions as that of, say, justice. John Rawls's discussion of the institution of punishing is an effort to rescue the morality of officers in institutions, such as McCloskey's Sheriff in a southern town who must decide whether to let an innocent man be lynched or to let a race riot tear the town apart.[2] In this respect, the system of nuclear deterrence, if it is to be meaningful and effective, must be as embedded in an institution as is the system of justice. The system would not be desirable if it depended on the autonomous commitments of a single actor.

---

2 John Rawls, 'Two Concepts of Rules,' *Philosophical Review* **64** (1955), 3-32; H.J. McCloskey, 'An Examination of Restricted Utilitarianism,' *Philosophical Review* **66** (1957), 466-85; for further discussion, see Russell Hardin, 'The Utilitarian Logic of Liberalism,' *Ethics*, forthcoming, especially the section 'Institutionalization of Rights.'

Hence, much of the discussion of the morality of retaliating once deterrence has failed is remarkably wrong-headed or beside the point. Retaliation will not be left up to a philosophically grounded moral chooser in the relevant moment, it will have been almost fully arranged in advance in the complex sense that all the institutional and physical requirements for it will be in place. Therefore one cannot reasonably separate the issue of retaliation from the large policy of deterrence. If there are decisions to be made, they are all one, which is whether to deter at the risk of retaliating. Certainly this is the issue for citizens as policy makers who will not themselves be in control of events at possible moments of retaliation. This is the heart of the moral problem of deterrence and it may not become fully clear without much of the following discussion.

Understanding may often be led astray by the persuasive mis-definition of 'threat' in this context. Curtis Lemay and Nikita Khrushchev are well known for asserting that their nations would retaliate and destroy the other side if provoked. Khrushchev, however, proclaimed his threat already at a time well before the Soviet Union was capable of carrying it out. To one who knew better, therefore, Khrushchev's 'threat' was meaningless. The meaningful threats that both sides pose today require no proclamations: they gain their meaning and therefore their force from the fact of the clear existence of physical capability and apparent organizational will. Because of these, an American president probably could not successfully retract the American threat. The American deterrent has a life of its own that is not simply subject to anyone's will or action – although it may be that its misuse could be subject to someone's will.

In utilitarianism it is a standard move to consider a whole package of actions and their implications, typically in comparison to alternative whole packages. In action-based moral theories it generally is not. Rather, each separate action is judged as though it were independent of any other. Hence, action-based theorists all too often argue against the system of deterrence in a way that is analogous to the way they think utilitarians must argue against the system of justice. They suppose that individual choosers cannot morally carry out the decisions that might fall to them and that therefore the system of deterrence is morally wrong. A utilitarian can reach such a conclusion only after comparing the expected results of the sys-

165

tem of deterrence to the expected results of plausible alternatives. Or perhaps a utilitarian would wish to argue that it is both right to set up the system of deterrence and wrong of relevant individuals to carry out some of the actions it requires.

The Focus on Individuals

Action-based moral theories are concerned with what an individual does, with the natures of actions and individuals, with the relationship of actions to character rather than to consequences more fundamentally.[3] In some ways such theory seems self-indulgent and egocentric and, in its focus on clean hands, it is egocentric when it concludes that what matters is what *I* do rather than what happens. Some of this concern in the work of non-theological moral theorists may be a residue of Catholic concern with salvation, for which what *I* do may be of paramount interest. But traditionally the concern with what *I* do governed kinds of choices very different from those we face with nuclear weapons.

Most of contemporary action-based theory is generally Kantian in its content but often intuitionist rather than rationalist in its arguments. Kantian theory is paralleled, even overlapped, by Catholic theory. Contemporary Kantian and Catholic philosophers have contributed substantially to the debate over the morality of nuclear weapons. The action-based quality of Catholic theory is somewhat

---

3 Unfortunately, our vocabulary here is not as perspicuous as we might wish. I am not happy with the distinctions as I have drawn them. I wish to highlight the difference between judgments of actions as kinds *tout court* and judgments of outcomes. In the latter, what is of interest in motivating behavior is also actions, but the character of the action that matters to us is the effects it has, not its type as determined by some other criterion. In *The Rejection of Consequentialism: A Philosophical Investigation of the Considerations Underlying Rival Moral Conceptions* (Oxford: The Clarendon Press 1982), Samuel Scheffler speaks of agent-centered versus consequentialist moral theories.

ambiguous, especially in the just-war theory, which is rather more institutional than individual.

Presumably because their prescriptions are typically for individual action, many deontological accounts of deterrence tend to focus on decision makers and their actions at relevant moments. Jeff McMahan argues that certain of these accounts are misguided in their interpretation of the wrongness of certain contingent intentions and he goes on to suggest that the relevant issue for these deontological critics of deterrence is what policy citizens of a democratic polity should want their nation to adopt.[4] This is an artful effort to make a moral theory for individuals relevant to institutions. Given the plausible structure of an institution for deterrence — and many other public policies — action-based theories will be lost without such an artful effort.

The only alternative to McMahan's kind of effort would be to argue about what one might do if one happened into a significant role in the deterrent system. Even this will be irrelevant to the morality of the American and Soviet deterrent systems, however, because it is implausible that any one individual role holder could make a significant difference in preventing the use of their weapons in retaliation. Hence, a deontological argument against nuclear deterrence must focus on the large number of prior decisions by all those who might influence whether a deterrent system is put in place or maintained. On the American side, at least, this leads in part to McMahan's concern with democratic citizens.

As a citizen what is it right for me to do? Alas, the individualist focus of action-based theories leaves us in a quandary here. It might be right for me qua individual not to participate in retaliation for an attack on my nation. But in the collective decision would it be right for me to impose on my fellow citizens the risk that we not participate in deterrence of such an attack?

What is it that I as a citizen in a representative democracy am responsible for? Very indirectly and conditionally I may be in part responsible for whatever policy my nation adopts. If the issue when

---

4 Jeff McMahan, 'Deterrence and Deontology,' *Ethics* **95** (1985), 517-36

I vote or participate in politics were solely whether I should defend my own life by threatening to kill millions of innocent Soviet citizens in a nuclear retaliation in order to deter Soviet leaders from killing me,[5] debate would not last long. But that is, of course, not the issue: which is whether millions of other innocent people should be protected by such a threat at the risk that it be carried out. My vote whether my nation should erect or maintain a system of nuclear deterrence is inherently other-directed in large part. If I believe that not having a system of nuclear deterrence invites the destruction of some of my fellow Americans much more than having such a system invites destruction of them as well as of many Soviet citizens and others, how am I to decide what an action-based morality demands of me in the polling booth or in political activity? Both these groups are innocent. In plumping for or against deterrence, I am plumping for the risk of killing innocents, merely different innocents and different risks. The only questions at issue are which innocents and at what relative risks.

This conclusion cuts both ways in current policy debates. Many critics of deterrence suppose that certain new weapons systems that are supposedly defensive only are therefore morally preferable to current systems for massive retaliation against innocents.[6] This conclusion cannot follow simply from the fact that the weapons are directed against weapons rather than against cities. One must also be able to assert that the new weapons would lead to fewer expected deaths and other harms overall. But this is, of course, a fundamentally utilitarian calculus. It is impossible to escape the task of consequentialist calculation here. Given the inherently institutional and interactive nature of the deterrent system, we cannot consider the problem of killing innocents as unambiguously the problem of the one or the other policy.

More generally, the problem of fixing responsibility for various outcomes in a large polity makes action-based arguments very com-

---

5 Ibid., 535

6 James Turner Johnson, *Can Modern War be Just?* (New Haven, CT: Yale University Press 1984)

plicated. For example, one might ask what is my responsibility for residual racism in the United States. Suppose I have done something toward solving that problem, but I have not dedicated my whole energies to it. Just how much must I do?[7] Independently of this question, which seems to plague any hortatory moral theory such as many deontological theories and utilitarianism, deterrence poses another that particularly plagues recent deontological accounts. Supposing responsibility for any policy my nation adopts is partly mine, we may then ask, 'Toward whom am I acting when I support or oppose an American deterrent?' My action is necessarily directed at Americans and Russians as well as many others.

It is a peculiar fallacy of composition to argue as though I were only acting toward Russians and to reach judgments about my action from analogies to how I should act on my own behalf toward another. My own interest counts as nothing in the face of potential nuclear war. Although my concern for my family might actually motivate me to take a stand one way or the other on certain issues of nuclear weapons, I doubt that my own direct interest otherwise even matters to me in this context. Beyond the interests of my family, I will be motivated exclusively by fairly general sympathy and reasoned generalization from sympathy. If this is true, as I suspect it is of almost all who are grievously concerned with the threat of nuclear war, then a direct assessment of my actions will be misguided if it is posed in the typical manner of action-based moral theories.

Intention

The notion of intention obviously runs afoul of institutional and strategic considerations in the context of nuclear deterrence. There are two separate issues which come together here. First, it is often hard to know what it means for a nation, an institution, or a collectivity

---

7 See further James S. Fishkin, *The Limits of Obligation* (New Haven, CT: Yale University Press 1982); and Martin McGuire, 'The Calculus of Moral Obligations,' *Ethics* **95** (1985) 199-223.

to have intentions at all. Second, it is hard to know what is being intended in the contingent future of a strategic interaction in which one party's action is defined as dependent on another's. The latter consideration applies as well to individuals as to institutions. Let us consider each of these issues in turn and then bring them briefly together.

Institutions and Intentions

First let us consider the institutional problem of what it means to say that the intention behind the American nuclear weapons is, say, to deter the Soviet Union from attacking. There is no one person whose intentions matter in this issue. Nor can we easily read from legislative and administrative records just what the weapons are intended by anyone to do. This is a problem common to governmental institutions. In the common law there is a special term, now obsolete in all other uses, for the intention of the law: the *intendment* of the law or of a law is not the intention that went into its design but rather the interpretation that the courts read out of its words as embodied in legislation or past cases dealing with it. As Lon Fuller notes, 'Any private and uncommunicated intention of the draftsman of a statute is properly regarded as legally irrelevant to its proper interpretation.'[8] If we have an understanding of what it means for an individual to have an intention (and we may not), we cannot immediately translate this understanding into a notion of collective or institutional intention.

We can probably safely read from the actual institutional arrange-

---

8 Lon L. Fuller, *The Morality of Law* (New Haven, CT: Yale University Press 1969, revised edition), 86; Fuller (86n) illustrates his point with a lovely chastisement of Lord Nottingham, who said in a case, 'I had some reason to know the meaning of this law; for it had its first rise from me.' Campbell's *Lives of the Lord Chancellors of England*, vol. 3 (third edition, 1848), 423n, retorts, 'If Lord Nottingham drew it, he was the less qualified to construe it, the author of an act considering more what he privately intended than the meaning he has expressed.'

ments that American nuclear weapons are intended to retaliate to an attack, in part simply because they are virtually certain to do so. Whether they are also intended to be used by agents making active choices in other circumstances is much less clear. It seems likely that it will be hard for any agent to use more than a handful of the weapons without a rather massive and prior popular expression of support. It is possible, perhaps, that a provocative agent could launch a handful of warheads and thereby stimulate a counterattack that would motivate 'retaliation.' That such a sequence of events is counted as an accidental war suggests how far from the actual intendment of the weapons anything but retaliation is.

Much of the discussion of nuclear weapons may have been colored by the fact that their initial use in wartime is widely supposed to have been by the decision of President Truman. Not since the early days of the Eisenhower administration, however, has such a choice been faced by anyone with the autonomy to act to initiate nuclear war.[9] Once the weapons were sufficiently numerous and diverse and were faced by a credible threat from the Soviet Union they necessarily came under increasingly articulated institutional control.

It is a morally painful fact that the first use of nuclear weapons in war was perhaps a fully intentional act. And there may eventually be more such acts. But a full scale nuclear war between the superpowers cannot easily be such an act. Richard Nixon, as president, is supposed to have said, 'I can go into my office and pick up the telephone and in twenty-five minutes seventy million people will be dead.'[10] If he actually believed that, then, as was all too often true, his judgment was poor. He could not have initiated a full-scale

---

9 Eisenhower reputedly did face such a decision in the days just before the Soviet Union achieved the capacity to attack the United States with nuclear weapons. He considered making a pre-emptive attack but then rejected the 'concept' by the fall of 1954 (David Alan Rosenberg, 'The Origins of Overskill: Nuclear Weapons and American Strategy, 1945-1960,' *International Security* 7 (1983), 3-71, at pp. 33-4). Such an attack was similar to what Bertrand Russell had earlier advocated except that Russell rather more humanely proposed that the Soviet Union first be given an ultimatum not to develop nuclear

nuclear attack on the Soviet Union without massive, persistent, willful effort and perhaps not even then. If Watergate could bring him down in slow agony, nuclear macho would have brought him down instantly.

Someone in Nixon's position is not entirely irrelevant to what happens, but the world is not so simply organized as to respond instantly to an American president's whim in so important a matter. It would take long effort for a nascent Caligula or Hitler to pervert the system of institutional control over nuclear weapons. On the other hand, if the conditions for nuclear war came about, an American president could probably not stop its happening either. A president most assuredly could not stop retaliation for a massive attack on the United States.

Intentions and Strategic Interaction

Now turn to the fundamental question of intention in contexts of strategic interaction: What do we want when we want deterrence? Recall the discussion above of the nature of individual choosing in the setting of national policy.[11] All morally relevant action takes place prior to the moment of retaliation. For citizens it takes place more or less continuously as we try to influence or we ignore weapons policies.

What do I intend when I support a national policy of nuclear deterrence against nuclear attack on my nation? Primarily I intend to influence or support my nation's institutions in striving to protect a large number of innocent people from horrible consequences. I cannot plausibly intend myself to bring about their protection and I cannot plausibly intend myself to carry out retaliation in the event

weapons (Ronald W. Clark, *The Life of Bertrand Russell* [New York: Knopf 1976], 517-30).

10 John Krige, 'The Politics of Truth: Experts and Laypeople in the Nuclear Debate,' 67-85, in Nigel Blake and Kay Pole, eds., *Objections to Nuclear Defence: Philosophers on Deterrence* (London: Routledge and Kegan Paul 1984), 67-8

11 Under 'The Focus on Individuals.'

deterrence fails. Should the relevant moment come, there may be people who do intend the latter and who will do it, but they will be people who have been selected to be reliable in doing so. If I thought the consequences of the deterrent system were likely to be better than those of abandoning it, then, if there were a way to secure retaliation without dependence on actual people, I would prefer it if I thought it were more reliable in that it posed the lesser risk of harming anyone, east or west. Hence, the morality of the action in the moment it is taken is of little interest to our policy choice since the 'action' could be an automatic result that, like cancer, simply happens in the relevant moment. That is the kind of expectation we want in order to make our deterrent credible enough to be its most effective. (Of course, we might want a particular probability of retaliation of less than certainty. If, say, a fifty percent probability of retaliation against a full-scale strike would be nearly as effective as would be a virtual certainty of retaliation in deterring such a strike and, if it were no more likely to be used when it should not be, it would be a less harmful and therefore morally better system. We would want this system to be credibly sure to respond with the relevant probability insofar as its likelihood of working that way would secure its deterrent effect.)

In short, our intention is systemic and, as argued earlier, other-directed. We want to protect one set of innocents at the risk of harming another set of innocents. What we want overall is to harm as few as possible.

The clearest way to pose this issue analytically is to put it into game theoretic terms and to ask, 'What counts as the action I take in a game?' In a game in which one party is in strategic interaction with another, choices are only of strategies, not of outcomes. Of course, particular strategies are chosen for the purpose of influencing the joint determination of outcome. Nevertheless, it is simply false and misleading to say that I choose an outcome.

For example, in the ubiquitous Prisoner's Dilemma game of Table 1, I as the row player can choose one of two strategies, C or D, and you as the column player can choose between your C and D. The outcomes are here abstractly represented by the values we each place on them. In the usual RC (or *Roman Catholic*) convention, the *Row* player's valuation of each outcome is given first and the

Column player's valuation is given second, after the comma. In either case, 1 is the most preferred outcome, 4 the least preferred. It is obvious in the game that I cannot choose an outcome. If I tried to obtain the outcome that I value most highly, I could be relatively sure you would want to prevent that outcome by choosing your D strategy. Whatever the outcomes are in the way of objective events or states of affairs, I am powerless to decide which happens beyond narrowing down the set of possible outcomes. For example, If I choose my strategy D, the set will be narrowed down to the two outcomes which we jointly value at (1,4) and (3,3).

Table 1: Prisoner's Dilemma game

		Column	
		C	D
Row	C	2,2	4,1
	D	1,4	3,3

Philosophical discussions of action do not generally deal with the problem of strategic interaction except by treating specific cases in an ad hoc way. For example, Alan Donagan discusses a poker player's effort to maximize his winnings by betting in such a way as to lead others in the game to bet more than they would have done if he had accurately tipped the strength of his hand:

> Smith is playing stud poker with Jones and Robinson. His hole cards give him a hand that is probably stronger than Jones's whose face-up cards are stronger than his. At the second round of betting, he checks [that is, he passes on this round of betting], foreseeing that Jones will raise

heavily and that Robinson, who has marked Jones as a bluffer, will stay in the game. Jones does raise, and Robinson stays, enabling Smith to achieve his purpose, of winning a large pot.

Donagan concludes that 'An agent can intend, not only to cause certain events to come about, but to create situations in which others will act as he forsees, even though he neither can cause their reactions nor believes that he can.'[12] This is, in Donagan's discussion of intention, merely an aside to show that responsibility can be established even though cause cannot. In the usual context of social choices, however, this is not merely a side issue. It is the central problem.

Action in social contexts typically is inherently interactive. I cannot cause the outcome − (1,4) in the Prisoner's Dilemma of Table 1 − that I want, I can only hope to restrict the set of likely outcomes. If I can do as well as Donagan's poker player at foreseeing the reactions of others to my own actions, I may be able to make myself or both of us better off. My action, however, will be a choice of strategies, not of outcomes.

Where does this leave us in the superpower dilemma? Each side can only choose a strategy, which will include the relevant range of responses to the other side's strategy choices. What is chosen is an *expected* outcome, that is, some probabilistic mixture of various potential outcomes. Neither side alone can choose a simple outcome because the outcome that results from one side's strategy choice is necessarily contingent on the other side's strategy choice. To treat one side's strategy choice as though it were the cause of just one of the possible outcomes in that strategy would be unintelligible. Yet, that is what much of the recent philosophical discussion of deterrence does. What each side does is choose either a strategy of nuclear disarmament or a strategy of deterrence (this latter can be at any of many possible levels of armament, but let us simplify for the moment). Suppose we choose the strategy of deterrence. What is our moral responsibility?

---

12 Alan Donagan, *The Theory of Morality* (Chicago: University of Chicago Press 1977), 123-4

Return for a moment to Donagan's poker players. Smith took advantage of his knowledge of his fellow players to select the strategy that would maximize the pot he was likely to win. When American leaders follow a strategy of nuclear deterrence against the Soviet Union, they do something quite similar to what Smith does. They suppose that the leaders of the Soviet Union are relatively rational and would therefore not undertake any action that would guarantee their nation's destruction. Hence, the American leaders suppose that the policy of deterrence will very likely deter Soviet leaders from attacking the United States. In words analogous to Donagan's above, the American leaders will have created a situation in which others will act as they foresee, even though they could neither cause Soviet reactions nor believe that they could. The result will be mutual deterrence.

It is a necessary part of the rationality of creating the institutional arrangements to retaliate as a way of deterring the other side that each side assumes the rationality of the other and therefore foresees the other side's response. If this assumption were not credible, deterrence would be largely pointless. If it is credible, then it is an error to judge the action of retaliating *tout court* and to infer the morality of deterrence from that judgment. It is, of course, also a necessary part of the rationality of creating a system for deterrence that we suppose the likelihood of its failing for any reason at all is very low. Utilitarian criticism of deterrence policy often focuses on the factual validity of this supposition. It also might focus on the validity of the assumption that enough of the relevant actors on both sides are sufficiently rational as not to use the weapons. I think the latter issue is relatively easily settled in favor of the system of deterrence whereas the former is far harder to assess. Unfortunately, certain policy makers and advisors in the United States during the Reagan administration have given us to wonder about the latter assumption. But if it is valid, then, as in the action of Donagan's poker-playing Smith, our action of choosing to maintain a system of nuclear deterrence must be judged as the complex aciton it is, an action that includes certain expectations of how others will react to our readiness to retaliate for a nuclear attack. To ignore this consideration and to look solely at part of the larger set of possible outcomes of our strategy is to make a mistake analogous to that of many actors in an economy who suppose that only they will be smart enough to react to others' actions while all others will simply act without reflection on how anyone else will react to their actions. Assuming that others will not react to one's own actions makes sense in a market context with very large numbers of equivalent actors but not in contexts in which the number of those with whom one interacts is very small.

Philosophers writing on deterrence from a deontological perspective typically focus not on strategies as actions but on contingent outcomes of strategy choices as actions. As with other fallacies discussed above, this is not a move that can simply be assumed to yield results consistent with usual accounts of action theorists or moral philosophers. It may yield a correct result in a particular case but, if so, the correctness of the result desperately wants argument. But it is a wrong move in principle because action theory for social choice is inherently more complex than much of philosophical action theory typically is. Failure to deal with the relevant complexity makes many moral accounts of nuclear deterrence irrelevant. (Of course, the issue is far more general than this: it arises in principle in all complex social choice contexts.)

It is interesting that the fallacy of reasoning from contingent outcomes of strategy choices in interactive social contexts is typically not treated as a general problem but is only addressed in such asides as Donagan's. It would be wrong to claim that it has not been recognized as a problem, but its general significance seems typically to be overlooked. In a similar vein one may note that the problem of strategic interaction in general had not been well analyzed until very recently with the advent of the theory of games. Ryle notes that 'There is, anyhow at the start, an important sort of unfamiliarity about such generalizations of the totally familiar. We do not yet know how we should and how we should not operate with them, although we know quite well how to operate with the daily particularities of which they are the generalizations.'[13] Theoretically, perhaps the most distressing aspect of a new generalization about

---

13 Gilbert Ryle, *Dilemmas* (Cambridge: Cambridge University Press 1954), 30

the totally familiar is that it must eventually remake many of our other understandings, even those which have been developed extensively and articulately. The generalization that is the theory of games has, even in its merely verbal grasp of the nature of strategic interaction, been undoing and remaking our understandings for a generation, but clearly the work is far from done.

One can only hope that the slow entry of game theoretic reasoning into social and moral philosophy will be accelerated. Unfortunately, however, game theory seems to smack enough of consequentialism that it does not appeal to many deontological moral theorists. But it is deontological theory that will be the loser if it cannot be made more rigorously to address the issue of what counts as an action in social choice contexts.

Institutional Intentions and Strategic Interaction

Finally, consider just how complex the notion of intention is in a context of strategic interaction especially when it is complicated by institutional considerations. A system of deterrence requires a command and control structure to do two things: to insure retaliation in a relevant moment and to prevent launch of missiles at all other times. Unfortunately, these two tasks must be handled by one structure, which must therefore be a compromise between those which would best accomplish the one and the other.

To loosen central control in the future is to increase *present* control over future events in one way and to decrease it in another. It increases control in that it makes wanted retaliation more likely in the event that central command structures fail or are destroyed. It decreases control in that it makes unwanted attack more readily possible. The value of the increased control over wanted retaliation is that it makes the deterrent threat more credible and therefore reduces the likelihood that there would ever be ground for retaliation.

These two effects cannot be fully separated: to reduce the likelihood of unintended attack is to decrease the likelihood of wanted retaliation and quite possibly therefore to increase the likelihood of there ever being occasion for retaliation. This is a problem that has long worried American strategic planners.[14] In the early years of relatively primitive weapons on the Soviet side, the more worrisome prospect was unintended attack, so that tight control was perhaps the easy choice. In recent years, the capacity of Soviet strategic weapons to decapitate American command and control has become increasingly worrisome and control has presumably become much looser.

This is a general problem of many control and enforcement systems. How do we prevent such enforcers as police and tax collectors from intimidating those who are honest while encouraging the enforcers to track down all who are dishonest? In the system of deterrence we accomplish both positive and negative control by building in redundancy as though to achieve regression toward the mean. We set up land-based missile controls so that action by each of two people is necessary but not sufficient to launch at each of two or more levels each of which is sufficient but not necessary to launch. No one person has much control either positively or negatively. Even if several people acted wrongly in helping to launch missiles, there would be only a limited number they could launch. In a variant of this system, each submarine in the strategic force has enough warheads by itself to devastate the Soviet Union but no submarine's missiles can be launched without the concurrent actions of several officers any one of whom might block that submarine from launching.

In relevant moments those who set up this system, including, of course, the general populace insofar as their democratic participation has mattered, would be unable to affect its behavior significantly. In certain moments, the President and the Joint Chiefs of Staff could not stop it. While dozens of people acting morally might refuse to assist in retaliation once deterrence had failed and retaliation seemed useless to their own fellow citizens but grievously harmful to others, we can probably confidently expect that enough others would act to cause substantial retaliation. Indeed, the system is suffi-

---

14 Paul Bracken, *The Command and Control of Nuclear Forces* (New Haven, CT: Yale University Press 1983)

ciently large and it involves sufficiently many people that it is difficult to believe it could be set up to be credible without virtually guaranteeing that it would work to retaliate under certain circumstances. Too many people would have to participate in subterfuge for the system to be designed not to work to a substantial degree and still be credible.

How tight should we want our control to be? This is not a question that admits of a deontological or action-based answer. But if we want deterrence at all, we have to answer it. Hence, either we have no deterrence or we choose the level of control of unwanted and wanted attacks according to the likely effects of that level on the success of the deterrent system and of the damage it risks. Even if we want deterrence for deontological reasons, then we must be consequentialist in constructing the system for it.

The Doctrine of Double Effect

One way in which the nature of the 'action' of nuclear deterrence has been addressed in recent work is by supposing that it is somehow a complex action which either does or does not run afoul of the doctrine of double effect. The principle that underlies the doctrine of double effect is Aquinas's assertion that 'moral actions are characterized by what is intended, not by what falls outside the scope of intention, for that is only incidental... .'[15] The words 'double effect' refer to the intended good effect of an action and the unin-

---

15 Germain Grisez, 'Toward a Consistent Natural-Law Ethics of Killing,' *American Journal of Jurisprudence* **15** (1970), 64-96, at p. 73; cf. Donagan, *Theory of Morality*, 164. Donagan (163) holds that the doctrine is either otiose or wrong in its implications for actual cases. H.L.A. Hart thinks the doctrine is legalistic theology that distinguishes cases in which 'There seems to be no relevant moral difference ... on any theory of morality' (*Punishment and Responsibility: Essays in the Philosophy of Law* [Oxford: Oxford University Press 1968], 124). But here we need be concerned only with its relevance and application to nuclear deterrence, not with its acceptability more generally.

tended bad effect. The two may or may not be causally inseparable.

Under this doctrine, I am exonerated from blame for, say, accidentally running over and killing a child while driving my car so long as it was no part of my intention to run over the child and I was driving with due care. My intention was only to get from home to a restaurant to enjoy a good meal. Now if I am to be held responsible for every causal result of what I do, I am as guilty of killing that child as would be a child murderer. The doctrine of double effect not only exonerates me from culpability in this case, it more fundamentally permits me to undertake such simple actions as driving my car even though I can be quite sure that there is a realistic chance that doing so will cause great harm: I may drive so long as doing such harm is not my intention in driving my car. We also need to include the condition that, in general, driving is not likely to be massively injurious, that the good that comes from doing it outweighs the bad. As Aquinas stipulates, 'an action beginning from a good intention can become wrong if it is not proportionate to the end intended.'[16] Hence, the doctrine involves a mixture of deontological and consequentialist principles: some actions are prohibited merely on the ground of their intentions and others are prohibited despite good intentions on the ground of their disproportionate bad effects.

Elizabeth Anscombe gives the doctrine a particularly strong role. Without it, she says, 'anything can be – and is wont to be – justified, and the Christian teaching that in no circumstances may one commit murder, adultery, apostasy (to give a few examples) goes by the board ... and without them the Christian ethic goes to pieces.' The doctrine is a 'necessity' to buck up our resolve to pass up an opportunity to 'do evil that good may come.'[17] Unfortunately she does not take up the complicating character of deterrence but addresses only such actual actions in war as obliteration bombing, ac-

---

16 Grisez, 'Toward a Consistent Natural-Law Ethics of Killing,' 73

17 G.E.M. Anscombe, 'War and Murder,' 51-61 in Anscombe, *Ethics, Religion and Politics* (Minneapolis, MN: University of Minnesota Press 1981), 58-9 (this essay was originally published in 1961)

Russell Hardin

tions that many supporters of deterrence would also condemn. Her rationales for the doctrine are also often theological and not relevant to the present discussion.

Here again we find that a traditional view does not address the fundamental nature of the problem of deterrence. In order to generalize the traditional concern to our present problems, Germain Grisez speaks of 'the unity of action' and cites several instances of actions that necessarily include evil effects with the intended good effects, actions that cannot be separated into two 'distinct human' acts. For example, he supposes that committing adultery to gain the release of one's child would constitute two distinct acts while interposing one's own body in the path of a ravaging animal to protect one's child would constitute a single act.[18] Grisez supposes that 'only the definite intention to act at the last ... stage can make' the nuclear deterrent threat effective, so that the deterrent inherently entails a dual action.[19]

To speak of 'double actions' rather than of 'double effects' of a single action probably confuses the issue. The program of nuclear deterrence does not so clearly involve two separate actions, one evil and one good. It does not entail deterring on the one hand and retaliating on the other. Our system of deterrence, as devised by many people over many years, involves the disciplined response by others or even the nearly automatic electronic response to certain events. Is it two distinct acts if the system leads eventually to an actual retaliation, or is the creation or maintenance of this system inherently unitary even if it leads to retaliation? The American threat to counterattack that deters the Soviet Union from attacking the West is not simply an action in its own right. What deters is the existence of a credible system for counterattacking. Its deterrent effect depends on its credibility, which in turn depends heavily on its likely actuality. One cannot meaningfully separate the threat from the potential retaliation. (That is why various bluff strategies proposed by clean-hands moral theorists are irrelevant to the problem

---

18 Grisez, 'Toward a Consistent Natural-Law Ethics of Killing,' 90

19 Ibid., 92

of nuclear deterrence.) Institutionally speaking, there is only one action at issue: maintaining the deterrent force.

Where does the Thomistic doctrine come in? Unfortunately, it is not clear. That doctrine is applied by Aquinas in an example in which the use of force takes its traditional form in defeating the attacker upon actual attack.[20] A defender of deterrence may suppose sensibly that the purpose of creating the system of deterrence is only to deter attack — if that were not the purpose, it would be pointless to create the system. Then if, as in the case of my driving, the likelihood that the system will go awry is small enough, so that the deterrent system is proportionate to the end intended, its creation is morally permitted under the doctrine of double effect. For deterrence to be rational requires that its risk of failure be very small; for it to be utilitarian presumably requires that this risk be even smaller; for it to pass the test of Aquinas's doctrine may require that it be still smaller. The first two assessments have to be relative to the risks of alternative policies, as might Aquinas's assessment also if we interpret his concern with proportion and measured force reasonably.

Against the defender of nuclear deterrence, Grisez, Anscombe, and many others may also sensibly insist that maintaining a deterrent system is to have a conditional intention to kill millions of people. One may well wish to conclude with them that this system is evil because it threatens and arranges for an evil result under certain contingencies. But then one should argue why that is distinctively wrong in this case despite its complexity as compared to usual cases in which one actually *does* evil that good may come. At that point, we seem to be up against a plausibly irresolvable problem in the notion of an intention in contexts of complex strategic interaction.

One other way the doctrine of double effect has been generalized in contemporary moral theory is to distinguish letting something happen and causing it to happen, as in letting someone die

---

20 Moreover, Aquinas takes care to apply his principle only to actions by individuals, not by public authorities acting for the common good (ibid., 74) but we may choose not to follow him here.

versus killing someone.[21] This distinction might seem compelling for many of the problems to which it has been applied. But no matter where it stands on the issue of typical cases of individual killing versus letting die, a moral theory that is centrally concerned with the difference between letting a large part of humanity be destroyed and causing it to be destroyed seems trivially beside the point. The person or policy who would knowingly do either is beyond the moral pale. As Robert Tucker says, 'the prospect held out by nuclear war threatens to make of the issue of intent a grotesque parody.'[22]

If we bring our analysis to the level of the individual voter in deciding on a policy, as discussed above, the very distinction between causing certain deaths from nuclear war and letting others happen collapses. Which of my possible actions as a voter is passive and which active: supporting the maintenance or supporting the elimination of the American deterrent force? In which case do I cause and in which do I let a result potentially occur? Oddly, the doctrine of double effect with its focus on individual actions − with a consequentialist constraint on proportionality − loses its meaning in an account of the morality of individual citizens in their choice of public policies.

Just-War Theory

The Pauline injunction that we not do evil that good may come has spawned, in addition to the Thomistic doctrine of double effect, the Augustinian just war theory. As does the doctrine of double effect, just war theory builds from a combination of consequentialist and deontological concerns. The traditional doctrine of the just war, of *bellum justum*, is typically seen to deal with two distinct issues: first,

---

21 Philippa Foot, 'The Problem of Abortion and the Doctrine of the Double Effect,' 19-32, in Foot, *Virtues and Vices* (Berkeley, CA: University of California Press 1978)

22 Robert W. Tucker, 'The Morality of Deterrence,' *Ethics* **95** (1985), 461-78, at p. 472.

with *jus ad bellum*, or with when it is just to engage in war; second, with *jus in bello*, or with what it is just to do while engaged in a war. As Tucker notes, earlier notions of when it is just to enter war have given way in our time to only one generally plausible justification: 'war is no longer a means generally permitted to states for the redress of rights that have been violated... Armed force remains a means permitted to states only as a measure of self-defense against a prior and unjust attack.'[23] Hence, in contemporary concern, the doctrine of just war is almost exclusively a matter of *jus in bello* after an unjust attack.[24]

It should immediately be clear that the doctrine of *jus in bello* cannot simply apply to the system of nuclear deterrence without considerable casuistry to argue why our insights or intuitions about warfare once underway translate into valid insights about deterrence of war. After such casuistry one might conclude that deterrence is indeed unjust, but without such casuistry there is no reason for us to suppose simply from traditional *jus in bello* arguments that it is unjust. These traditional arguments are about what it would be just to do once attacked.

The peculiar difficulty of deterrence is that it is a move taken in advance of any attack that might justify warlike action but that what it threatens would no longer make sense after the fact. Indeed, unthreatened retaliation would clearly be immoral on virtually any moral theory. To justify deterrent moves in advance of any attack, supporters might argue that they respond to a reciprocal threat, whether explicit or implicit, made in advance. This would be analogous to a *jus ad bellum* argument for responding to 'attack.'

To discuss the morality of actually retaliating to a nuclear attack, however, is seemingly to be concerned with *jus in bello*. If we were faced with the simple decision whether to retaliate with a nuclear

---

23 Ibid., 463

24 For further defenses of this view, see David Hollenbach, *Nuclear Ethics: A Christian Moral Argument* (Ramsey, NJ: Paulist Press 1983), 39; John Courtney Murray, *Morality and Modern War* (New York: Council on Religion and International Affairs 1959), 9-11; and William V. O'Brien, *The Conduct of Just and Limited War* (New York: Praeger 1981), 19-27.

attack, the issue would be clear and easy: if it were not part of a larger program of deterrence, retaliation after the fact would be immoral. But it would be facile to conclude from this that the system of deterrence is immoral. Since almost any supporter of deterrence would agree — perhaps only after argument — that unthreatened retaliation would be immoral, critics of deterrence who base their opposition merely on what would happen if deterrence failed will not persuade supporters. Indeed, such critics will seem to fail to grapple with the relevant distinction.

What advocates of deterrence claim is that the prior threat, because of its effects, is what would make retaliation moral, but only as part of the whole system of deterrence. This is at first glance such an odd position that its point often does not even get across. A harmful action is rendered moral only if it is first threatened? Not quite: it is the whole system of threat and fulfillment if and only if the conditions of the threat are met by action on the other side that is moral because that system is supposed to produce better results on the whole.

In this respect, the present system of nuclear deterrence is radically different from traditional forms of conventional deterrence. For practical purposes we have already taken whatever action we are going to take before action is called for. Military preparedness has presumably always been a strong deterrent to attack. Hume writes of Edgar, one of the ancient kings of Anglo-Saxon England, that, 'He showed no aversion to war; he made the wisest preparations against invaders: And by this vigour and foresight, he was enabled, without any danger of suffering insults, to indulge his inclinations towards peace... The foreign Danes dared not to approach a country which appeared in such a posture of defence.'[25]

The conventional deterrence that Hume describes involved preparation for action, not action in advance. It required accurately directed action to stop particular aggressors while nuclear retaliation is likely to be massively directed against populations who have

---

25 Daivd Hume, *The History of England*, vol. 1 (Indianapolis, IN: Liberty Classics 1983), chap. 2, 96-7

taken no recent steps of aggression. Nor did the morality of Edgar's preparations for defense require that he threaten the foreign Danes before responding to an attack. Had his forces been secretly hidden and ready for attack they would have been morally acceptable — although one might suppose that open declaration to deter attack would have been morally better. A secret arsenal of nuclear weapons for retaliation would be reprehensible — it would also be stupid since it would not deter attack on one's own nation. Unlike Edgar's defense forces and plans, the superpower nuclear deterrents require open acknowledgement to make them effective and to make them putatively moral.

Etymologically, to deter is to provoke terror, which is to cause to tremble and flee. That is the purpose of the nuclear deterrent. While traditional defense establishments might have provoked terror and caused Danes and others to tremble and flee, just-war theory is concerned with them only at the point at which they have failed to deter, at which they are put to use against attacking forces.[26] The creation of a defense establishment for the purpose of deterrence, of provoking terror that enemies might flee without first attacking, is simply not a part of the theory.

In Hume's account of Edgar's reign, deterrence of the foreign Danes was not the purpose of preparations to defend against them but was a causal effect of those preparations. At least since the late fifties, the superpower nuclear arsenals have principally — I wish one could confidently say 'entirely' — been created for the purpose of deterring one another. It would probably be foolish to suppose that no one had ever thought of the idea before our time, but it is probably also true that any program of deterrence before nuclear weapons was an afterthought, a derivative realization from the principal purpose of defense systems, which was to defend against actual attacks. In the nuclear era, the afterthought has become forethought and principal intention or intendment.

One way to put this issue in current strategic jargon is to note

---

26 Just war theory originally was broader than this, since it saw it as morally permissible for a state to attack another for reasons other than direct defence against prior attack.

Russell Hardin

that deterrence may take at least two forms. First, traditional or conventional deterrence is 'based on *denial*, which requires convincing an opponent that he will not attain his goals on the battlefield.' Second, 'Deterrence based on *punishment* is associated usually with nuclear weapons.'[27] Hume may well have grasped this distinction. The passage from him quoted above continues, 'The domestic Danes saw inevitable destruction to be the consequence of their tumults and insurrections.'[28] Surely nothing deters so effectively as inevitable destruction, although the sense of this notion has now surpassed what Hume had in mind.

The strategic considerations that complicate the just-war analysis of nuclear deterrence need not confuse a just-war analysis of deterrence by denial if the latter would, in the event of the failure of deterrence, not entail *jus in bello* violations. In that case we could analyze the problem as though its parts – prior preparation and threat and eventual retaliation – were decoupled. If neither of the parts would be wrong, the two parts taken together would not be wrong. But analyzing the system of nuclear deterrence, in which denial of an attacker's objective is not possible, as though its parts were decoupled will not do. In this system, a moral analysis must address the fact that the parts are inherently coupled just as the consequentialist justification of the punishment of miscreants generally depends on the prior establishment of a criminal justice system.

Intuitionist Reasoning

Arguments in moral theory are often grounded in intuitions of rightness and wrongness and of goodness and badness, with actions counting as either right or wrong and outcomes as either good or bad. Because the issue of nuclear deterrence is so unlike anything we have previously faced we are apt to find our intuitions not very

---

27 John J. Mearsheimer, *Conventional Deterrence* (Ithaca, NY: Cornell University Press 1983), 15, emphasis added.

28 Hume, *History*, vol. 1, 97

well supported by experience in their application. Conspicuously, we have contrary intuitions about it as we increasingly often do for other new issues, such as those that arise from new medical technologies. The belief of many intuitionists, such as Prichard, that we share moral intuitions is clearly undercut by our debate over moral positions on these issues. It will be useful to state cases for and against the reliance on intuitions in moral reasoning to see how we stand on nuclear deterrence.

As Prichard supposed, much of our moral knowledge or beliefs at the level of routine practice is quite secure, and to know whether we have an obligation we need merely let 'our moral capacities of thinking do their work.'[29] Contrast with this our highly contested knowledge of abstract moral principles, such as Kantian imperatives, the basic utilitarian intuition that utility is right-making, Alan Gewirth's principle of generic consistency,[30] and so forth. Therefore, one might suppose, we can be more confident of our direct apprehension of the moral rightness of an action or the goodness of a state of affairs than of any theoretical assessment of these. This is essentially the view of Butler and of those who follow what Sidgwick calls the method of intuitionism in ethics.

Against this quick conclusion, note that the principles which make sense of the physical universe are abstract and, to most of us, very insecurely held. Indeed, our commonsense knowledge at the level of practice seems to be violated by the abstract principles of theoretical physics. For example, the theoretical account of the structure of the table at which I now work sounds utterly lunatic to anyone but a physicist. Nevertheless, it would be foolish to conclude that the confidence of our commonsense intuitions about these matters should call into doubt our abstract principles.

Unfortunately, as Hume, Gilbert Harman,[31] and others argue,

---

29 H.A. Prichard, 'Does Moral Philosophy Rest on a Mistake?' 1-17 in Prichard, *Moral Obligation and Duty and Interest* (London: Oxford University Press 1968 [1912]), 17

30 Alan Gewirth, *Reason and Morality* (Chicago: University of Chicago press 1978)

31 Gilbert Harman, *The Nature of Morality: An Introduction to Ethics* (New York: Oxford University Press 1977), 3-10

the abstract principles of physics can be supported by experimental tests whereas our abstract moral principles stand on their own without the possibility of test. Hence, it is not clear that our abstract moral principles should trump our direct intuition of moral rightness and goodness. We are forced into a form of reasoning back and forth between practical and abstract principles with rigor only in tests for consistency. In this standard form of reasoning in moral theory, our effort is to achieve what Rawls, with his gift for apposite labels, calls reflective equilibrium, in which we test our abstract principles against our substantive intuitions and our substantive intuitions against our abstract principles.

How we weight the intuitions and the principles is, of course, the fundamental issue. In a letter to Hume, Gilbert Elliot of Minto writes, 'I often imagine to myself, that I perceive within me a certain instinctive feeling, which shoves away at once all subtle refinements, and tells me with authority, that these air-built notions are inconsistent with life and experience, and, by consequence cannot be true or solid.' Hence, he concludes, there must be 'something in the intellectual part of our nature' that determines the truth of the practical principles instinctively.[32] Hume's response to what he labels Elliot's 'correcting subtlety of sentiment' is somewhat ambiguous since he allows sentiment a role in moral reasoning.[33] But, he notes, some have argued 'that it was neither by reasoning nor authority we learn our religion, but by sentiment: and certainly this were a very convenient way, and what a philosopher would be very well pleased to comply with, if he could distinguish sentiment from education. But to all appearances the sentiment of Stockholm, Geneva, Rome ancient and modern, Athens and Memphis, have [not]

---

32 John Hill Burton, *Life and Correspondence of David Hume,* vol. 1 (New York: Burt Franklin, undated reprint of original edition published in Edinburgh in 1846), 323-4

33 Ibid., 324; David Norton relies on this passage to support his claim that Hume is a 'common-sense moralist' but a 'sceptical metaphysician' (David Fate Norton, *David Hume: Common-Sense Moralist, Sceptical Metaphysician* [Princeton, NJ: Princeton University Press 1982], 50-4).

the same characters.'[34] Locke speaks of practical principles that are 'borrowed,' saying that one 'may take up from his Education, and the fashions of his Country, any absurdity for innate principles.'[35]

While Sidgwick is generally critical of the method of intuitionism, he argues forcefully that utilitarianism is based on 'a first principle – which if known at all must be intuitively known – that happiness is the only rational ultimate end of action.'[36] In essence he finds intuitions about goodness more acceptable than those about rightness. But then for him rightness is a characteristic of means and is therefore contingent on the relationship of various means to the end of goodness. Since under even a very rich description any kind of action could be a means to both good and bad, kinds of action are not right or wrong *tout court*.

Despite all these contrary arguments, I think a consequentialist can make serious claims for intuitive apprehension of the rightness of actions, at least prima facie, that is, subject to rational criticism. One ground for accepting Rule-utilitarian principles as adjuncts of Act-utilitarianism is that our knowledge often comes directly at the level of rules or relatively abstract generalizations – it is not aggregated from numerous particular instances. This is perhaps especially true of social knowledge, that is, knowledge of social facts. But as Wittgenstein's discussion of our knowledge that Mont Blanc is, say, 4000 meters high suggests,[37] even many everyday facts about

---

34 Burton, *Life and Correspondence of David Hume*, vol. 1, 326; Hume continues thus: 'and no sensible man can implicitly assent to any of them, but from the general principle, that as the truth in these subjects is beyond human capacity, and that as for one's own ease he must adopt some tenets, there is most satisfaction and convenience in holding to the Catholicism we have been first taught. Now this I have nothing to say against. I have only to observe, that such a conduct is founded on the most universal and determined scepticism, joined to a little indolence; for more curiosity and research gives a direct opposite turn from the same principles.'

35 John Locke, *An Essay Concerning Human Understanding* (Oxford: Clarendon Press 1975), Peter H. Nidditch, ed., I.III.26, 83-4

36 Henry Sidgwick, *The Methods of Ethics* (London: Macmillan 1907 seventh edition, reprinted by Dover Publications, New York), 201

37 Ludwig Wittgenstein, *On Certainty* (Oxford: Basil Blackwell 1969), ¶170

the physical world are highly articulated deductions from abstractions that are grounded in a system of social construction so that no one individual may know such facts fully by direct observation. Nevertheless, the facts count as known by any reasonable canons.

All of us most of the time must simply begin from such facts without testing them. Wittgenstein remarks, 'My life consists in resting content with many things.'[38] His contentment may partly derive, as Hume says, from 'a little indolence,'[39] but without indolence in certain quests, life could not go on. Similarly, my moral life consists in my resting content with many things, although as a moral theorist I may increasingly question these. Many of us could test the utilitarian beneficence of various moral rules by violating them and observing the consequences in a few circumstances. Or we could carry out relevant thought experiments. (The deontologist, of course, has no such recourse available, because the deontologist's rules are not merely means.) But it is a mark of good sense that we generally follow many of these rules without seriously testing them in such fashion.

A deontological defense of moral rules will be different from this consequentialist justification, at least in large part. It might be simply that one can apprehend rightness directly. To that claim, I have nothing to say apart from an expression of disbelief and of the suspicion that what is apprehended is little more than what Hume and Locke deride. Alternatively, the defense might be that one derives moral rules for action by reasoned argument from first principles, as Kant and Gewirth attempt to do.

Virtually all deontological arguments about deterrence seem to follow the first tack. As in the just-war theory, they simply assert that it is wrong to kill innocents and that this rule cannot be violated. Hence, Grisez writes, 'When I say that the deterrent is morally evil, I do not mean that we ought to dismantle it if and when world amity is established. I mean that we ought to dismantle the deterrent immediately, regardless of consequences. The end simply does

---

38 Ibid., ¶344

39 Burton, *Life and Correspondence of David Hume*, vol. 1, 326

not justify the means.'[40] This is the most extreme view one might take in asserting the inviolability of a deontological principle that stands on its own without foundation.

If the principle of not killing innocents were rationally derived, one would still want to say why it follows that deterrence as a system for protecting certain innocents is condemned in the interests of other innocents. If it is not rationally derived but is a directly apprehended intuition, however, it runs up against the problems of specifying who is the agent and what is being done when a deterrent system is maintained. It may be that one's directly apprehended intuitions would survive intact through all of these changes in circumstances from those in the ordinary life of an individual. But if one does not even seem to acknowledge the difference in circumstances in this proscription and in that against ordinarily killing an innocent, one cannot expect to have one's intuition taken at face value. In Locke's rude term, the principle here seems 'borrowed.' It is at best assumed by analogy to the usual principle, but then the analogy wants spelling out. Or is it plausible that we have meaningful intuitions about something that was inconceivable only a generation or two ago?

Earlier generations could swear with impunity to do justice though the heavens might fall — it was not conceivable that they would have to make the choice. We may be forced to make the choice. Alas, we may be caught with our slogans in the lurch and with the mistaken but firm belief that our inherited slogans are unshakable moral truths.

Received February, 1986
Revised June, 1986

---

40 Grisez, 'Toward a Consistent Natural-Law Ethics of Killing,' 93

CANADIAN JOURNAL OF PHILOSOPHY
Supplementary Volume 12

On Defense by
Nuclear Deterrence

JAN NARVESON
University of Waterloo
Waterloo, Ontario
Canada N2L 3G1

War winning, however, is impossible precisely because of the fact that there is no defense now against all-out nuclear use and probably not for the foreseeable future. A nuclear war could therefore be controlled and won only if one side consciously chose to lose the war, an event as unlikely in the future as it has been rare or nonexistent in the past. It is not necessary to win a nuclear war in order to deter it; one has only to ensure that both are likely to lose it.[1]

---

1 Robert Art, 'The Case for the Mad-Plus Posture,' *Ethics* **95** (1985), 499

Jan Narveson

I The General Situation

It takes (at least) two to make a war, and of those combatants, one (at least) must start it. If nobody starts the war, there won't be a war. This is as true in the nuclear era as it ever was. But if any given party is certain that he would lose any war initiated by him, then presumably he would not initiate a war. One way for A to make certain that B would lose any war B starts is by having an unstoppable superpowerful weapon of retaliation at hand. Then making sure that such a war would not start is a matter of making it clear to B that A does indeed have, and is willing to use, such a weapon. Such is the current situation between today's superpowers.[2]

Of course, if neither of these parties would start a war even if they were sure that they would win, the situation would be rather different. If A was this party, and B was certain that that is what A thought, then what? Evidently, there would be no point in B's having the weapons with which he would retaliate if A would start the war in question. It would be a waste of money, at least so far as the immediate purpose of expenditures on those weapons was concerned. Evidently, neither of today's superpowers believes this of the other. Each professes to be concerned only with defense — but this doesn't stop him from maintaining an extraordinarily expensive and dangerous military establishment. If this profession is sincere, then those expenditures would be irrational unless each believed that the other *would* initiate a war if he thought he would win. Yet the expenditures are made.

Something, therefore, is wrong. Either (a) at least one of the parties is telling less than the complete truth when he claims to be concerned only with defense, or (b) at least one is incorrectly estimating the other's intentions. So much is clear enough. But which? Obviously there is no publicly acceptable answer to this question. Hence, we might suppose, the 'arms race.'

---

2 This was originally written prior to Mr. Gorbachev's disarmament initiative of early January 1986, American response to which had not been announced at the time of writing.

II Defense and Arms Races

But it doesn't follow. An arms *race* is not a necessary outcome in this situation. An arms race is a situation in which (1) at least one party, A, is seen to be attempting to gain a military advantage over another party, B; and (2) B believes that A really would have such an advantage if B's arms weren't at least equal to A's, and so (3) B makes an effort at increasing B's armaments in response, this effort in turn being (4) sufficient to motivate A to respond by increased effort of his own. The situation would not become an arms *race* in the absence of any one of these conditions. Thus, consider condition (1). If no one believes that A is trying to gain an advantage, no one will have anything to respond to. Regarding (2): if either believed that the other's expenditures are futile, again, neither would respond with an effort of his own. Then about (3), if B didn't in fact increase his own armaments in response, A wouldn't have anything to respond to in turn. Finally, (4) if A didn't in turn respond to B's response, B would have nothing to re-respond to.

Of course, all this is assuming that the parties are acting rationally. And obviously, they just might not. In what way and to what extent this can or should be taken into account is an important question. But it is essential first to find out what would be done by parties acting rationally – especially since one of the most potent criticisms we can make to a given party is that he is not acting rationally.

Since we have been in the midst of an arms race,[3] it is evident that all of these conditions are being met. Each side evidently does believe that the other is attempting to gain an advantage. Let us suppose that both are in error about this, though neither is readily persuaded of that.

But what about condition (2)? Apparently both sides believe that expenditures on nuclear weapons research, development, and deployment, in response to the supposed threat, are *non-futile*. Why

---

3 This was also written prior to the American Congress' recent resolution to cut down on budget deficits, which will have the effect of halting arms-race effects from the American side for the time being, at least.

would they believe this? We may divide the possibilities into two kinds: technical and non-technical.

(1) On the technical side, I see only two sub-possibilities: (a) fear of a successful 'first-strike' capability on the part of the other side, and (b) concern about escalation. Let's briefly consider each. (a) If it appears that the other side might be able to carry out a successful first strike, then increased effort on one's own side might be necessary to ensure that such a strike could not be successful. Whether a disarming First Strike is possible is a technical question, but it is hardly an open question: the belief that either side could successfully conduct such a first strike, in anything like current technological circumstances, is not credible. As a case in point, consider the American administration's belief, professed over the past several years, that the USSR's ICBM force might destroy the entire American land-based ICBM force at one blow. Such a blow would require accuracy bordering on 100 percent, and everyone knows that this is not possible. In any case such a strike would leave American submarine and other forces intact; yet those forces are enough to mount an unacceptable counterstrike even if the ICBM-destroying strike were feasible. (b) The escalation idea is that one of the parties might begin a military action of, perhaps, a conventional sort, and then when it ran into opposition would employ small nuclear weapons, and then if the attacked side had no small nuclear weapons to reply with, it would be faced with the choice between massive retaliation and surrender and might prefer the former. Yes: but of course, if it does have those weapons, then if it used them the attacker would surely retaliate with larger ones and eventually the same choice would have to be made. And if this spirals up to massive reply, why wouldn't it in the first place − especially since its policy would have been based on that all along? It is not plausible that side A could improve its security by endlessly increasing its weapons at the intermediate stages.

(2) What about the 'non-technical' reasons? Presumably these have something to do with the psychologies of the parties − but what? Perhaps it is that A must not only have sufficient forces but must also have forces that the public *believes* are sufficient; and the public might not believe it. We have here a question about the term 'reason.' If A *knows* that his current force is technically sufficient,

why should he pay any attention to the undiscerning public? In particular, why should A spend incredible amounts of money and effort responding as though this were not an illusion? Why not instead spend a small fraction of that money and effort pointing out that it is an illusion?

This reply, I suppose, might be thought naive, especially in a democracy where those who make the laws must worry about getting elected. I shall consider that possibility in conjunction with a point that will arise later in this argument. Provisionally, I conclude that in current circumstances the belief that increasingly large nuclear expenditures by superpowers are currently *useful* is irrational — sufficiently so that one cannot plausibly credit either side with it.

Meanwhile, let me return to the opening line of argument. There is an arms race, and we would wish there wasn't one. So we must ask which one of the four conditions to go to work on. The four, recall, are as follows.

(1) party A is seen to be attempting to gain an advantage over B, *and*

(2) B believes that A really *would* gain such an advantage if B doesn't make an effort at least to 'catch up,' and so

(3) B makes this effort in response; and

(4) A's perception that (3) obtains is sufficient to motivate A to respond by increased effort of his own.

People will argue about who, among the current superpowers, is A and who is B in my sketch. But perhaps this does not matter: let us hope that we can generate sound advice for both parties, advice that at least one of them might take. If so, perhaps the falsification of one of the conditions could be achieved, and thus an end to this depressing situation. The obvious premise to work on for this purpose is (2), which describes a belief that we have excellent reason to think is misguided. If A has, say, 30 percent more missiles than B, then A does not have a real advantage and B has in fact no reason to catch up. And if A sees that B will make no effort to catch up, then, presumably A will not make a still further effort.

Why won't he? There are different possibilities, and it matters which. One is that A thinks he now has an advantage sufficient to mount a first strike after all. This would be a major disaster, but is in current circumstances totally irrational. Much more likely is that A's concern that he was behind is now completely removed, since he is in fact manifestly 'ahead.' Why A should have wanted to *be* ahead is puzzling; but what matters is that it doesn't matter.

III Morality and Defense

If both parties are, as they ought to be, interested only in defense, then there is a ready piece of moral advice for both parties: the right thing to do in this situation is to *stay behind*. The party whose nuclear force is clearly less extensive − less numerous and less powerful − than the other's is doing the right thing. He is not in fact in any more danger, since his retaliatory capability is ample − 'less powerful' is nevertheless very, very powerful − and yet he is clearly doing the nonprovocative thing, for the 'inferior' party cannot be thought by anyone to be contemplating the first attack necessary for beginning a nuclear war. Power A would also save itself, with any luck, a good deal of its people's money. If only one of our two parties follows this, the arms race would shortly cease. If both parties follow it, the results are even better: for we would now have a reverse arms-race: A, seeing that B was inferior to it, would scrap enough weapons to make it the inferior party, and thus B would have to scrap still more, and so on until eventually, it is assumed, total disarmament would obtain.[4]

Good though this advice may be, it is to be presumed that neither current superpower will take it. After all, neither party has, and yet the facts are well enough known. (Or are they? Perhaps people in the Reagan Administration actually *believe* in the 'window of vulnerability,' contrary to the advice of their own military experts. If

---

4 My argument for this is spelled out more fully in 'Getting on the Road to Peace: A Modest Proposal,' *Ethics* **95** (1985), 589-605.

so, the world can do nothing but sit tight until that government re-
tires.) But let us go as far as we can and suppose that in terms of
sheer numbers, there is some conceivable point in not being behind.
Thus equality or parity becomes the goal. Among the things we
know about the current situation, however, is that even if both parties are reasonably sincere, a mutual effort at parity will amount to
an arms race, for there is so much difference as to what constitutes
'equality' that what is seen by A as an attempt to regain equality
is interpreted by B as an attempt to get ahead. What are we to do
when this is the case?

At this point, we can reconsider the suggestion made above, that
the right thing to do is to stay behind. The rationale of this is clear
enough: it is to make the purely defensive character of one's armaments unmistakable. The idea is that inferiority would assure people of this.

And so it should; but because of the aforementioned difficulties,
perhaps another approach is required. Suppose there was a weapon
which could not plausibly be thought to be usable for the first strike
which would be necessary to get a nuclear war going, but was
nevertheless perfectly usable for defensive (retalitory) purposes?
Then another idea would be to switch the character of one's weaponry to this type.

IV Reflections on Cruise Missiles

A currently available weapon seems possibly to exemplify the idea
in question: the so-called 'cruise' missile. Cruise missiles are guided, jet-powered missiles, in contrast to ballistic missiles, which cannot be altered in course once their rocket motors are exhausted. They
are slow (about 500 mph or so); extremely difficult to detect because
they fly low and are made to be as radar-proof as possible; they are
small, and thus highly portable and easy to conceal. Nevertheless,
they are capable of carrying very potent warheads. They are also
highly accurate, again by comparison with their ballistic counterparts. This superior accuracy has been thought by many to imply
that they could be used for a First Strike. But this is completely coun-

teracted by their slow speed, combined with the imperfect nature of their radar-resistant properties. A First Strike requires the ability to hit *all* of the enemy's missiles before he can retaliate. But no missile moving at such a leisurely rate could manage that unless it were not merely difficult but virtually impossible to detect. The enemy's missiles are distributed over a huge area, the distance from the nearest to the farthest being several thousand miles. An attack by several thousand cruise missiles over such a vast area would have to be coordinated in such a way that all hit their targets simultaneously. Even if this were possible, which it plainly is not, no such attack, however well coordinated, could escape detection: a very large number of missiles would be in the air for hours before reaching their targets, giving the enemy ample time to detect at least a few — but that's all he needs! What this means is simply that the cruise cannot be used for a First Strike. The leaders of a state thinking to depend on a First Strike attack by cruise missiles with a view to disarming the enemy would have to be clinically insane.

As a retaliatory weapon, on the other hand, the cruise is just fine. Because they are hard to detect, no enemy could count on being able to destroy all or even most of them before they reached their targets, despite their slow speed. And because they can nevertheless carry potent warheads, not very many would have to get through to inflict unacceptable levels of damage. The small size and portability of the cruise also make it essentially invulnerable to attack, at least from the air. The enemy could not target one's cruise missiles, for by the time he had targeted any one, it or some others would be somewhere else and he'd have to start all over again; but he wouldn't easily be able to find where else it had gone, due to their portability. Nor is it plausible to suppose that three or four thousand cruise missiles could be simultaneously attacked by saboteurs. Thus the cruise missiles would seem to be a weapon eminently suitable for deterrence and equally eminently unsuitable for a disabling first strike, the kind of attack required in order for a nuclear war to begin by intentional means. But, as was observed above, if nobody starts a nuclear war, there won't be one.

Meanwhile, the cruise missiles, if employed instead of today's ballistic missiles for deterrence purposes, would also greatly reduce the likelihood of unintentional conflict. Their slow speed means that even if one were somehow accidentally fired, or fired by a ground crew gone berserk, it would be possible for the people in charge on that side to warn the target country of what had happened and to give it precise information about its location so that it could be shot down. And also, it would in principle be quite possible to build in reversability, so that the weapon could be recalled even if it did begin its flight. These features mean that the possibility of unintentional nuclear exchange is virtually eliminated.[5]

The moral I would draw from this is that any state sincerely claiming to be maintaining its nuclear weapons establishment only for defensive purposes ought to junk its ballistic missiles, which are clearly the only weapons that could be used for a First Strike, and replace them with cruise missiles, which cannot. If a state were to do that, it seems to me that it would be in a vastly superior moral position vis-à-vis any opponent state that did not follow suit. For the rest of the world would then be able to identify that state unambiguously as the aggressive party.

Critics of this argument might suggest[6] that the cruise would increase the probability of wars beginning by the 'crisis' route: escalations from relatively minor causes in, say, Third World countries. But it seems to me that the stumbling block to that route is the same as it always has been: anyone escalating such a crisis to the point where superpower interests become seriously at stake knows that he is running the risk of armageddon down the line, and not terribly far down at that. No one has dropped a single nuclear weapon of any size on any enemy since the second World War — not incidentally, the last time any party had a monopoly on such weapons. Surely the risk of escalation — due to our very clear perception of what happens at the end — has figured among the reasons, though

---

5   This assessment of the cruise was first broached in my 'Why Doves Should Love the Cruise,' *Policy Options* **6** (Toronto, Canada 1985), 4-7. A shorter version was published in *Concerned Philosophers for Peace* **11** (April 1985) (Box 42393, Portland Oregon 97242, U.S.A.).

6   Two have done so already: see Conrad Brunk, 'Why Doves Should Loathe the Cruise,' *Policy Options* **6**, 4 (May 1985); and Douglas Lackey, *Concerned Philosophers for Peace* **12** (December 1985).

there are no doubt others. The advent of the cruise wouldn't change that situation, so far as I can see.

It would, of course, cast a pall over this scenario if, as has been hinted, a very fast version of the Cruise is developed. This would diminish the margin of response-time for the enemy to somewhere in between what it is now (almost zero) and what it would be with the current cruise (several hours). Fortunately, there is a severe limit to this development because of the extreme difficulty of lengthy supersonic flight in the atmosphere, but it still a worry of some magnitude.

This suggestion comes under the heading of 'Hardware Solutions' to political problems. 'Put not thy faith in hardware!' might well be emblazoned on the banner of doves as their principal motto. And there is some plausibility to this slogan — though after all, nuclear war is an issue because of the existence of hardware! Hardware problems *can* have hardware solutions; we ought not to knock such solutions a priori when proposed. I shall return to this important matter; but meanwhile, since it raises fundamental issues, we had best review those to begin with.

V Defense: The Moral Basics

In the foregoing reflections I have deliberately not considered the option of unilateral disarmament, nuclear or otherwise. I have accepted the very plausible assumption that there is no defense against nuclear weapons except the threat of similar retaliation, i.e., nuclear deterrence. And I have accepted the moral hypothesis that a nation threatened with nuclear attack would be entitled to employ nuclear deterrence to defend itself, this being the only means by which it could do so. More than a few words of justification here are doubtless in order.

First, I should point out that these are not completely independent claims. Obviously one possible response to a threat of nuclear attack would be simply to give in to whatever demand the enemy was threatening to achieve by way of attacking. Another would be to tell him to go to hell, and that we would fight to the last individual before he got his way. Few demands that would be made by any remotely normal enemy would be plausibly bolstered by a nuclear threat under these circumstances: you can't enslave the enemy if he's dead, or convert him to socialism, say; and you can't move in yourself if you have just rendered his territory uninhabitable by exploding two hundred megatons of nuclear weapons over it. I concede all this, and agree that these are alternatives to be carefully considered. What I deny is that we *must*, morally, accept anything so extreme in preference to making a threat of nuclear retaliation.

What would make participation in a nuclear war begun by the other party immoral? There are two replies to this worth considering. First: some would say that it is immoral because it raises the prospect of eliminating all life on earth. I agree, naturally, that this would be a very undesirable outcome. But it does not follow that we have no right to threaten actions that *might* promote that effect as retaliations to such an attack. Certainly other means should be employed if it is possible for other means to be sufficient for the defense of what is under threat. But our assumption is that there is no such other means. What does follow is that perhaps a state considering a nuclear attack should bear that in mind. For what it will be worth, it will be his fault, and not ours. In doing *the only thing open to us* by way of defense against his contemplated actions, we are acting within our rights if the right of defense means anything. And a world in which there was no right of defense would not, I think, be worth living in.

It is interesting that this possible eventuality — the extinction of the human race — is considered to be of such supreme importance by so many people. Indeed, the continuance of the human race is often claimed to be of 'infinite' value. But why should this be so? The image seems to be that in doing what terminates the lives of all those now living, we would also be terminating the lives of all future persons as well. But that is not so, of course. Since there would be no future persons brought into existence, there are no future lives to terminate. Extinction of the human species would deprive *us* of that future, a future in which, for instance, those presently here would perhaps be remembered with fondness (or otherwise), a future in which other people might realize many of the outcomes we presently are very keen on — maybe someone would have discovered a really good Unified Field Theory, for instance. But extinction does not deprive any of the people who would have done those things of any experience whatever. There would be no such people in the first place, and thus no one to be 'deprived' of anything at all.

The other reply is of more fundamental importance, I think, and is certainly much-discussed; namely, that in threatening such an action, we are threatening to kill innocent people. I agree with that, in a sense: that is, we are threatening to do something which we know will have that result. And I agree, of course, that it is extremely regrettable. No doubt we can accept Eric Mack's dictum that 'Insofar as an act is *an act of self-defense*, it must be directed at an aggressive threat. Insofar as an act strikes out at nonaggressors, its status as a defensive act is at least questionable.'[7] Again, however, I am afraid that that is a charge for the attacking party to live with, and for the same reason: it is he who puts us in the position of having to do this. He can avoid this outcome by the simple expedient of leaving us alone. The right of defense is surely a right against blackmail and extortion while it's at it.

It is worthwhile, in this connection, to consider a recent article against deterrence by Professor Lackey, long one of the ablest writers on these matters. His argument is that in undertaking a policy of nuclear deterrence, the U.S. is *increasing the risk* of of nuclear death to some innocent parties, as compared with the policy of U.S. nuclear disarmament.[8] There are two questions to ask about this: (a) Is it true, in any sense in which it matters? And (b) How much does it matter, even if it is true?

Whether it is true depends on at least two things. In the first place, we have the question whether increasing the risk of nuclear death *imposed by Americans* is the only thing that matters. Lackey is here explicitly assuming a 'deontological' ethical position, at least for the sake of argument. And some versions of deontology no doubt maintain that all that matters is one's *own* actions — that it is, for instance, wrong to kill the innocent, whether as end or means,

---

7 Douglas Lackey, 'Immoral Risks,' in *Social Philosophy and Policy* 3 (1985) 154-75

8 See the same two as in note 6.

regardless of what comes of it. Contrasting with this is supposed to be the Utilitarian position, which allows any means provided the net good achieved at least equals that of any alternative. But of course these alternatives are not exhaustive. One could have an ethical view rejecting the 'side constraints' view, the strong Double Effect principle *and* the utilitarian view. In fact, several serious writers have in fact advocated such views, myself included. What we will want to know is not whether a policy increases the risk of American nuclear attack, but whether (for instance) it increases the risk of attack by anybody. American leaders have certainly claimed that their policies are in effect preventing unprovoked attack by the Soviet Union on many States, not just the U.S.A. And so they would insist that American policies are not increasing the risk of nuclear attack on innocents *simpliciter*, even though of course they are increasing the risk of *American*-imposed nuclear deaths of innocents.

More fundamentally, there is a question about the assessment of this particular kind of risk. Talk of the 'risk' of Nuclear attack is perfectly in order if we consider accidental firings and the like. Here the question is indeed whether the parties concerned are doing their best to minimize such risk. Each has an enormous interest in doing so, and the argument that such risk is 'negligible' is eligible as part of the justification of the general policy. To talk, however, of the 'risk' that we or anyone would intentionally begin such a war is quite another matter. If everyone in a deterrent situation is acting rationally, and the parties doing the deterring have done their homework properly, then what is the risk of nuclear war? The correct answer to this rather narrow question, given even approximately the current estimate of the interests of the parties concerned, is: zero. Each party being deterred will then calculate that what it stands to lose from an attack is greater than what it could possibly gain; and so, insofar as each is acting rationally, neither will begin the conflict. Talk of 'risk' here is out of place. There is risk that some party will go temporarily insane, no doubt. But this is another of the accidents which each has a great interest in minimizing the risk of, and presumably each has in fact highly effective procedures for preventing temporarily insane persons from initiating acts of war. The argument that the risks in question are negligible is an eligible one, at any rate.

The most fundamental question, however, remains the second one: even if we grant that deterrence increases the risks in question, is this a sufficient reason for rejecting the policy? Lackey discusses the suggestion that the risks of which he speaks are about the same as those involved in driving automobiles. He agrees that this is risk which can plausibly be viewed as being neglible in comparison to the advantages of driving, but argues that the risk of nuclear annihilation stemming from deterrence policies is by no means neglible. But the question is whether they are worth taking *in relation to the advantages gained*. In the case of automobile driving, what we gain is transportational efficiency and convenience. What do we gain from a policy of nuclear deterrence, assuming it to be both necessary and successful? The presumed answers are: national independence and the retention of our political systems. It is certainly important to ask whether these are worth risking serious wars for, indeed. But how much room is there to question whether people have the right to defend these things *if*, upon due consideration, they are so inclined? And if they have the right, then what is to be said if the *only* way of so defending them is by a system of nuclear deterrence, with its attendant risks? The innocent persons are put at risk to some degree is hardly to be doubted. And that weapons exist which make it possible for many nations to put people at this risk — the risk, that is, imposed by their opponents' defensive actions — is perhaps the worst single feature of the modern age, from the moral point of view.

But what are victims of nuclear blackmail to do, if indeed this is the only way out? There are two obvious answers: (1) They must do all they can to persuade those whose aggressive actions are responsible for the situation to re-think their policies; and (2) they must do all they can to ensure that the situation is not the result of mistakes or misunderstandings. Thus they ought to take seriously any peace initiatives, to make the most serious possible efforts at mutual reduction of forces, and to follow the policy of assuming that others are innocent of evil intention unless the facts compel the conclusion that they are guilty. It is, perhaps, the necessity of these actions (and attitudes) that people are getting at when they reject 'hardware solutions.' Fair enough.

But to ask any more: for instance, that they refrain from using the only system which could secure their defense from what they reasonably judge to be threatened aggression, is to ask the absurd, humanly speaking. Rational beings do not surrender cherished values unless they are either compelled to or persuaded of their untenability, and any moralists who insist that they refrain from defending themselves must surely be asked what they think they are doing. Meanwhile, it is unfortunately true that everyone is to some degree at risk. And an implication of this is that everyone should bethink himself or herself whether he or she does not bear some responsibility, by virtue of putting up with regimes which would utilize such things as nuclear weapons for their ends. Possibly the answer is that they can do nothing. Very well: but then, the peoples threatened by those regimes can say the same.

VI What, Then?

Again, critics may be expected to point out[9] that my proposed advocacy of courses such as replacing ballistic missile with cruise missiles will fall upon deaf ears. The American military people have every intention of continuing to increase their already monstrous collection of missiles of all kinds, ballistic *and* cruise. What's more, it seems, they are currently determined to carry the American military program into space as well. True enough. I do not suppose that one small voice in the wilderness, or even quite a few of them, will make much of an impression on American military thinkers, not to mention their yet more intransigent counterparts in the Soviet Union. My argument is only that some such courses would be the *right* thing for them to do, and that any party which does not do it is under the circumstances liable to a charge of insincerity in his claims to be interested only in defense. The superpowers, if I am right,

---

9 Eric Mack, 'Three Ways to Kill Innocent Bystanders: Some conundrums,' *Social Philosophy and Policy* **3** (1985), 1

are liable to that charge. I also insist that it is a mistake to infer from this that peace movements should, as they have in the past, continue their policy of objecting to any and all nuclear weapons deployments. The powers who develop these weapons have too good a reply if the basis for objection is merely that nuclear weapons are evil (of course they are — as are all weapons, so far as that goes), or that war is evil (of course it is). But the superpowers will *not* have a good reply if we can now object to *certain* weapons (and not others) on the ground that the former are usable for attack while the latter, though satisfactory for purely defensive purposes, are not. They can hardly shuck *that* off as a utopian, misty-minded, or ideologically biased reply. Facts are facts. If a purely defensive policy that cannot be mistaken for an aggressive one is really possible, at the nuts-and-bolts level, then we are in the position of being able to level an accusing finger at those whose hardware includes the wrong sort of nuts and bolts. It is important to be able to do this, and my argument is designed to enable us to do so.

VII Postscript

If we ask why military and political authorities persist in the sort of policies they currently pursue, there are two answers to consider. One is that they are insane. I do not think this is a satisfactory assessment, nor a particularly effective bit of rhetoric. Another is that those in charge of defense around the world are into a particularly effective if particularly abhorrent bit of boondoggling. Each side justifies to its public the expenditure of enormous amounts of the people's money by pointing to the danger presented by the other, a danger easily substantiated by the character of current military hardware and easily exaggerated by minds not accustomed to an unprejudiced look at the facts. Yet each side can pretty confidently expect that its little game will not lead to the kind of ultimate danger everyone fears, that of nuclear war. Nobody really *wants* a nuclear war, needless to say, and a great deal of effort — fortunately, successful so far — is expended by both sides to ensure that one does not come about. So both sides are pretty confident that it won't happen, and thus that they can expand their bureaucracies without real fear, either of their leading to the evil everyone is concerned about or of their being found out. The ultimate truth about the nuclear age is probably better explained by referring to Parkinson than to Satan. But if this is so, perhaps to recognize it may also do some good. Goodness knows, the world has better things to do with its time and money.

Received January, 1986
Revised May, 1986

CANADIAN JOURNAL OF PHILOSOPHY
Supplementary Volume 12

Individual Responsibility, Nuclear Deterrence, and Excusing Political Inaction*

STEVEN C. PATTEN

'The circle of responsibility is drawn around all who have or should have knowledge of the illegal and immoral character of the war.'

--Richard Falk

I

Jonathan Schell's *The Fate of the Earth*, is in a large part an earnest, aphoristic essay on individual responsibility in these times. Con-

---

* This article was accepted for publication by the editors of *Praxis International* and is published here with their kind permission.

sider a representative passage: 'With the generation that has never known a world unmenaced by nuclear weapons, a new order of the generation begins. In it, each person alive is called on to assume his share of the responsibility for guaranteeing the existence of all future generations.'[1] I have no doubt that many people in most countries — citizens of representative democracies in particular — know this call and feel in some dim and tentative way that there must be special individual responsibilities that have evolved with that defensive, strategic and political doctrine we know as nuclear deterrence. And how could we expect otherwise? There are certain to be times for many of us when the risks of nuclear deterrence will seem so momentous and the conflict to be avoided such a staggering calamity, that we will believe that something approaching the heroic should be the norm: our responsibilities should be those of protest, and civil disobedience, and political reorganization, and ... How could we expect to spend our days in less decisive ways?

At least this is the way the problem appears to us at some times, that there are singular if not heroic acts to be done and decisions to be made that are unique to these times and that are very much our responsibility as citizens living in representative democracies. Yet in other moments nothing seems clearer to us than that there are no responsibilities that we have as individuals that are a special function of the present day situation. At such moments when we ask, 'What should I be doing?' we get back the reply, 'Nothing much.' For isn't nuclear deterrence a guarantee of peace? And hasn't it avoided major destruction in war since World War II?[2]

Throughout this paper my comments are sympathetically directed to those individuals who ask 'What should I do?' or 'What can I do?' and in posing these questions are expressing doubt whether there is any sense in which they are responsible for deterrence doctrine and about whether they can be effective in changing the doc-

---

1 Jonathan Schell, *The Fate of the Earth* (New York, N.Y.: Alfred A. Knopf 1983), 173

2 At least this is the familiar historical claim. For an insightful critical account see Trudy Govier, 'Nuclear Illusion and Individual Obligations,' *Canadian Journal of Philosophy* **13** (1983), 475ff.

trine. More specifically, I shall be concerned to put forward a line of argument that is intended to show that a model of responsibility that is commonly put forward to excuse individuals from responsibility in war or warlike times, cannot possibly function as an excuse for our political inaction in those times.

As agents concerned to be ethically and politically responsible, reflecting on contemporary nuclear deterrence doctrine is — at least sometimes — a matter of seeing our predicament as a combination of terror at the prospect of nuclear war and a feeling of political impotence in military matters. For when we think of what is at stake in the matter — conditional strategies that threaten the physical existence of the populations of the superpowers and their more or less ideologically aligned allies — and when we reflect on the scale and nature of the weapons, the complicated systems of intelligence and command and delivery, the various strategies for response and targeting, most of all when we think of the massive human slaughter threatened, with all of these things we think of our situation as one of war, or of war being prepared for, and in doing so the responsibilities we expect of individuals tend to appear to be those we associate with those of citizens of countries at war, or of countries preparing for war.

The point I want to insist on first in this essay is that there are attitudes toward personal responsibilities that are appropriate, natural and understandable in times when war is being prepared for or waged *and* which often function as excuses for us when we come to suspect that our country is preparing for, or waging an unethical war, or preparing for or engaging in unethical practices in war.

Consider the attitude that is often appropriate for residents of democracies in a state of war. It is a fact that patriotism often becomes the supreme value in a time of war.[3] Whatever other functions patriotism may have (e.g. in promoting the most efficient war effort) it serves in a handy way to encourage an attenuated — or as Michael Walzer has it — a *realistic* set of individual responsibili-

---

3 John Sommerville puts forward a gripping picture of the role of patriotism in the period following the Cuban missile crisis in 'Patriotism and War,' *Ethics* **91** (1981), 568-78.

215

ties that are to be expected in representative democracies during times of war.[4] The realistic view is one that accounts for the distancing and limiting of individual responsibilities that occurs in war.

> The state that goes to war is ... governed at a great distance from its ordinary citizens by powerful and often arrogant officials. These officials, or at least the leading among them, are chosen through democratic elections, but ... political participation is occasional, intermittent, limited in its effects, and it is mediated by a system of the distribution of news which is partially controlled by those distant officials and which in any case allows for considerable distortions. ... It is no longer as easy to impose responsibility as it is in a perfect democracy. One doesn't want to regard those distant officials as if they were kings, but for certain sorts of state action, secretly prepared or suddenly launched, they bear a kind of regal responsibility.[5]

It is not my point to recommend this form of responsibility, and as Walzer points out, for certain classes of state action (e.g. atrocities in war) and for certain groups of individuals (e.g. those who have influence) it is totally inappropriate. Instead, I wish to suggest that when we consider the strategic side of deterrence theory, it is natural (though mistaken) to see the relationship of citizens to government in representative democracies as very much like, if not exactly the same as, the realistic one of war. And, given the realistic view of individual responsibility, it is understandable (and not necessarily mistaken) that the political leaders come to be viewed as supreme in power and knowledge and the individual citizens are seen as politically impotent or nearly so. From this perspective the individual is confronted with the terror of nuclear war but the political means for dealing with it are withdrawn; and yet from this perspective the individual is at least partly excused from responsi-

---

4 Michael Walzer, *Just and Unjust Wars* (New York, N.Y.: Basic Books 1977), 301f.; the idea of the realistic view is a normative notion, not an epistemological one. The suggestion of the realistic view is that we should be realistic — i.e. not severe — in judging the political acts of individuals when their government is at war.

5 Ibid., 301

bility, partly (at least) excused from the requirement of engaging in political means to change things. For how could the individual – barring heroic effort – ever get *close* enough to affect change? In what follows I shall be arguing that it is a mistake to think that the realistic view either partly or completely excuses us from political action in altering deterrence doctrine.

II *(a)*

We can look on the work of Jonathan Schell as proposing to lead us away from the realistic view of individual responsibility that I have described by arguing that it is a mistake to fix the responsibility of individuals confronting nuclear deterrence doctrine anywhere in the ordinary political processes, whether or not one views one's country as in a state of war or a warlike state, or in a state of peace. On Schell's account the problem of distancing created by the realistic view rests on the mistaken idea that we can satisfy our individual responsibilities only by the means provided for by the modern nation state, irrespective of how resourcefully democratic that state might be. On Schell's account the responsibility generated by nuclear deterrence strategy is to bring about the abolition or radical transformation of the modern nation state.

His argument moves first from an insightful suggestion that the bare possibility of ending life on earth through nuclear war entails a moral imperative to prevent it.

> ... Although, scientifically speaking, there is all the difference in the world between the mere possibility that a holocaust will bring about extinction and the certainty of it, morally they are the same, and we have no choice but to address the issue of nuclear weapons *as though we know for a certainty* that their use would put an end to our species.[6]

This moral certainty leads Schell to suggest that it is the responsi-

---

6 Schell, 95, my emphasis

bility of individuals to work to bring about complete disarmament. But not just that. Schell shares the view of the Harvard Nuclear Study Group that nuclear weapons cannot disappear, even with nuclear disarmament. For the knowledge of the means and methods for constructing these devices will always be with us. Thus, Schell's reading of our moral responsibilities extends to eliminating the very source of the sort of antagonism that encourages the temptation to arm with nuclear weapons: we must abolish the nation state or constrain its war making powers in some way. Thus, 'if ... disarmament is not accompanied by a political solution, then every clash of will between nations will tempt them to pick up the instruments of violence again... '.[7]

No one will gainsay the importance of the tone and temper of Schell's reflections on the threat of deterrence strategy and the debt that contemporary debate owes to him. Nonetheless he has been severely criticized for his solutions and his rendering of individual responsibility. The individual who is in the grip of the threat of nuclear disaster can hardly be encouraged by the weighty suggestion that one must first dismantle the weapons, then get rid of or completely restructure the nation state *and then* go on to establish some sort of fraternal world order. To say that Schell's account entails no rest for the virtuous is to say far too little. To recommend the reinvention of politics and the reinvention of the world[8] in the face of what many see as an impending calamity is, practically speaking, to encourage apathy and alienation and a new set of excuses for political inaction.

Yet the most serious fault in Schell's account of individual responsibilities is not its utopian character, but the fact that it rests on empirical claims about the nature of nation states and the character of history that are dubious at best. First, the claim that nation states are essentially aggressive or that they must relate aggressively under conditions of tension, misses recognition of all the various pacific relations that can and do occur between nation states and the

---

7 Ibid., 221

8 Ibid., 226

large variety of instances when nation states have managed to construct peaceful solutions to their differences.[9] One suspects that Schell must be in the grip of a Marxist-like definition of the state — that the nation state is nothing more than a set of police and military forces. Second, to make use of Karl Popper's terminology, there is a strong whiff of historicism in Schell. Even if there is a trend or tendency in nation state relations to be aggressive, it is a fallacy to suppose that there is any necessity in this, and it is dangerously misleading to suppose that such trends or tendencies represent laws.

Third, it is empirically naive to suppose that the abolition of the nation state in favor of some new 'fraternal' forms will eliminate sources of aggressive conflict. In Western history the nation state is an entity that evolved in the late middle ages, but there was no shortage of military conflicts prior to that time, encouraged by factors such as religious, ethnic and economic differences. (And consider the ever present threat of civil wars within some recognized nation states.)

Fourth, and finally, if it is granted as I have suggested that the presence of the nation state cannot explain the tendency toward military conflict, and if we assume with Schell that the aggressive conditions for such conflict inexorably will lead to picking up nuclear arms, then we have every excuse for avoiding the task of denationalizing the world.

Jonathan Schell has marked out important new territory in the debate over deterrence strategy. Yet he has not provided us with an alternative account for our individual responsibilities that plausibly prompts us to move away from the distancing of the realistic view.

II *(b)*

In *Living with Nuclear Weapons*,[10] the Harvard Nuclear Study Group,

---

9 I was reminded of this point in another context by Trudy Govier.

10 Albert Carnesale, Paul Doty, Stanley Hoffman, Samuel P. Huntington, Joseph S. Nye Jr., Scott D. Sagan, *Living With Nuclear Weapons* (New York, NY: Bantam Books 1983)

as they have decided to call themselves, implicitly put forward an account of individual responsibility that is traditional in representative democracies. It is one that leads us away from the realistic view by playing down the terror of deterrence doctrine and emphasizing a key element in the ordinary political process. Embedded within their detailed accounts of international relations, strategy and weaponry we find a belief — enunciated in a words-of-one-syllable tone that tells us a great deal about what they think of their audience — that the first, if not final, responsibility of individual citizens is to be factually informed. There is nothing wild about this sort of understanding of individual responsibility. It is the very viscera of the sort of careful, responsible preparation that protects us against individual and governmental excess in matters of public policy. If we want to make the right decision on which of two routes for a new highway is best, then we must know the facts. And if we want to make the best choice of alternative candidates we must have all the information before us. But what if the public are concerned with whether or not a highway should be built at all or whether or not any of the candidates should be elected? And what if they are concerned with the possibility that they will not be allowed any significant political say in such matters? In either case the kind of information required for individual decision making and effecting political change must be of a different order than that provided to make choices between more or less acceptable alternatives.

I am suggesting that the person who asks 'What should I do?' or 'What can I do?' as an expression of despair about the political effectiveness of individuals, is asking a question about individual responsibility that is far deeper and much more profound than anything the Harvard Nuclear Study Group seems willing to face. Individuals who ask such questions are seeking alternatives to deterrence strategy, perhaps its complete replacement, perhaps a significant modification, at least an explanation why it cannot be altered.

How could the Group completely miss the weighty nature of the problem of individual responsibility, especially in a book which aims to put individuals on the right track? It is because, unfortunately, they assume with practically no argument that present deterrence strategy is the best of all alternative strategies. In fact, they seem to take it as clear that nuclear deterrence hasn't a strong ethical case against it. Consider:

> Most people judge the morality of actions on their intentions and their consequences. Moreover, in deterrence our intentions are not to do evil. Our threat is intended to avoid both the horrible outcome of nuclear war and aggressive behavior by the other side. Our intent in making the threat is not immoral, and the consequences depend in part upon the intentions of the other side. On the contrary, to remove the threat altogether … might indeed have disastrous moral effects, if it incites one's adversary to take greater risks, and thereby make war more likely.[11]

In assessing this sort of passage it should be apparent first that the Group does not recognize or acknowledge the usual way of representing nuclear deterrence in contingencies such as first use or massive retaliation − that under certain conditions it is the intention of the Alliance to use nuclear weapons in response to a conventional attack and that under other conditions it is stated policy to cause massive destruction through counter city retaliation. To say, without argument, that this is not an intent is misleading at best. Second, to give the Group its best case, and grant that occurrences such as first use or massive retaliation would be unintended consequences, still will not serve to remove the prima facie moral pressure against deterrence strategy, at least not without profound argument. For whether or not the consequences of a nuclear exchange come about knowingly or intentionally the ethical problem remains the same.[12] Finally, the suggestion that removal of the threat of deterrence might be the morally worst alternative is far too glib. Whatever we might end up saying about the merits and shortcomings of unilateral disarmament it can hardly be dismissed out of hand. And even if we could shoulder unilateralism aside, there are

---

11 Ibid., 247-8

12 For criticism of attempts to establish a moral difference on the basis of this knowingly/intentionally distinction in other contexts, see Steven C. Patten, 'The Case That Milgram Makes,' *Philosophical Review* **86** (1977), 359-60 and James Rachels, 'Active and Passive Euthanasia,' *The New England Journal of Medicine* **292** (1975), 78-80.

a large variety of alternatives that fall short of it that deserve serious consideration.[13]

The Harvard Nuclear Study Group removes the remoteness of the realistic view by altering the problem. For the group, nuclear deterrence is a serious, but ordinary political problem, one among many. The person confronted by the dreadfulness of present day deterrence strategy and who asks for direction on what individual responsibilities should be assumed in the face of it, will find little in the way of direction from the Group.

II *(c)*

Richard Wasserstrom[14] does not deny the realistic view in considering nuclear deterrence. Yet, on his account, the danger of deterrence strategy is so great that the excusing force of the supposed remoteness of this strategy is greatly mitigated. He argues that the responsibilities of individual citizens in this period of nuclear deterrence are particularly pressing, and more or less specifiable, because of the unusual features of the conflict that would result should deterrence fail. His case is the striking one that, at least within the representative democracies, the obligations of the ordinary citizens are to deal with those compelling questions that one would confront during a war that is ethically questionable. Thus, to those individuals who ask, what are my responsibilities at this time when the threat of nuclear aggression and retaliation is always before us, the student of Wasserstrom would reply that those responsibilities are primarily those demanding individual decisions that we must

---

13 I have in mind, for example, unilateral modifications of alliance doctrine such as denial of first use and large scale partial disarmament such as that suggested as a unilateral step in the writings of George F. Kennan.

14 In 'Moral Issues of the Nuclear Arms Race,' unpublished manuscript, presented at a conference on Philosophy and Nuclear Deterrence at the University of Dayton, Dayton, Ohio, Fall 1983. See 'War, Nuclear War, and Nuclear Deterrence: Some Conceptual and Moral Issues,' *Ethics* **95** (1985), 424-44.

expect when one's nation is at war and the morality of its action is in question.

The argument that Wasserstrom puts forward moves from reflection on main features of the nature of the conflict that would result between the superpowers should nuclear war come about. There are three such features: (1) There would be very few decision makers, and very few participants — there will be nothing for the bulk of us to do in the waging of such a war.[15] (2) There would be little duration in time of such a conflict. 'Depending upon the location and speed of the components of the "delivery" systems, the destructiveness would commence and its full short term effects would be experienced between 7 minutes and a day or so after the war commenced';[16] and (3) most of the citizens will die.[17] What then follows in respect of individual obligations? Wasserstrom says this: 'All of the decisions and actions that individuals might want to make and to take in respect to nuclear war have to be made and taken, if they are to made and taken at all, before the war occurs.'[18] What are these decisions and actions? Here is a sample list: (1) Those that result from deliberations on questions concerning the justification of waging the war and the means used; (2) Those that come about as the result of reflection on questions concerning one's own status in the war, especially conscientious objection; (3) Those that culminate in decisions about whether or not to protest the war; and (4) Those that emanate from self-scrutiny about whether one is culpable in designing or participating in the manufacture of the means of war.[19]

How then does the argument proceed? It moves first from recognition of the empirical nature of nuclear war and the fact that this entails a limited if not a non-existent role for individuals during the conflict. Second, it encourages appreciation of what probably is a

---

15 'Moral Issues...', 16

16 Ibid., 14

17 Ibid.

18 Ibid., 16

19 Ibid., 20

fact — that individuals in a democracy have an obligation to question the correctness of their nation in going to war and the way it is pursued, and connected obligations to decide on their own place in the conflict (combatancy or not; public protest or not). Let's then grant Wasserstrom's assessment of the nature of nuclear war and grant too that we have obligations to question the justification of our government in going to war and in waging war, how does it follow that we have an obligation — that it is our responsibility — to ask these questions about one's responsibilities in a country at war *right now* at this time? Wasserstrom says that, 'In a nuclear war all issues such as these are foreclosed and, of necessity, relocated in an earlier time and context.'[20] At another place he tells us that such questions (e.g. combatancy or not) can have no meaning or place during an actual nuclear conflict. Granted. But someone might wish to respond in this way: how does it follow from the fact that such questions of personal responsibility that apply when one's country is at war will be foreclosed or without meaning during a nuclear war, that they are sensible and pressing right now? For surely, if one's country is not presently at war we cannot meaningfully protest its decision to wage war or the means it uses in doing so. If it is meaningless to contemplate making personal decisions whether or not to support one's country during a nuclear way, it must be equally empty to attempt to make those same decisions when one's country is in a state of peace. This objector insists that from the probable shortness of a nuclear conflict nothing follows about the kinds of responsibilities one is confronted with right now.

The counter to this objection involves appreciating the full force and ingenuity of the argument schema Wasserstrom is committed to in constructing his case for individual responsibility in this time. It moves from the following premises: (1) That nuclear war is an ever present danger; (2) If we are to protest against nuclear war it is now or never; (3) It is certainly better to protest against nuclear war now rather than never. So, (4) our responsibilities are ... (thus and so).[21]

---

20 Ibid., 16

21 This formulation is due to Cheryl Misak.

But my main concern, now and throughout, is with the thoughtful but acquiescent individual, who will be inclined to accept the premises of Wasserstrom's schema, yet deny the conclusion, deny that any responsibilities of a personal sort follow at all. My concern is with the individual who is captured by the grip of the realistic view: 'I will grant that there is a danger of nuclear war,' this person will say, 'and this consequence would be dreadful to say the least. But it is an unfortunate truth that none of this speaks in any clear way to my responsibilities. For the political, strategic and defensive policy of deterrence has been created by and is sustained by a few distant political leaders working in secret that I can in fact influence only by the most determined and heroic acts. What can I do? What possible responsibilities can I have beyond the obligation to perform a few trivial acts that serve primarily to gesture support and fellow feeling toward my friends and neighbors? Whatever political power I may have in the usual matters of public policy cannot reach to the tables of high strategy, even on a good day. In exchange for my political ineffectiveness in this matter I have at least the comfort of knowing that I am not culpable. The remoteness of strategic deliberations on deterrence assure me of that. And in the meantime I'll gamble with you, that deterrence will work.'

The proposal that follows is intended as a supporting ammendation on Wasserstrom's important work. The argument is that a set of unique facts in addition to those cited by Wasserstrom provide strong support for the claim that individuals are not excused from responsibilities of a political sort with respect to nuclear deterrence doctrine by the distancing effect of the realistic view.

III

Thus far we have considered three different attempts to account for what many claim to be a peculiar or unique set of individual responsibilities when living with nuclear deterrence, three different ways of dealing with the political impotence that is the natural result of the distancing effect of the realistic view. The first recommendation (Schell's), that we should acknowledge an obligation to transcend, overcome and replace traditional forms – indeed that we should go so far as to dismantle the modern nation state — is not only impossibly unrealistic but is based on a set of mistaken premises. The second, that we should avoid excess by coming to grips with the problem of living with nuclear weapons by understanding them and their means of use, fails, I think, in that it is based on an impoverished understanding of the ethical questions raised by the presence of deterrence strategy. The final solution, that of Wasserstrom, comes closest to a satisfactory recommendation about how we should view our responsibilities in this time by fixing on features of deterrence doctrine that are unique. Nonetheless, or so I have argued, this account will fail to touch those many individuals who view deterrence strategy as a creation that has a political and strategic life of its own removed from their political hands.

My suggestion for understanding individual responsibilities takes its inspiration from Wasserstrom in fixing on features of deterrence doctrine that are unique in comparison to other periods of war build-up in this century, enough so in their nature that they take us beyond the normal conception of political responsibilities that we are said (under the realistic view) to take on as ordinary but reflective citizens in time of war or in preparing for war. My claims rest in an essential manner on the obvious empirical fact that the doctrine of nuclear deterrence is a matter of public knowledge in an astonishingly detailed way. In fact this may even be a matter of necessity. For nuclear deterrence cannot work without fear, and fear cannot come about without ever-present knowledge of what is to happen under certain contingencies, *and* detailed public promulgation functions as a resolute guarantee to the other side that one is completely serious about the intent. I say that knowledge of deterrence doctrine is detailed in that it specifies a named enemy and the means to be employed against this enemy (nuclear devices of varying sizes) as well as an enormous amount of information on the expected effects to millions of people, combatants and not, third parties and not. Taken in all, deterrence doctrine is a public doctrine that is to be understood as a conditional intention to commit unparalleled massacre. Furthermore, although it is not essential to my case, I take it as obvious — and certainly determinable from public facts as well — that deterrence doctrine is a conditional intention to carry out a completely unethical set of actions.[22]

What follows from this set of facts, what is entailed by the fact that deterrence doctrine is public knowledge of a conditional intention to commit massacre? I am arguing that because of the public nature of deterrence, not only military leaders and elected and appointed officials, but also ordinary citizens of representative democracies are in on the planning for nuclear war. Of course, the citizens don't sit in on the private strategy sessions, nor is their advice sought from facilities such as the targeting centre at Omaha, but I am insisting on a denial of the defences of the realistic view that entails a strong case for the claim that the bulk of the citizens in democratic countries within the Alliance, which either acquiesce in present policy or support it, share in planning responsibility in an important sense. First, they know the score (they know the basic strategy and its implications). Second — barring a sound empirical argument to establish political impotence in such matters — these same citizens can bring about changes in strategy and weaponry by appropriate political means. It is precisely here, I am claiming, that the perplexing problem of fixing individual responsibility begins to find an answer: because of the public nature of deterrence doctrine and the fact that the power to influence change is available, competent individuals in representative democracies cannot be excused from responsibility for its continuation and form by the distancing of the realistic view of individual responsibility. And to the person despairing of political effectiveness who asks 'What should I do?' or 'What can I do?' (once we add Wasserstrom's condition that our responsibilities cannot be discharged during nuclear war) what I am calling the 'strong case' answer is this:[23] seek to exercise the appropriate political means to alter the doctrine.

I want to press this point, especially against those who may find it too tame in the face of the threat of a nuclear holocaust. The ob-

---

22 I follow others, especially Trudy Govier in 'Nuclear Illusion and Individual Obligations,' 484, in taking it to be obvious that a nuclear war would be immoral, irrespective of what we might say about threats and intentions to engage in such a conflict.

23 The idea of the 'strong case' is explained below.

Steven C. Patten

jection I have in mind is that the individual responsibility I am claiming to make a strong case for, by denying the realistic view, is
nothing more than the sort of responsibility of a *collective* of individuals to be found when a government acts in the name of its citizens.[24]
For example, we might say that the British people in the early 40s
were responsible for obliteration bombing or that the Canadian people are responsible for thousands of highway deaths each year. There
is nothing infelicitous in saying that those distinct collectivities are
responsible for the untoward events and even in asserting that they
are to blame for them. But we would not, should not, on that account say that individual citizens A and B are also responsible and
to blame. Likewise, or so the objection will have it, collectivities such
as the people of the Alliance countries – or the American people,
the British people, the French people – might be responsible for
the conditional intention to commit nuclear war and be blamewor-
thy to boot should that war come about (in the sense that they haven't the excusing condition available under the realistic view). But,
to apply the analogy involved in this objection, this does not entail
responsibility on the part of *specifiable* individuals. If any individuals are responsible, this objector will have it, they can only be those
in leadership positions.

This objection, I maintain, fails to appreciate the unusual implications entailed by the public promulgation of the nuclear deterrence
doctrine: that the doctrine is a matter of public knowledge, that it
is underwritten by public opinion, that it is a conditional intention
to wage devastating war, that it can be altered by appropriate political means, and (Wasserstrom) that there will be no opportunity for
political influence once a nuclear war begins. It is these features,
I think, that provide a strong case for responsibility and blame. It
is this set of facts – that taken in sum deny the distancing excuse
of the realistic view – and not that some government, or set of
governments, acts in the name of the citizens, that is essential to

---

24 This way of talking about certain forms of collective responsibility comes from
Peter A. French, 'Morally Blaming Whole Populations,' in V. Held, S. Mor-
genbesser and T. Nagel, eds., *Philosophy, Morality and International Affairs*
(London: Oxford University Press 1974), 282f.

my case. The set of criteria I have in mind — in particular those of prior knowledge (knowledge of the precise nature of the war prior to its occurrence) and the power to alter strategic policy by appropriate political means — is precisely that set in place by the military tribunal at Nuremberg. Consider:

> If a defendant did not know that the planning and preparation for invasions and wars in which he was involved were concrete plans and preparations for aggressive wars and for wars, otherwise in violation of international laws and treaties, then he cannot be guilty of an offense. If, however, after the policy to initiate and wage aggressive wars was formulated, a defendant came into possession of knowledge that the wars to be waged were aggressive and unlawful, then he will be criminally responsible if he, being on the policy level, could have influenced such policy and failed to do so.[25]

And again, when considering the culpability of individual members of the German armed forces the Tribunal says: 'It is not a person's rank or status, but his power to shape or influence the policy of his state, which is the relevant issue for determining his criminality under the charge of crimes against peace.'[26]

The insight of the Tribunal is the correct one. If an individual is aware of a plan to commit murder and so knows, inter alia, that a moral wrong is in the offing, and that individual also has the means to inhibit or stifle the act, then the individual is culpable to some degree should the act come about. But it will be noted that in laying down its criteria for crimes against peace the Tribunal specifically insists that culpability must be a function of not only prior knowledge, but also of one's position in government — one must have knowledge and be at 'the policy level.' Whatever the Tribunal may have had in mind with the notion of a policy level we can find sense in their restriction of liability to top leaders on a number of grounds. For Germany was, for all intents, a country at war well

---

25 Quoted by Sanford Levinson, 'Responsibility for Crimes of War,' *Philosophy and Public Affairs* **2** (1973), 254.

26 Ibid.

prior to declared hostilities against Poland, France and Britain, so that at least the realistic model of responsibility with all its 'regal' power for its leaders would have to be assumed. More to the point, it is trivial to remark that Germany was a closed society with respect to effecting political change. It would have been impossible for the Tribunal to find individual citizens culpable for crimes against peace given that ordinary political channels were not open to them. Furthermore, being a resident of a country, even in the worst of times, and being one of its heroes, are distinct notions: being heroic cannot be an ordinary obligation, since it is not one of one's obligations at all. Also, in the usual case, one must suppose that given the kind of emergency created by a short gap in time between the design of a plan and its implementation, the ordinary citizen, thwarted by a hobbled political system, would not have any opportunity to influence the alternative political means to inhibit the deed. But none of these defeating conditions can apply to citizens of representative democracies at this time. For we are not at war, we are not members of a closed society, and we are not in a situation of emergency: we have both prior knowledge and the power to influence change (even if the causal chain is complicated). Thus, I would insist that the spirit, if not the letter, of the Nuremberg set of criteria in determining crimes against peace, apply to individual citizens today.

In order better to see the force of my claim, consider the familiar case of the My Lai massacre. As one of the most highly publicized atrocities of the Vietnam war, the responsibility of individuals in bringing it about has been discussed extensively both within and without the courts which tried Lt. Calley. But let us suppose a somewhat different situation than what actually happened. Let us suppose that well prior to the outbreak of hostilities, some country A threatens for deterrrence purposes to commit an atrocity or set of them of the My Lai type against country B (we are supposing that country B, for whatever reason, is especially fearful of such acts). We can even imagine that this 'atrocity strategy,' because of its deterrence function, is in the public eye for a period of years — it is embellished and refined, it is the subject of open debates, political leaders take stands on it in getting elected and so on. Now can we say that individual members of country A are not responsible for the form and existence of this policy? I think that the individuals are responsible — barring unique circumstances cited in rebuttal — in the sense that they cannot be excused from political inaction since they are aware of the strategy and can effect change and influence change without resorting to heroic means. As well we have a strong case for saying that those same citizens — at least those who don't object and those who support the policy — must be said to be responsible if this atrocity strategy is put into play.

To be sure it will be suggested by some that my portrayal of individual responsibility for deterrence doctrine is based on a naive understanding of the obligations that citizens can reasonably be said to have within representative democracies. Here it will be claimed that I have the facts wrong. Here it will be suggested that when it comes to responsibility for deterrence strategy something like the realistic model really is most appropriate — deterrence, and everything it involves, is the more or less private preserve of a select and distant group of political and military leaders. This is an empirical claim and I have argued that it is false; but should it prove to be true in the sense that ordinary citizens lack political influence then it would seem that for essentially the same reasons as before (especially, detailed prior knowledge) it is now the responsibility of individual citizens to influence alteration of the process. And if the claim is that the majority of citizens support the policy of deterrence, then one's obligations become those of influencing change in the collectivity. At least this will be so barring a knock-down empirical case to show that the collective of individuals cannot be moved. (This would be one way in which what I have been calling the strong case for individual responsibility might be rebutted.)

If I am right in my basic claims — that the public nature of deterrence strategy at a time when democratic means for influence remain intact entails (in conjunction with Wasserstrom's condition) a strong case for individual responsibility for deterrence strategy, then a set of crucial consequences also receives support. First, that the nearly canonical way of discriminating combatants and non-combatants — in terms of political innocence[27] — has doubtful ap-

---

27 What I refer to here as political innocence is the fourth sense of innocence outlined by Richard Wasserstrom in 'On the Morality of War: A Preliminary

plication to those who defer to deterrence strategy or those who actively support it. Of course this fact can make little difference of a practical sort in the event of nuclear war since by all reasonable calculations there will be few individuals left to stand up and proclaim their innocence. And no one will seek ethical refuge in the fact that it is doubtful that a Nuremberg type tribunal will ever deal with the matter later on. Still, recognition of this case for loss of innocence should serve effectively to underscore the degree of responsibility of individual citizens in representative democracies. Few of us will wear the charge of culpability and non-innocence with sanguinity.

Second, I have been attempting to provide foundation for a claim made by Jonathan Schell[28] that individual responsibility for deterrence strategy properly applies only to citizens in representative democracies and not to those of the closed societies of the Warsaw pact countries and the U.S.S.R. Certainly, citizens of the latter countries have as much public knowledge as the rest of us, but given the fact − as standard accounts insist − that they have little in the way of political means to influence public policy on key matters, and given too that their political systems cannot be altered in the way of democracies, it follows that the responsibility of individual citizens in these countries is greatly mitigated by comparison; enough so, I should think, that these people can properly by judged to be politically innocent.

Third, it is a consequence as well that most political leaders in representative democracies are no more (or less) responsible (in the sense of the strong case) for the existence of the war making capabilities of deterrence than individual citizens. It is a dodge, and a dangerous and stultifying one that owes its heritage to unthinking

---

Inquiry,' *Stanford Law Review* **21** (1968), 1652. It is a notion of innocence that is '... concerned with culpability rather than causality per se' (1652).

28 This is the sort of view that motivates this kind of claim: 'The Government leaders who are now talking about and planning for nuclear war are violating the principles of the Nuremberg War Crimes Tribunals. Is there a way to try them as "war criminals"?' Panel Discussion in T.L. Perry, Jr., ed., *The Prevention of Nuclear War* (Vancouver, B.C.: Physicians for Social Responsibility, B.C. Chapter 1983), 159; see also Schell, 229-30.

acceptance of the realistic view, to think that the destructive fission and fusion of deterrence are in the hands of a few elected and appointed leaders. For if they are mistaken in the way they deal with deterrence and its threats, the denial of the realistic view suggests that appropriate means are available to change their minds. And if their thinking cannot be changed then the appropriate political means are available within representative democracies to have them replaced.

It is traditional when talking about preparing for war and waging war to ponder especially the responsibilities of those who work in industries that make the missiles and bombs and the complicated components of the systems of delivery. I do not wish to trivialize this concern, nor the sort of soul searching that might well be the lot of people who work in such industries, but I do believe that centering our attention on the status of those who provide the means of war distracts us from the main issue in individual responsibility. For if the question is one of combatancy or non-combatancy status, and if this is to be determined by reference to political innocence, then individual citizens have less innocence, and they are more culpable, than those who provide the means of war. And if the question is one of relative responsibility for deterrence doctrine in the present day my answer must be the same: those who can influence policy – individual citizens in their political functions – have far greater responsibility than those who act at the direction of the policy. (Although it should be noted that at certain times refusing to participate in the construction of missiles might well be the most appropriate political act.)[29]

Thus far I have spoken only to the conditional intention to wage nuclear war and the individual responsibilities we have for that. But some will be quite happy with these reflections in that, or so they will insist, it tells just part of the story. I am thinking of those who are convinced of the peace securing functions of deterrence planning. More specifically, I have in mind those who insist that the 'real' or 'primary' intention of the doctrine of deterrence is to protect and

---

29 Cheryl Misak pointed this out to me.

keep the peace whereas one intends only secondarily − or, in the words of the Harvard Study Group, pictures as an unintended consequence[30] − a full scale nuclear war. On this account one might well accept the model of responsibility on the part of individuals that I have been arguing for, but then go on to insist that what they are responsible for under the strong case proposed here is a policy that provides for peace, and − to put it bluntly − there is no loss of innocence in that. Few of us have the sort of background and stamina that make us entirely at home with the kind of stacking, splitting, shuffling and shrouding of intentions that is involved in this version of what one is responsible for in deterrence planning. Yet even under the most pacific reading, Alliance policy does recommend first use and massive retaliation. And it does involve as well the very real possibility of accident. And it does, in its present form, involve the possibility of an 'unintended consequence' that could end life on this planet, bring about disastrous side effects such as nuclear winter, and even when it is construed as a very limited exchange, it could cause untold suffering for uninvolved third parties. Those who are defenders of deterrence strategy have an equally strong case for individual responsibility to use political means to make deterrence doctrine safer and less reckless and destructive than it is at present.

IV Conclusion: Review, Critical Reflections

In this essay I have been concerned with the problem of whether or not individual citizens have responsibility for deterrence strategy, and with the problem of whether or not those same citizens have responsibilities that arise from the existence of that strategy in its contemporary form. I have construed these problems as raising one central question: Does the realistic view of individual responsibility with its distancing function serve to excuse individual citizens from

---

30 Albert Carnesale, et al., 245

political inaction? Indeed, I have been assuming that the individual who asks 'What can I do?' or 'What should I do?' as a way of expressing political impotence in considering deterrence doctrine is implicitly making claim to the excusing force of the realistic view.

I have argued that certain key and unique features of contemporary deterrence strategy — prior knowledge, the power to influence by appropriate political means, in conjunction with Wasserstrom's insight — preclude appeal to the realistic view as a means of excusing political inaction. I have been pressing the claim that the kind of defense for inaction available to individual citizens before and during World War II, and reasonably at hand for American citizens during the early stages of the Vietnam conflict, is not available to ordinary citizens in these times. I have taken this as the 'strong case' that individual citizens have responsibility for nuclear deterrence strategy (in a way that ordinary British subjects did not have responsibility for the strategy of obliteration bombing), and I have construed it as the 'strong case' that individual citizens today have the responsibility to alter deterrence strategy (in a manner that American citizens during the early stages of the Vietnam conflict probably did not have responsibility for altering aggressive strategy). I have argued that the denial of the realistic view *involves* a 'strong case' for individual responsibility. I have adopted this way of talking rather than the more familiar expression 'prima facie case,' since I think it is justifiable to attempt to shoulder something close to entailment of responsibility from the denial of the realistic view. For it is traditional, if not canonical, in the literature, and in ordinary discussion, to measure individual responsibility by the presence of knowledge of what is going on in preparing for and waging war, and in the power to influence change in policy. But, of course, the strong case is not the same as entailment. The strong case is always open to rebuttal by those willing to take on the burden in a serious and reflective way. For example, if one had sound empirical evidence of Freeman Dyson's prediction that nuclear weapons will be outmoded and useless on technological grounds very soon, say next month, then the strong case for individual responsibility would be rebutted. One's actions would be superfluous, otiose, unnecessary in that case.

So much for the main argument: the denial of the realistic view entails the strong case and the strong case entails (ceterus paribus) that individuals have responsibility to influence change in the doctrine of nuclear deterrence. But how much influence? Influence change to what degree? For there is nothing in the argument of this essay to suggest a scale of individual responsibility, a weighting scheme for determining degrees of political engagement. In fact, it might be objected that the account offered here, with its talk of 'influencing change' by 'appropriate political means' requires too little from us, given what is at stake. My first answer to this objection is short: the argument of this paper requires the minimal amount from all of us. But the minimal amount is all that is needed to alter the strategy. My second answer is only slightly more complex: the argument of this paper does not preclude acting beyond the minimum on grounds other than those provided here. The main argument here constitutes a finding, something like a verdict in law; determining the penalty, fixing the degree of responsibility, can proceed on other grounds. Given the abundance of information available that argues for the gravity of the danger of nuclear deterrence strategy we have sound reasons to believe that the degree of individual responsibility is far greater than the minimum implied by the case of this paper.[31]

31 Earlier versions of this essay were read at the University of Prince Edward Island in August 1984; at the Conference on Philosophy and Nuclear Arms, University of Waterloo, September, 1984; and at An International Conference on Issues in Nuclear Deterrence, Inter-University Centre for Post Graduate Studies, Dubrovnik, Yugoslavia, June, 1985. Work on this paper was completed while assisted by a research fellowship to the Calgary Institute for the Humanities, University of Calgary. I have learned from the comments and criticisms of Maryann Ayim, David Copp, Philip Koch, Cheryl Misak, Robert Ware and Ron Yoshida. Trudy Govier, Leslie Wilson and Anne Williams patiently introduced me to the topic of individual responsibility for deterrence planning some time back. I am grateful to Sharon Prusky for a timely reminder about the importance of thinking about deterrence and especially to Mark Patten who was acting long before many of us were thinking about whether it was responsible to do so.

CANADIAN JOURNAL OF PHILOSOPHY
Supplementary Volume 12

Weapons Research and the Form
of Scientific Knowledge

IAN HACKING
University of Toronto
Toronto, Ontario
Canada M5S 1A1

From time immemorial all weapons have been a product of human knowledge. Today the relationship is reciprocal. A great deal of the new knowledge being created at this moment is a product of weaponry. The transition occurred in World War II, and, in the West, was institutionalized by the new ways of funding research and development put in place in 1945-47 in the U.S.A.

Presumably this makes some difference to what we find out. Brains and equipment are dedicated to the production of knowledge and technologies useful in time of war. Our *Physical Abstracts, Chemical Abstracts, Biological Abstracts, Indexus Medicus* — our repositories of references to new knowledge – would look very different if we had different research priorities. That means that the *content* of our new knowledge is much influenced by the choice of where to deploy the best minds of our generation.

Outspoken people who urge us to find out more about living than dying deplore this distribution of research resources. But the picture that is suggested is rather like a menu: we cannot afford (or eat) all three of the entrees: meat, fish, and vegetarian. So we settle on one, but our choice does not affect the menu. Choosing meat today has no consequences for fish tomorrow, unless the restauranteur did not purchase enough fish, guessing we would go for meat again. But that defect can be cured in one more day, and the menu is restored. Thus today we order up fibre optics communications that resist the Electromagnetic Pulse which wipes out standard signals systems upon a nuclear detonation. Tomorrow, however, we could order up a solution to the death of the Great Lakes by poisoning, if we used comparable brains and comparable material resources.

I do not quarrel with the menu view, except that it deflects us from the menu itself. It implies that there are all those things out there in the world, waiting to be known, and we choose which to know. But is there not the possibility that the very form of the menu may change, and in the case of knowledge, change irrevocably? May not new knowledge determine what are the candidates for future new knowledge, barring what, in other 'possible human worlds,' would have been candidates for knowledge? May not a direction of research determine not just the content of our *Abstracts*, but the very *form* of possible knowledge? There is a nagging worry that 'science' itself is changed: not just that we find out different facts, but that the very candidates for facts may alter. In romantic but familiar terminology, we may live in different worlds for two different kinds of reason. One is material. Our soaring triumphs and our poisons exuded by technology equally change the face of the material earth. So we live in a different world, thanks to our knowledge, from that of 1930, say. But we may also live in a different world because our conceptions of possibilities are themselves determined by new knowledge – a theme familiar from T.S. Kuhn.

One of my tasks in what follows is to provide examples of how the boundaries of knowledge are formed by the direction of actual knowledge. The boundaries of knowledge lie between the possible and the unthinkable, betweeen sense and nonsense, not between possibility and impossibility. I think that we are creating these boundaries all the time. I believe that when so much knowledge is created by and for weaponry, it is not only our actual facts, the content of knowledge, that are affected. The possible facts, the nature of the (ideal) world in which we live itself becomes determined. Weapons are making our world, even if they are never exploded. Not because they spin off new materials, but because they create some possibilities and delimit others, perhaps forever. How are we to think about that? Such is my problem in what follows.

I

I am thus concerned not with the use of knowledge but with its creation. My questions will often be abstract, compared to brute facts about our use of knowledge – such as the fact that the nations of the world have spent 17 trillion on weapons since World War II. My topic is, however, not unrelated to that. It arises from the fact that we generate much of our new knowledge in order to make better weaponry.

Where it makes sense to distinguish public from private financing, as in the United States, the bulk of public funds for research and development is dedicated to weaponry.[1] The proportion of total R&D money spent on weapons in the U.S.S.R. is far greater than in the U.S.A., for it is a poorer country. In fact few nations spend much on R&D, but of those who do, Japan is the only one in which weapons do not play a primary role.

It is a rule of thumb, to which there have been notable excep-

---

1 Estimates of R&D spending are notoriously inaccurate. For an extreme version, consult the *Bulletin of the Atomic Scientists* **42**, 3 (1986), which, using a National Science Foundation Report (USA) 85-322, estimates that military R&D now accounts for 72.7 percent of total American public R&D investment.

tions, that the more talent and the more material resources devoted to an investigation, the more we find out, and the more quickly we find out. The sheer amount of investment in weapons research virtually insures that that is where much of our new knowledge is brought into being.

There is of course an important if obscure distinction between basic and applied research so that 'R&D' covers a multitude of practices. Before the advent of the Strategic Defense Initiative, which is profoundly changing the structure of research investment,[2] the U.S. Department of Defense spent about 20 percent of basic research money on in-house laboratories, contracted out about 40 percent to private industry and the remaining 40 percent went to universities. This does not include nuclear weapons research, which comes primarily from the Department of Energy. It was a deliberate policy, regularly stated in congressional hearings, not to insist that all of this was 'mission-oriented.' In particular, the university workers should be allowed their heads, without too much direct control. All the same, the DoD would be paymaster, and select the projects and the directions in which they should proceed. So when I speak of much basic research being devoted to weaponry, I acknowledge self-conscious policies of using military funding to create knowledge that is held to be both basic and not mission-oriented. Other nations have different policies. I refer to the U.S.A. because it is so much more open than any other nation, including my own. To find out what happens in Canada, it is often more expedient to ask an American to obtain access to American archives on Canadian affairs, than to go to our own ministries.

Many would urge that the most successful growth of knowledge since 1945 has been in molecular biology, whose British, French and

---

2 In the current fiscal year, SDI has about the same budget as the National Institutes of Health, a little less than $5 billion. The latter is projected to decrease a little in future years, while the former will increase substantially. Once again, figures must be regarded with caution. In 1986 many of the sums for SDI will be paper transfers, in which work already funded will be transferred to SDI accounts, thus ensuring responsibility to the military for work not previously held to be in that domain.

American founders had, in the beginning, precious little of anyone's money. So much better endowed today, molecular biology continues on non-military funding. There are indeed endless projects that rely on non-military money, and many that survive on almost no money at all. Sometimes these are the best. But many of our momentous achievements, with innumerable peaceful spinoffs, were systematically created from military accounts. The laser is an example. We now think that almost anything can be made to 'lase' yet quite likely no substance in the whole universe ever 'lased' until our own lifetime. This is a remarkable achievement. It is sometimes thought that lasers and 'Star Wars' are a recent marriage in which a peaceful enquiry is put to military purposes. What could be more peaceful than using a laser to treat a cataract of the eye, or totally transform music reproduction in the form of compact discs? Nothing. Yet the basic research leading up to the laser was not 'peaceful.' It was strictly made on DoD contracts, as a possible successor to radar and microwave technology. I shall give a few details in II (4) below.

I hold that despite the notable counterexamples, and despite the exciting peaceful spinoffs, much of our new knowledge is being made in the pursuit of new weapons. This conclusion raises vast issues both for morality and for policy. I deliberately avoid them. Many readers will be convinced that it is evil to spend the national treasure of brains and resources on new agents of death. Others will hold that in today's political situation it is essential that present directions for research should continue. Still others will be shamelessly pragmatic: many a young scientist will reason that one must ride the crest of militarism in order to get someone to pay for basic research. 'Star Wars' is a bonanza for a whole generation of new American PhDs in computer science or in physics.

The moral issues are philosophical and they concern science, but there is no reason to think that a philosopher of science – as the term is professionally defined on this continent – will be well qualified to discuss them. Philosophy of science falls under metaphysics and epistemology – what there is and how we find out about it – while I have been citing familiar issues in ethics and policy. There are philosophers of science who write essays defending torture as an instrument of public policy, and others who disagree, but qua philosophers of science they are no better qualified to discuss such

241

Ian Hacking

matters than an able truck driver or a Xerox repair person. Likewise philosophers of science should claim no more expertise on the ethical issues than, say the man with an office adjacent to mine, who is a classical archaeologist; less, perhaps, since he is the world expert on ancient Mediterranean archery.

Rather than discuss the ethical issues (about which I have strong opinions, but claim no rights as an expert) I shall bring to bear the most pressing and yet the most obscure of questions in contemporary philosophy of science. It takes us through the gamut of that fashionable idea of 'the social construction of scientific facts,' and the antique problems of scepticism and realism.

Before proceeding I should clarify what I mean by weapons. our obsession with nuclear weapons tends to make us think of a bomb as the paradigm weapon. A moment's reflection reminds us that the essential part of weaponry is most often not what actually kills or destroys, but the euphemistically styled 'delivery system.' The so-called sturdy yeomen who won the battle of Agincourt in 1415 did so not because of their arrowheads but because of their hi-tech long-bows (and their deployment). The most brilliant military-scientific complex ever formed before the Manhattan project — Napoleon's group of mathematicians — was brought together to solve problems in ordinance, namely, how to ensure that the cannonball both travelled far and hit the target quite often. The Manhattan project is almost the only example in which the killing device — the atomic bomb — was the sole object of research, while the delivery system was a routine bomber on a routine flight. The Soviet triumph in atomic and nuclear warfare was not, as is commonly thought, the rediscovery of how to make the bomb, but the development of crude but unbelievably powerful rocketry. It is sometimes forgotten that the hardest problems to solve in 'Star Wars' research involve not missiles and lasers, but guidance systems and fifth (or later) generation computation.

When I speak of weapons, then, I include a whole gamut of military technology. Certainly I do not restrict myself to sensational weaponry in the news. I also have in mind the computational and artificial intelligence knowledge required for the windowless helicopter gunship, which would be very handy for counter insurgency work. Even philosophers who write about the principles, the logic,

242

or the statistics of perceptual systems can now get contracts for that sort of research.

II

That old nag of a distinction, form and content, still has some life in it. I am concerned with the way in which the forms of parts of scientific knowledge are affected by the fact that knowledge is brought into being with a view to military efficiency. Much of this essay will discuss examples, not in general military, in order to bring some clarity to a question about the form of knowledge.

I might well have used in my title the phrase 'conceptual scheme' rather than 'form of knowledge.' Quine has, however pre-empted the former term, meaning by it a structured set of sentences held for true. I think of a scheme of concepts as more like a framework for what can or may be true. By a *form* of a branch of scientific knowledge I mean a structured set of declarative sentences that stand for possibilities, that is, sentences that can be true or false, together with techniques for finding out which ones are true and which ones are false.[3] Note that this is closely connected to Kant's idea of the origin of synthetic a priori knowledge. It is, however, very much of an historical a priori, to use the phrase of Michel Foucault. Thus what may be deemed possible at one time may not be held to be so at another. But a form of knowledge represents what is held to be thinkable, to be possible, at some moment in time.

My account of a form of a branch of knowledge is deliberately nonjudgmental. The editor of this supplement to the *CJP* rightly noted that according to me, any set of declarative sentences, together with a Ouija board and a psychic, could count as a form of knowledge. Exactly so. It is only a matter of historical fact that it does not. The various possibilities envisaged in the doctrines of the trinity − including unitarianism − did constitute and do still for

---

3 These ideas are developed in my 'Styles of Scientific Reasoning,' in J. Rajchman and C. West, *Post-analytic Philosophy* (New York: Columbia University Press 1985), 145-64.

some people constitute a form of knowledge. They are not possibilities for me. Neither they nor their denials are part of my web of belief. In this respect my account parallels Quine's for conceptual schemes, who would have to take all the sentences declared true by a psychic, and accepted by her associates, as a conceptual scheme. Likewise for the trinity or the transubstantiation of the host; likewise for the arcane sentences of Paracelsus.

As nuclear weapons are the favourite topic in weapons philosophy at the present, let me take for example the nucleus of the atom, without which there is no nuclear bomb. We can witness the coming into being of the nucleus, as a real possibility, in the years 1890-1912. I would say that in 1870 it was not thinkable that an atom should be constituted by an infitesimally small concentration of mass in a void at whose outer limits there are the remaining parts of the atom. It is true that Maxwell said there must be structure in molecules (by which he meant atoms), but Rutherford's atom was unthinkable. Certain possibilities for us did not exist, and only gradually entered the field as electrons came to be postulated and then known. Even when Rutherford did have the nucleus in 1911, he was very slow in talking about it, and did not at first much draw attention to it at the small congresses of the day. It really took him two or three years, not to countenance the nucleus as a fact, but to think of it as a possibility. The fact that the atom has a nucleus was less of a problem for Rutherford than transforming a form of knowledge to make an atom with a nucleus a possibility (and simultaneously a fact).

Quine's aversion to modal concepts makes the idea of possibility, and hence of a form of knowledge, unattractive to him. Yet my procedure is almost alarmingly nominalist, verificationist and positivist. I am speaking of nothing more than declarative sentences whose truth values can be determined and of the ways in which they are determined. The importance of the idea is that it gives us some general way to discuss the organization of constraints on directions of research, constraints which arise from an historical, a priori, absence of possibilities. Note that I do not say the exclusion of impossibilities. Slightly to abuse Wittgenstein, I would call something that is impossible *sinnlos*, while something that is excluded as unthinkable would be *unsinnig*. The trinity, transsubsantiation, and much of my hero Paracelsus are, for me, *unsinnig*; so, I think, was an atomic nucleus, even for Maxwell, in 1870.

The notion of a frame of knowledge connects with many others that are at present well known, and it may even serve a useful deflationary purpose. Thus T.S. Kuhn, writing of scientific revolutions in a discipline or subdiscipline, speaks of changes in world-view, even of a revolution leading us to live in a different world. A less romantic way to indicate the general idea is to say that the form of a branch of knowledge has changed; a new space of possibilities has emerged, together with new criteria for questions to ask and ways to answer them. Whether or not there *are* incommensurable forms of knowledge is an historical question, but at least the meaning of an assertion of incommensurability is moderately clear; there is no common measure between the possibilities that exist in one form of knowledge, and those that exist in another. Note incidentally that Donald Davidson's animadversions against the very idea of a conceptual scheme (a set of sentences held for true) do not so evidently apply to my notion of a form as a set of possibilities together with 'methods of verification' – a crude but familiar label for a vast complex of ways for deciding questions.

Revolution sounds romantic. There are many more sedate ways in which the form of a body of knowledge can be historically determined, and might have been determined in other ways. I wish to steer away from grand talk of total conceptual schemes to more piecemeal things, and to steer away from talk of revolution to the manifold of complex ways in which not only the content but also the form of knowledge can be determined, altered or constrained. I shall do this by a string of very different kinds of example, and which will include:

1. Early intelligence quotients.
2. A now famous example from endocrinology.
3. Detectors in high energy physics.
4. Lasers.
5. Criteria of Accuracy for missiles.

None of the examples is my own. I deliberately take historical case studies made by other people. The examples are not in general from weapons research, although I will from time to time point out military connections. Each represents a different way in which a form of knowledge can be moulded. I wish to escape Kant's unifying idea that talk of the form of knowledge is talk of the one permanent form of knowledge. Since Hegel we have all become historicist, albeit in some cases kicking and screaming in resistance. Hegel denied the permanence of a form of knowledge, but not the unifying ideal. My talk of form is parasitic on a common idea of content. It does hold that at any time there are classes of possible questions bearing on some subject matter, and that ranges of possibilities change for all sort of reasons. A precondition for content is given by the form, the class of possibilities. But the determinants of these forms are multifarious. One of the reasons that the unity of science is an idle pipedream is that the forms of different bits of knowledge are brought into being by unrelated and unrelatable chains of events. Examples are needed to understand what this means.

1. *Intelligence Quotient*

The famous Stanford-Binet intelligence tests were set out along lines proposed by Alfred Binet, and then developed at Stanford University by Lewis Terman. There was a commitment to the idea that biological characteristics should be displayed upon a Gaussian or Normal probability curve. I ignore the long and tortuous nineteenth century origins of that idea. Binet devised questions which his subjects answered in such a way that scores shaped up on the familiar bell shaped curve. The trick was to get a set of questions which, when answered, had this property. Terman, with his able female assistants who administered most of the tests, discovered that women did better on his IQ tests than men. Since women 'couldn't' be more intelligent than men, this meant that the questions were wrong. Some of the questions that women answered better than men had to be deleted and replaced by ones on which men did better.[4] This procedure fixed, for some time, the form of knowledge

---

4 Lewis M. Terman and Maud A. Merritt, *Measuring Intelligence* (London: Harrap 1937), esp. 22f., 34; I owe the example to L. Daston.

about intelligence. There were particular items of content, 'How intelligent is Jones,' whose sense became fixed by the finalized method of verification, deliberately established by the investigator and his ideas. There also came into being certain synthetic a priori truths — and I mean this in exactly the sense of Kant. It became a synthetic a priori truth that women are no more intelligent than men. In passing, I emphasise that like so many of my other examples, this work had no military motivation or connection whatsoever. Yet war is always just around the corner. The Stanford-Binet test was legitimated and made both popular and semi-permanent by its use in screening American recruits.

In speaking of forms of knowledge we appear close to questions of scientific realism. Since Kant, 'realism' has usually meant anti-idealism. The recent flurry of discussions about scientific realism and anti-realism have commonly focused on questions of idealism, as to whether electrons exist, whether science aims at the truth or merely at instrumental adequacy, and so on. Such rather tedious debates do not concern me here. Talk of a form of knowledge (despite owing much to Kant) takes one back to an earlier sort of realism, whose opposite is nominalism. The realist, in the sense that matters here, may well echo the first half of Wittgenstein's first sentence in the *Tractatus*: 'The world is made up of facts.' The nominalist retorts that *we* have a good deal to do with what we call a fact. The world of nature does not just come with a totality of facts: rather it is we who carve up the world into facts, which are, in a contemporary phrase favoured by modern nominalists of the Edinburgh School, 'social constructions.'

The realist/nominalist controversy need not detain us. There is enough in common between the two for each to admit the phenomena I shall present. The attitude to the phenomena will be different, and the background talk about the phenomena will be different, but not enough for us to pause. For example, the nominalist says that the structure of the facts in my world is an imposition upon the world. The world does not come tidily sorted into facts. People construct facts in a social process of interaction with the world and intervening in its affairs. Importantly, says the nominalist, forms of knowledge are created in a microsociological process. Well, the realist will be offended by this description, but if attracted at all by

247

the notion of forms of knowledge, he has an alternative background tale. It is this. The world is far too rich in facts for any one organization of ideas to trick it out uniquely in *the* facts. We select which facts interest us, and a form of scientific knowledge is a selector of questions to be answered by obtaining the facts. A rival, and if possible incommensurable, form will elicit different facts. The facts are not constructed although the forms of selection are. In what follows, it does not matter which variant of these two extremes you find most attractive.

It is easy to see that both nominalist and realist may give accounts of the IQ tests. The nominalist will say that it is an unusually clear-cut example of a social construction. The realist may say that the Stanford-Binet test is objective (and confirm this along Stearman's lines by factor analysis) but equally agree this is just one way of ranking the intellectual abilities of people, attending to some aspects of (objective) 'intelligence.'

I have inserted these remarks about realism and anti-realism because I am sure that the questions I am asking are prompted by some strand of anti-realism. But I think that is largely a personal matter. Although a realist may have little inclination to embark on my enquiries, little or nothing in what I say need offend a realist metaphysics.

2. *Endocrinology*

For a quite different example, consider the now famous book by B. Latour and S. Woolgar, *Laboratory Life: The Social Construction of a Scientific Fact.*[5] Acting as an ethnographer, or participant observer, in the Salk laboratories in San Diego, Latour was able to provide a first-hand account of a discovery in endocrinology that won a Nobel Prize. It seems a clear example of a discovery, one that even the most determined anti-realist must acknowledge. A certain hormone, or peptide, called thyrotropin releasing factor, seemed to play

---

5 Sage: Los Angeles and London 1977

an important triggering role in the hypothalmus, and thus be of importance to understanding mammalian endocrinology. Many laboratories competed but only two were successful, and they shared the prize.

Instead of completing a chemical analysis, both groups synthesised the substance TRF, which is now a standardly available substance from drug companies. How could one talk about social construction, except in the trivial sense that social organizations did the laboratory work?

I take only some things from the Latour and Woolgar book, for some aspects of it seem to me to be far-fetched or dated. But here are some interesting things. There is almost no TRF in the world to analyse. Five hundred tons of pig brains had to be shipped from the Chicago stockyards on ice, in order to distill a microgram of TRF. And what was this TRF? It was a substance that passed certain assay tests. But there was no agreement on what the assays should be, and different labs had different assays. The winning labs 'determined' the assays and so determined the practical criteria of identity for TRF. Second, when a certain peptide had been synthesised, and declared to be TRF, that was the end of the matter. A drug company that had sponsored much of the research patented and started selling synthetic TRF.

The question as to whether this really is TRF simply dropped out, with the sceptics turning their minds to other things. Synthetic TRF became a laboratory tool in its own right, and *Indexicus Medicus*, *Chemical Abstracts* and *Biological Abstracts* now have it as a heading listing numerous monthly reports of experiments using TRF to investigate something else. (Do suicidal women become less suicidal when injected with the stuff?) Also much of the original interest, as having to do with mammalian brains, may have been mistaken, as TRF plays a role in the chemistry of alligator's stomachs. And so on: a whole research field is created, but, argue Latour and Woolgar, not because we simply revealed a new fact, which we use as a stepping stone to the next bit of discovery. Instead, a social sequence of events fixes TRF as 'the' substance originally of interest, without it being clear that the experimental work had to conclude in this way. Indeed, once certain events occurred, there is no doubting the 'reality' of the synthetic substance, TRF. Moreover, no one will ever challenge the system of assays that determine what TRF is, because they now define TRF. Certainly the research work will not be 'repeated' − who will collect another 500 tons of pig brains to distill a microgram of whatever it is?

This example may seem to concern the content of scientific knowledge rather than its form. The fact that TRF is a certain tripeptide would naturally be called part of the content of endocrinology. But facts do not just pile up blindly. They are used to determine the form of future enquiries. It is not just that the formula for TRF becomes a fixed benchmark in the science. The substance is manufactured and becomes an investigative tool, for it allows for certain new questions to be addressed, and certain new techniques to be deployed. This example has nothing to do with the idea I mentioned earlier, of form being a byproduct of scientific revolution. Nor is this case at all like the operations of Terman. Why I speak of form here is that certain issues have been closed off, and certain others opened up. An incredibly rare hypothesized substance is translated into an easily manufactured synthetic substance, which defines what is going on in your head. Nominalists Latour and Woolgar call this fact constructed. A realist need only say that among all the possible facts to be discovered in the endocrinology of the hypothalmus, this particular structure has been singled out, and will determine the future possible structures to be discovered, shutting off others from the screen of possibilities.

3. *Particle Detectors*

I turn to a stronger example of the way in which the form of a science may be altered. It is well described by Peter Galison.[6] The bubble chamber has been a chief detection device in high energy physics for over twenty years, although of course not the only one. It consists of liquid hydrogen under high pressure. When a very fast par-

---

6 'Bubble Chambers and the Experimental Workplace,' in P. Achinstein and O. Hannaway, *Observation, Experiment and Hypothesis in Modern Physical Science* (Cambridge, MA: Bradford Books 1985), 309-73

ticle goes through this substance, it releases bubbles, which serve as a track of the particle, and also of tracks of colliding particles, decaying particles and so forth. It has the great merit that it is very 'fast,' allowing an enormous number of tracks to be observed in very short periods of time, whereas in older devices one had to wait a while between one good observation and the next.

The bubble chamber permanently changed high energy physics. First, liquid hydrogen is incredibly explosive. That meant that a new level of staff had to be introduced into high energy laboratories: safety engineers and the accompanying controls on scientists. Research physicists could not just wander around the lab any more. Second, for the first time, very many more data were produced than any team of individuals could process. At first a new layer of observers, photographers and counters, was introduced, but this has all been replaced by magnetic tape and computer scanning. Moreover, in order that different laboratories could even understand their results, the tapes and their methods of interpretation had to be standardized. This was done at international conventions. A detecting device, the bubble chamber, did not merely enable one to detect what had not been seen before. It determined the form of the questions to be asked in high energy physics in the world's laboratories. The inventor of the bubble chamber, Donald Glaser, was so appalled at the way his child changed the day-to-day practice of physics that he left, Nobel Prize in hand, and took up molecular biology.

Most high energy physics in recent years has had precious little military pay-off. In a larger view, it is widely agreed that the militarization of funding for science research in WWII was what made possible much big science such as high energy physics. All the same, many who work in the field feel that they are outside the arms race. Only in the early development of the atomic bomb were high energy physics and weaponry intimately and necessarily related (e.g. the first plutonium used to fire up Fermi's pile was made in the Radiation Lab and cyclotron at Berkeley, whose engineers also designed the calutrons at Oak Ridge, for preparing enriched uranium). But even though I happily call the bubble chamber 'peaceful' it was made possible in its day by weaponry. It required a great deal of liquid hydrogen technology, known as cyrogenics. This cyrogenic knowledge and material just happened to exist – in Colorado, where it had been prepared for Edward Teller's model of the hydrogen bomb. Teller's version was superceded, so it was possible to conscript liquid hydrogen technology and technicians for the first large bubble chambers.

This happy turning of swords into ploughshares has not been uncommon in high energy physics. But it is also to be remembered that the rersources of equipment and of talent were made available out of Department of Defense funds, largely because of the old collusion between high energy and weaponry established during the Manhattan project.

4. *Lasers*

Lasers are perhaps the best known ingredient in the three level Strategic Defence Initiative known as Star Wars. Despite this, it is entirely possible that they will be the first to drop out. Certainly the biggest investment for some time is likely to be in the direction of advanced computation, in part as a way to subsidize the American computing industry into its next generations of computing power. Acknowledging that lasers may merely be the sensational tip of a vastly more complex programme, it is still worth while telling a little bit about where lasers came from.[7]

Shortly before 1939 British scientists developed a primitive but valuable radar system for the detection of incoming bombers. (Even then they fantasised about 'death rays' on the side.) Radar was, for a short time, as close to a defensive weapon as you could imagine. It quickly became used for offensive purposes, for example in locating enemy warships and in particular submarines that had occasionally but regularly to surface. Throughout the second world war there was intensive development of numerous microwave techniques, which continued unabated after the war. A collection of projects was begun which are aimed at producing exceedingly stable and relia-

---

7 Here I rely heavily on a preprint by Paul Forman, Smithsonian Institution, 'Behind Quantum Electronics: Elements of the Military Context of Physical Research in America, 1940-1960.' His paper was read at the XVII Congress for the History of Science, Berkeley, California, August 1985.

ble high frequency emissions, and the solution gradually proposed was to use artificially stimulated resonances of molecules themselves. Work on the maser was entirely funded by the department of defense. So were the two earliest programmes to construct a laser (Harold Townes at Columbia and Gordon Gould at TRG Inc.). In the three years following the first demonstration of lasing, the DoD dumped 100 million 1985 dollars into research. Private industry also quickly responded, and soon was putting more into laser R&D than the DoD. It was, however, the DoD that gave us this phenomenon – a remarkable gift; for although the phenomenon of lasing is becoming ubiquitous all over the industrialised parts of our planet, it existed (with all probability) nowhere in the universe before 1950.

Peaceful applications of lasing are legion. Moreover, it will long continue to be a topic of profound basic research, particularly as it is an unusually accessible and manipulable instance of a non-linear process. Assuredly we should express gratitude for this gift of the Department of Defense.

Why should I group it under the heading of a form of scientific knowledge? Let us suppose that there has been a pretty steady weapons thrust underlying laser research, a thrust that brings us to Star Wars research. Does this not represent simply the steady investment of public funds in military research, churning up new discoveries that may have military application, and certainly have peaceful ones? On the form/content spectrum, is this not squarely on the content side?

I shall give two connected answers, one practical, and the other embedding that answer in a current philosophical tradition. The practical answer (given here from a realist standpoint, but susceptible to nominalist rewriting) is that there was no prior inner necessity, in the development of post-war physics, for lasing to be discovered. There are endless aspects of molecular structure on which to work. The choice of problem was directed by the military. That done, we had another benchmark situation. This fundamental discovery served as a 'paradigm' of inquiry – not due to any revolution, but because other fields of questioning were screened off by this monumental success. For a substantial period of time to come, a wide range of possible questions will be formulated according to this paradigm.

The significance of this commonplace can be partially understood by connecting it with Lakatos's notion of a research programme. I avail myself of the difference between American and British spelling. A research program is a familiar beast, often described in an initial proposal asking for money from a patron. You say, we are going to do this, this and this, and if we are lucky we'll do that, and then try for such and such. A research program is pretty specific, should be flexible, and is finite. It may be replaced by another successor program in three years or three months.

Lakatos's research programmes are quite different. His own examples include programmes that last a century and are driven underground, forgotten for decades while they lie fallow in a field of counter-examples. His research programmes have a structure of positive and negative heuristics, of hard cores and protective belts, they may be progressive and degenerating, both theoretically and empirically.

A research program, as I understand it, is an inquiry that takes place *under* a form of knowledge, although its upshot may change that very form. There are certain questions, and certain ways of trying to answer them. When the program first surfaces as a proposal for scrutiny, it is supposed that the questions are intelligible and their answers at least partially attainable by the proposed techniques. The aim of a program is to increase the content of our knowledge and its uses.

A Lakatosian research programme, on the other hand, is not so far from my idea of a form of knowledge. Part of Lakatos's idea of positive and negative heuristics is that of the questions that can be asked, and those that cannot. Lakatos would have resisted my word 'form' with its Platonic and Kantian overtones. But Plato and Kant were for fixed forms within a unified scheme; it will be clear from my previous examples that I markedly am not. I propose even more ways of changing programmes than Lakatos ever got around to discussing. I am not unhappy to think of a Lakatosian research programme as one of the ways in which to come to grips with my groped-for concept of form. I would not identify the two, any more than I would identify Kuhnian revolutions with the creations of forms of knowledge. This is because I want a more flexible and many-valent concept. I don't think there are many Kuhnian revolutions or Lakatosian research programmes in the history of science, which has got on very well, much of the time in many places, without either notion being instantiated.

At any rate, it will now appear that in my thinking, programmes and programs are fish and fowl, oranges and apples, or perhaps as different as fish from apples. But radar-microwave-maser-laser-SDI gives me pause. This is certainly no short term program, written up in a few proposals and funded by the U.S. Army Signal Corps or whomever. It needs little stretching of Lakatos's own definitions to see this development as the working out of an identifiable research programme, starting, indeed, with the only partly jocular thought of the British pioneers thay they might devise a 'death ray.'

Yet such stretching of Lakatos would belie some of his own intentions. He wanted research programmes to be part of his philosophical theory of a purely internal, autonomous account of the growth of knowledge. Political, social and psychological factors were to be excluded. A dominant feature of 'the laser programme' (if there was one) would be that despite its endless civilian spinoffs, which burgeon apace today, there was one and only one major paymaster, the Department of Defense. That is, there is an entirely external account of what directed the programme and got it moving.

5. *Missile Accuracy*

Here I shall allude only briefly to Donald MacKenzie's essay, 'The Social Construction of Missile Accuracy,'[8] in part because in certain ways it so resembles our first example of IQ. At first blush it may seem that missile accuracy is an entirely objective concept; the missile either hits the target or it does not. On second thought, it obviously isn't 'objective,' and that for several reasons. First, as in archery, accuracy must be graded, with top marks for the bull, and

---

8 This paper is also in the preprint stage. It too was read at the Congress cited in footnote 7.

diminishing marks for increasing deviation from target. The grading depends upon the point of the exercise. If killing is the aim, the warhead will determine part of the measure of accuracy. For example, in a defense of Western Europe against an imagined tank attack, consider two missiles. *A* carries a relatively small amount of conventional explosive; *B* is a very low yield fission bomb. To be 'accurate,' *A* must detonate very close to the tank that is its target. The constraints of accuracy on *B* are different; it can be somewhat off the center of a tank battalion to wreak havoc. On the other hand, in the jargon of the army, small towns in Germany are only a kiloton apart, and if part of the object is to be of some help to the locals, the missile *B* should be as close as possible to half a kiloton away from any village. Problems of accuracy for *B* are a good deal harder than for *A*; luckily they become increasingly moot with improved 'missile accuracy' for *A* type missiles. Evidently questions of missile accuracy become more complex for strategic as opposed to tactical nuclear weapons.

So there is a problem in defining how close one is to a target. The second problem is that one is not talking about the accuracy of an individual missile (which is fired only once). One is concerned with a kind of missile, and missile accuracy becomes a statistical concept, which is open to a good many interpretations.

MacKenzie argues that there was once an extensive debate on missile accuracy which has gradually stabilized into a set of measures and comparative standards. Every manufacturer and every branch of the armed services had its own standard of missile accuracy, often giving wildly different characterisations of the relative 'merits' of different missiles. By what the nominalists call a microsociological process, concensus has been reached. This concensus determines in part the very construction and design of missiles (because you have to achieve accuracy within the designated limits, whereas another measure of accuracy would have called for a different design). It matters to arms control negotiations and much else. There appear to be many formal comparisons between this example and that of IQ. In crucial cases, answers to the question, 'Is this missile more accurate than that one?' are determined by the assay criteria on which the community has decided. These become part of the form of possible knowledge, defining the contentual answers to questions that at first seem independent of any 'form.'

These five examples serve to put some flesh on the skeletal idea of a form of scientific knowledge. It is all very well to say a form is a structured class of sentences that are all capable of being true or false. That is but to pose a question; namely, how do such classes come into being and how are they changed? My answer is manifold. It includes deliberation, as in IQ or missile accuracy. It includes the establishment of assay techniques as definitive. It concludes the making of a substance synthetically that defines a part of nature. It includes the creation and standardization of detectors. It includes research programmes and the external forces that give them direction. It does of course not exclude Kuhnian revolutions. Nor does it exclude that most general kind of form of knowledge that Michel Foucault called an *episteme*. The roots of the present essay may be detected in some of Foucault's ideas of what makes positive knowledge possible.

III

Alas, I have no simplistic conclusions. My aim has been to connect traditional philosophy of science and the weapons research question. I have attempted to open a debate, not to close one. The paper is in part a response to three commonplaces. (1) We have enjoyed remarkable spinoffs, of great benefit to humanity, from weapons research and military funding. (2) The human race learns more in times of war and of rumours of war than at other times. (3) Knowledge can be put to good uses or evil ones; the use of knowledge is a matter of public policy, not science.

I have been at pains, in my examples, not to deny the first saying. It is not that I have asserted it, but I have provided illustrations, some unfamiliar, that could be used to defend it. However, the claim about spinoff knowledge is not particularly germane to the concerns of this paper. Insofar as there is a viable form/content distinction, (1) is about the spinoffs from particular contents of knowledge.

257

The second statement, about the fertility of research in times of war, is connected by its proponents to the spinoff doctrine (1). However, it seems to be false. It is true that prosperous wartime and war-preparation economies (such as ours at present) provide ample funds and motivation for discovery. It is true that wartime shortages also invite invention, such as that of artificial rubber (after loss of colonial Malaya) or sugar from sugar beets (after, in the Napoleonic wars, effective loss of the French West Indies). But it requires some talent to list war-related discoveries in the warrior nations of Europe 1914-1918. Rocketry, nuclear power and microwave technology are among the adventures accelerated by 1939-1945, but the greatest scientific achievements of our era, in terms of knowledge, are surely (to take the interwar years) the new quantum mechanics of mid-twenties Weimar Germany, or the early postwar triumphs of molecular biology (made, in many cases, by men who had wasted six years in 'war work'). Platitude (2) isn't true, but if it were, it too would be about content, not form.

I have no doubt that in many respects the third proposition is true: in the case of nuclear weapons, the great powers could without inconvenience eliminate them in a few years. It is a political choice, which may be wise or foolish, not to do so. Should the creators or possessors of the knowledge that makes the weapons and the delivery systems possible, be part of the political scene? That is an issue that in this paper I have forsworn.

Like (1) and (2), the third commonplace operates at the level of individual matters of fact. There is this knowledge, crafted by human minds and hands. This knowledge may then be used by other minds and hands for good or evil. This statement (3) and the corresponding ethical problems are stated, quite appropriately, at the level of matters of fact, of content.

All three commonplaces are governed by that very picture encapsulated by Quine, of knowledge as a conceptual scheme, of a set of sentences held for true. That cheerful empiricist picture of a holistic structure of sentences says nothing of questions, except in the form of whether items in the scheme are, after all, true. It says nothing of what questions are possible for us to ask at a time, and of how the arrangement of possible questions can be changed. It says nothing of how it will be altered by a radically new invention (the bubble chamber) or how making a new substance sets up strategies for attack on old questions in a new way. It says nothing about how a program/programme can turn radar into the laser and give us the Strategic Defence Initiative (as well as many goodies on the side).

The conceptual scheme picture is one of autonomous knowledge living its own life, with its bosom buddies, the scientific investigators. The form of knowledge picture is one that admits that possibilities are constrained in a manifold of complex ways at a particular time. What we can think of, what we want to ask, what we want to do as investigators is an historical event. It is not rigid, but neither is it altogether fluid. Copper is malleable and ductile, but you can't do *anything* with copper; likewise, forms are malleable, but still operative. We have long had the fantasy that attending more closely to the forms of knowledge will somehow be liberating. That fantasy is not automatically to be dismissed when it is introduced into new and parlous territory. It is to be transformed into something more than fantasy, and one way to do that, in my opinion, is get a fairly rich diet of examples.

I would altogether deplore an inference from this paper, that forms of knowledge connected with research that is primarily funded by the military are wittingly created by those who are responsible for weapons research. Such ideological paranoia is absurd, if only on the ground that, contrary to what I write, the concept of a form of knowledge may be either inexplicable or when explained, empty. I am more concerned that we have no idea of what we are doing in the overall directions of our conceptions of the world. There is no monolithic military conspiracy in any part of the globe to determine the kinds of possibilities in terms of which we shall describe and interact with the cosmos. But our ways of worldmaking, to use the phrase of Nelson Goodman, are increasingly funded by one overall motivation. If content is what we can see, and form is what we cannot, but which determines the possibilities of what we can see, we have a new cause to worry about weapons research. It is not just the weapons — we can dismantle them in a few years with goodwill — that are being funded, but the world of mind and technique in which those weapons are devised. The forms of that world can come back to haunt us even when the weapons themselves are

Ian Hacking

gone. For we are creating forms of knowledge which — spinoffs or not — have a homing device. More weapons, for example.

Received February, 1986
Revised May, 1986

Notes on the Contributors

Noam Chomsky joined the staff of the Massachusetts Institute of Technology in 1955, and in 1961 was appointed full Professor in what is now the Department of Linguistics and Philosophy. From 1966 to 1976 he held the Ferrari P. Ward Professorship of Modern Languages and Linguistics. In 1976 he was appointed Institute Professor. During 1958 and 1959, Chomsky was in residence at the Institute for Advanced Study at Princeton. In 1969 he delivered the John Locke Lectures at Oxford; in 1970 he delivered the Bertrand Russell Memorial Lectures at Cambridge. In 1972 he delivered the Nehru Memorial Lectures in New Delhi, and in 1977, the Huizinga Lecture in Leiden. Chomsky is the author of a great many books and articles on linguistics, philosophy, intellectual history, and contemporary political issues.

Onora O'Neill teaches philosophy at the University of Essex in England. She writes mainly on Kantian questions and on problems of applied ethics. Her recent book, *Faces of Hunger: An Essay on Justice and Development*, like her contribution to this volume, explores philosophical difficulties that arise in reasoning practically about global issues.

James P. Sterba is Professor of Philosophy at the University of Notre Dame. He specializes in political philosophy and practical ethics. The books he has written or edited include *Justice: Alternative Political Perspectives* (1979); *The Demands of Justice* (1980); *Morality in Practice* (1983); and *The Ethics of War and Nuclear Deterrence* (1984). He is also general editor for Wadsworth's *Basic Issues in Philosophy* series.

Michael Dummett is Wykeham Professor of Logic, Oxford University, and Fellow of New College. He has held Fellowships and Readerships in Oxford since 1950, and he is a Fellow of the British Academy. In 1976, he was William James Lecturer at Harvard University. His publications include *Frege: Philosophy of Language; Immigration: Where the Debate Goes Wrong; Catholicism and the World Order;* and *Twelve Tarot Games*.

Alan Gewirth is E. C. Waller Distinguished Service Professor of Philosophy at The University of Chicago. His books include *Reason and Morality; Human Rights;* and *Marsilius of Padua and Medieval Political Philosophy*. He is a Fellow of the American Academy of Arts and Sciences and past president of the American Philosophical Association and the American Society for Political and Legal Philosophy.

Russell Hardin is Professor of Political Science and Philosophy, and Chair of the Committee on Public Policy Studies at the University of Chicago.

He is the author of *Collective Action* (Johns Hopkins University Press for Resources for the Future 1982) and the co-editor of *Nuclear Deterrence: Ethics and Strategy* (University of Chicago Press 1985). He is also the editor of the journal *Ethics*.

Jan Narveson is Professor of Philosophy at the University of Waterloo, where he has taught since 1963. He is author of *Morality and Utility* as well as numerous articles on ethical and political issues. He recently edited the anthology *Moral Issues*, and he is now writing a book on libertarianism.

Steven C. Patten, 1941-1985, was Professor of Philosophy at the University of Lethbridge and an Executive Editor of the *Canadian Journal of Philosophy*. He was the author of articles in moral philosophy, philosophy of mind, and the history of philosophy.

Ian Hacking teaches at the Institute for the History and Philosophy of Science and Technology at the University of Toronto. His publications include *Representing and Intervening* (1983); *Why Does Language Matter to Philosophy?* (1975); and work on probability, statistics and the history of science.

INDEX*

absolutist, 113
action guiding reasoning, 51
action theory, for social choice, 177
agency: and consequentialism, 48; individual agency as irrelevant to world affairs, 54; individualist conceptions of, 50; and institutional action, 48; 'thin' theory of, 51, 56; 'thin' theory of institutional agency, 62
Anscombe, E., 183
Aquinas, Thomas: 83, 180; Thomistic doctrine, 184
Archimedean vantage point, 45
arms control, 18, 32
arms race, 24, 129, 147-50, 196, 251
autonomy and sovereignty, 59
Axelrod, Robert, 151

ballistic missile, 209; see also ICBM
ban on testing and development: as reducing likelihood of first strike, 25; 1963 treaty, 151
bluff, 103; and the achievement of deterrence, 11, 100; as not credible, 119, 120, 180; bluff of massive nuclear retaliation can be justified, 101; not possible to institutionalize bluffing, 100, 120; see also intention
Baier, Kurt, 82
Beiner, R., 50
Beitz, Charles, 59, 60
'body politic', 59
Bracken, Paul, 2n., 18, 179
Braybrooke, David, 151

*Prepared by Steven Hetcher

build-down, 36

Catholic philosophers, 166
Catholic theory, ambiguity in just war theory, 167
Chernobyl, 2n.
chivalry and just war, 112
civil liberties, 26
clean hands, 51, 52, 55
cold war, as system of global management, 30-3
collective punishment, 58
collective responsibility, 48
conditional intentions, 11, 183; and wrongs, 122; to commit unparalleled massacre, 226; see also intention
consequentialism: act consequentialism, 112; consequentialist, 5, 49, 50, 113, 114; consequentialist calculation and nation-state, 49; consequentialist reasoning, 49; consequentialist reasoning and agency, 48; foreseen consequence, 87; formal structure of consequential reasoning, 50; game theory, 178; and retaliation, 15
conventional war, 98
Counterfactual Test, 87
counter-force: as second strike, 4; strategy, 4, 119; and consequentialism, 15n.; see also counter-value
counter-value, 114
cruise missile: 3, 201; as first strike, 202, 209

defensive policy, 210

263